Debunk

DEBUNKING THE BULL

FOR SEEKERS OF ANOTHER TACK

Sarah Honig

gefen publishing house
JERUSALEM • NEW YORK

Copyright © Sarah Honig
Jerusalem 2013/5773

All rights reserved. No part of this publication may be translated, reproduced, stored in a retrieval system or transmitted, in any form or by any means, electronic, mechanical, photocopying, recording or otherwise, without express written permission from the publishers.

Cover concept: Sarah Honig
Cover design: Benjie Herskowitz, Etc. Studio
Typesetting: Irit Nachum

ISBN: 978-965-229-607-8

2 4 6 8 9 7 5 3 1

Gefen Publishing House Ltd.
6 Hatzvi Street
Jerusalem 94386, Israel
972-2-538-0247
orders@gefenpublishing.com

Gefen Books
11 Edison Place
Springfield, NJ 07081
516-593-1234
orders@gefenpublishing.com

www.gefenpublishing.com

Printed in Israel

Library of Congress Cataloging-in-Publication Data

Honig, Sarah, 1946–
　[Essays. Selections]
　Debunking the bull: for seekers of another tack / Sarah Honig.
　　　pages ; cm
　ISBN 978-965-229-607-8
　1. Arab-Israeli conflict—Influence.　2. Arab-Israeli conflict—1993—Peace.　3. Palestinian Arabs—Politics and government—1993–　4. Israel—Politics and government—1993–　5. United States—Politics and government—2009–　6. United States—Foreign relations—Middle East.　7. Middle East—Foreign relations—United States.　8. World politics—21st century.　I. Title.
　DS119.76.H663 2013
　956.05'4—dc23
　　　　　　　　　　　2012042849

For Nicky

Contents

Ode to Sarah ix
Foreword xi

What's in a Name 1
The First Day 6
What's That about Daughters? 13
The German "Robbed Cossack" 18
Obama of the Open Mic 24
Sabina's Misrepresented Murder 30
With Intent to Deceive 34
Good Manners and High Morals 39
Banana Noses and Freckles 43
The Nudnik's Oft-Kibitzed Refrain 47
Optimism Was Compulsory 51
Boycott Is Beautiful 55
Remember the Tsunami of 1949 60
Don Abbas Makes an Offer 65
Roger Waters' Jarring Music 69
Ibrahim and Ibn-Rabah 72
Memo to Kibitzers and Kvetchers 77
Isolation I – How Not to Be *Ill* 81
Isolation II – My American Cousins 86
Musings on Skillful Salami Slicers 89
Edgardo and the Quarterbacks 94
Symptom of Craziness 98
Putty in His Hands 102
The Good Cop Goes to Auschwitz 106
If Ahmadinejad Attended Harvard 111
Fond Jane and Mr. Braun 115
It's Not the Settlements, Stupid 119

Tall Tales from the Has-Been Bunch	124
(Trans)Jordan *Is* Palestine	128
Self-Exiled by Guilt	132
In the Footsteps of Sam Lewis's Suck-Ups	137
Poster Child of Razzmatazz Land	141
Drenching Little Srulik	145
Haggling over the Price	149
Nitpickers That We Are	153
Not a Spiritual Santa	157
Don't Dream On	161
The Craftiest of Sophists	165
The May Day Massacre	169
The Forward Position	174
First Peacenik, Forgotten Founder	178
Saving Labor from Itself	183
Ma'alesh, Inshallah, Bukrah, Bakshish	187
Judah Macabee Was Your Father	190
Obama's Conquest and Beilin's Confession	195
Pius's Pious Pretension	199
Long Live MAPAI	203
Then What's the Alternative?	208
The Sergei Connection	212
The Wooden-Headedness Factor	216
My People Love to Have It So	220
Buried with Kalonymus	224
A Masjid Grows in Brooklyn	228
Where His Heart Is	232
Three Days and Sixty Years	236
Vague and Not Uncommon	240
Where Penitents Stand	244
About the Author	248

Ode to Sarah

For more than four decades – that's half the *Jerusalem Post*'s existence – Sarah Honig's name has provided prestige to the pages of Israel's top English-language daily.

As a political correspondent, she made a name for herself in the corridors of power, serving delicious scoops fed by the close contacts she forged with the country's top politicians.

And these politicians, from Left to Right, read her copy daily, often learning things from her juicy news items and benefiting from her sharp analyses of the ever-changing exigencies of political life in the Jewish state.

Later, as a regular columnist, Sarah gained a huge fan club, here in Israel and around the world. It was, perhaps, a combination of her fresh insights and her well-researched historical context, her pithy prose and delightful descriptions of her subjects.

Above all, Sarah is a supreme storyteller. Anyone who knows her cannot avoid the conclusion that she was born to spin yarns. She has a mind for fine detail, a flair for flowery language and the moral integrity to tell the whole truth as she sees it.

Sarah takes you back in history and makes you feel that you were there. And then she propels you forward, jolting you with a clear message that is just as relevant today as it was then.

Hers is the genre of ageless journalism that will be relevant forever, and should be taught in schools. Her columns are really superb slices of Israel's history, each one unique and precious.

They can be read over and over again, just like the best literature. And each time, new gems are revealed. Her love of language, life and Israel shine through her work, and with apparent ease, her sophisticated pieces weave together common threads into an overarching picture.

Elie Wiesel once said that God made man because He loves stories. And when it comes to Israel, no one tells a better story than Sarah Honig.

Steve Linde
Editor-in-Chief, the *Jerusalem Post*

Foreword

For the past four decades, Sarah Honig has been casting a giant shadow over Israeli journalism.

After beginning her career as a reporter, she went on to write brilliant editorials and excelled as a unique columnist.

Throughout, Sarah firmly upheld her ideals, beliefs and principles. This was not easy. Nevertheless, she was able to stand up against political pressure whenever it occurred and resist it regardless of its origin. In so doing, she earned and preserved the freedom of expression and opinion that characterizes all of her writing.

Her most outstanding contribution to the English-language daily has been her weekly column. It is labeled quite appropriately, "Another Tack," and frequently contains original ideas and firmly based interpretations of the status quo. The prevailing theme is Israel's national security and the dangers that might emerge from irresponsible territorial concessions.

She writes from the standpoint of a citizen who literally lives within range of the bullets, shells and rockets that might rain down on the country's coastal plain if a Palestinian state is carved out of Judea and Samaria – the area dubbed the West Bank when the Hashemite Kingdom's forces overran it during the 1948–49 War of Independence. (It was meant to differentiate it from Jordan's original East Bank.)

Few journalists invest the intellectual effort in composing their dispatches, articles and columns that Sarah Honig does. One of her uppermost considerations is the quality of her prose. The result is that reading it is an end in itself – an intellectual and literary experience that her readers cherish whether they agree with her conclusions or not.

Sarah Honig also has the rare ability to bring her personal

background and family relationships into her columns whenever they may bear on the issues at hand. She is not averse to quoting her daughter or revealing ideological clashes near and far, past and present. This is done in a way that personalizes Israel's endless political controversies and humanizes the contending parties.

Transcending all this is her unswerving belief in the Jewish people's historical and contemporary right to inhabit and govern the Land of Israel from the Mediterranean Sea to the River Jordan. In her view, territorial concessions there are out of the question – not only from the academic standpoint, but above all for the sake of the security and future survival of Israel's citizens.

That is why Sarah Honig's analysis and commentary go beyond vague generalization and simplistic slogans. She goes into the technical and tactical details of national defense and at the same time, makes her readers ponder the real-life implications they pose to rank-and-file Israelis. Using her vast literary talent as the vehicle for her concern for the personal safety of Israel's citizens, she transforms editorial discourse into a profound examination of the reality of life in the Jewish state.

Jay Bushinsky
Editor-in-Chief, Media Group International

What's in a Name

Word is that US president Barack Obama, remarkably free from introspection and unencumbered by healthy hints of self-doubt, assiduously attributes Israeli mistrust of him to his eminently Muslim middle name. For him that encapsulates it all.

Such simplistic, one-dimensional explanations typify his neophyte missteps on the treacherous turfs of foreign policy. Obama botches things up because of his predilection for facile grand gestures, which, alas, can't alter intricate realities. He hasn't got an elementary handle on our Israeli outlook and is likewise unable to navigate the tempestuous Islamic sea that swirls ominously around us.

He doesn't get us and he doesn't get them.

Obama's oversimplified presumptions about our perceived antipathy toward him (without stopping to consider his undisguised cold shoulder to us) are matched by oversimplified expectations that the Muslim/Arab world should cheer him. These too hinge on that eminently Muslim middle name. Being called Hussein should, in and of itself, create an affinity, make Muslims trust him and accept him as a kindred spirit.

This, of course, is every bit as simplistic as the notion that Israelis should harbor misgivings because of his name.

In both cases there's more than latent condescension in the notion that simpleton natives can be attracted or repelled with trivial outward accoutrements. Obama, the sophisticated enchanter, can manipulate them. Whether he captivates or chides them, they, like impressionable children, will play out his expectations, complying with considerations as silly as those encapsulated in a name.

The name accounts for everything. It explains away resentment of his policies as betokening prejudice against his extraction. It claims a special position vis-à-vis the Third World by boasting about connections unprecedented for an American leader. Obama banked on being recognized as a quasi-native son of non-Western cultures, who, with no other attributes than his African absentee father's distant heritage and his Asian stepfather's upbringing, could forge bonds unlike any previous White House tenant.

All this doesn't just convey unwarranted hubris, it also – and foremost so – causes misrepresentation, misconception and distortion. It presents things as they definitely are not and it triggers dismal consequences.

By not giving Israelis and the enemies who surround them more credit, Obama does what few before him have managed as incompetently. He alienates America's one committed comrade while earning the disrespect of all those he set out to endear with just his name and fawning flattery. Few have succeeded in doing as badly in as short a time.

The final fall of Egypt's Hosni Mubarak, sent for whatever time he has left to durance vile, underscores the Obama-esque folly more than the other Middle Eastern upheavals and sectarian conflicts falsely parading as democratic stirrings.

Obama never came close to criticizing Mubarak as a tyrant while Mubarak held the reins of power. Indeed as regional despots go, Mubarak didn't come close to being the quintessential ogre. His harshest measures were expended on plugging the bottle in which he contained the Muslim Brotherhood genie.

Mubarak was savable but Obama released the zealous Muslim genie with gaucheness even exceeding that of Jimmy Carter (his rival for the most-bungling-president distinction). Mubarak wasn't Israel's chum but he was a dependable keeper of the frigid peace. However, beyond that, he was the most pro-Western leader produced by modern Egypt to date.

With all of Egypt's diverse endemic woes, he was the leader who gave his impoverished country its greatest economic lift ever, garnished with diplomatic gravitas. Ironically, the brand of progress and Westernization Mubarak introduced and furthered, admittedly imperfect as it was, became his undoing.

It wasn't that the masses demanded more Westernization, as Obama disingenuously later sought to present it, with his equally disconnected secretary of state Hillary Clinton surreally chiming in. In actual fact, the rioters agitated precisely against Mubarak's Westernization.

Obama's belated spin either testified to his being dangerously out of the loop or to lack of elementary intellectual candor. Were Obama a tad more clued in or a tad more truthful, he'd acknowledge that Mubarak was in trouble because his adversaries didn't want anything resembling Western democracy rather than the other way around.

That doesn't only apply to the Muslim Brotherhood's blinkered preachers of regression but also to many Egyptian secularists. The latter don't necessarily hanker after liberality, freethinking and multicultural pluralism. Their hero is none other than Gamal Abdel Nasser, despite his repeated battlefield humiliations. Bizarrely because of his defeats, Nasser is regarded as a proud pan-Arab stalwart who confronted the West (never mind the unkind outcome).

A more forward-looking Egypt, still the Arab world's primary power but with a stronger economy and flourishing tourism, may have had its perks but it didn't instantly cure its population's festering afflictions and it certainly displeased the bearded fanatics. Mubarak was hard pressed from all sides. He had to be callous and pugnacious in order not to end up assassinated like his predecessor Anwar Sadat.

Therefore, Mubarak had compelling reasons for foreboding when Obama dashed to Cairo in June 2009, hot upon his electoral victory, to suck up to unspecified Islamists. Mubarak was undermined already in Obama's debut act of appealing with superficial naiveté to Muslim xenophobes and elevating their intransigence to undeserved equality with the West's carte blanche tolerance. The horror show elements of Obama's extravaganza were detected by a mere handful, Mubarak astutely among them.

At that pivotal point it should have been clear that the end is near for whatever remnants of delicate equilibrium still endured in this region. Obama ushered in chaos via what he hyped as a trailblazing new departure by a surprise soul-mate with an unexpected middle name. Mubarak significantly absented himself from the milestone sham. He was not in the audience as Obama extolled the virtues of Islam. He could sense the ill winds blowing.

But that was only the beginning of a convoluted path on which Obama seemed incapable of dodging any pitfalls. In the real world it's prudent to look out for long-term interests, which include reliance, where expedient, on the lesser of given evils in the absence of ideal alternatives. Mubarak was never the worst of options. Yet whereas Obama betrayed allies and quasi-tolerable hangers-on, he was incredibly hands-off toward the true villains of the Middle East piece –like Iran, Hezbollah, Hamas and, at least initially (and crucially), Syria.

For example, in 2009, following Iran's rigged election, thousands took to the streets in defiance of the theocracy that Carter pathetically enabled thirty years earlier. As pro-democracy demonstrators were killed in Tehran and as its ayatollahs furthered their designs to arm themselves with nukes, the current leader of the Free World spared no effort to stress the need to downplay the fuss.

Obama gave his own people a lesson in moral relativism: "It's important to understand that, although there is amazing ferment taking place in Iran, the difference between Ahmadinejad and Mousavi in terms of their actual policies may not be as great as advertised." Not unpredictably, Obama informed the unenlightened masses that he won't take sides: "I take a wait-and-see approach.… It's not productive, given the history of US-Iranian relations, to be seen as meddling in Iranian elections."

Given this, and given the irrefutable reality that colossal differences exist between Mubarak and the Muslim Brotherhood, one must wonder why Obama's administration couldn't wait before it took sides – this time against the ruling government.

Equally as unforgettable was Secretary Clinton's characterization (certainly with Obama's blessing) of Bashar Assad as "a reformer." This was when Assad's henchmen started slaughtering the junta's opposition.

With brash non-intervention in one instance and impetuous intervention in another, it appears that no principle or pattern guides Obama's responses. But on closer inspection, it's impossible not to conclude that Obama wasn't interested in destabilizing the anti-Western ayatollahs while he didn't mind destabilizing the pro-Western Mubarak.

In other words, painful as the bottom line is, Obama showed no loyalty to the West's allies – either on the streets of Tehran or in Cairo's presidential palace. If anything, his proclivities are anti-Western.

There's no chance that any Middle Eastern players would overlook this, much as Obama and his supporters may deny his apparent inclinations. All moralizing mantras about human liberty ring hollow as Obama is seen keeping his hands off the most rogue of Middle East autocracies while selling out professed teammates or opportunistic non-opponents.

If anything can conceivably discourage vulnerable local potentates (like the Saudis, the Gulf princes or Jordan's King Abdullah) from staking their futures on American promises, it's the evidence of their own eyes. Right now, all America's allies – Israelis among them – look like suckers liable to be left high and dry.

The ayatollahs, who were helped by Carter and not hindered by Obama, must be rubbing their hands in glee.

The circle is closed for us too. Carter was the one who twisted Menachem Begin's arms to cede the Sinai and contract the frosty peace with Egypt. We struck a risky bargain with a here-today-gone-sometimes-tomorrow regime. All Egyptian undertakings might disintegrate into the desert sands, leaving us on the precipice of a strategic calamity.

The word to the wise is to cut our losses and – no matter how hard Obama twists our arms – refrain from neurotically duplicating the same inordinate gullibility on our long tortuous eastern flank, where Mahmoud Abbas is more of a hollow-reed staff than any of our Egyptian interlocutors ever were.

Such wariness on our part has nothing to do with leeriness of Obama's middle name. It has everything to do with the recklessness spawned by his own exploitation of that name.

This is true both for Israel – America's one leftover genuine friend in this erratic region – as well as for Israel's inimical neighbors, whose innate acumen mustn't be underestimated.

They may be trapped in their own circuitous reasoning but their honed intuitions discern that precisely those in their midst – like Mubarak – who dared depart from nationalistic extremism or insular Islam are those whom America's president with the Muslim name let fall.

The First Day

"It is with great joy that I hereby close the Mandatory Police record book," wrote an anonymous duty officer at Tel Aviv's central precinct precisely as David Ben-Gurion recited the renascent Jewish state's Declaration of Independence.

Just below that spontaneous hand-inscribed historic annotation appears the first criminal entry ever in sovereign Israel's annals. It documents the capture of a thief. He stole a book, perchance pointing to preferences peculiar to the People of the Book.

Several hours later, the first ship docked in the new state. It began its journey furtively five days earlier in Marseilles when Israel was still under British rule. Its three hundred young passengers were outfitted with fake IDs, forged at the Hagana "laboratory" in France.

But the *Teti* would claim special distinction – it became simultaneously the last "illegal" aliya boat and the first legal one. The counterfeit visas proved superfluous. The vessel proudly hoisted the Israeli flag as the new day dawned. Because it was the Sabbath, the newcomers were issued their new country's entry permits only at sundown.

With such seemingly ordinary bureaucratic yet emotionally charged tasks, the Jewish state adeptly began the business of self-determination. In time, that would be presented to world opinion as inherently sinful. By its very brazen determination to be born, it would be asserted, Israel had displaced the Palestinians, condemning them to miserable refugee subsistence.

According to the Arab narrative, Jewish independence, in and of itself, constitutes aggressive belligerence. Incredibly, this perception sank sinister roots. It takes stronger hold abroad now than it did in 1948. We may speculate why. We may point to two millennia of merciless anti-Jewish hatemongering on religious and other mundanely lucrative grounds. But whatever the motive, our legitimacy, alone among the nations, is assiduously undermined.

Expediently forgotten is the fact that never, not for a single solitary day, were Israelis allowed to savor the elation of their newfound freedom. Behind the aforementioned two matter-of-fact exemplars of sovereignty, a frightening reality festered malevolently.

Israel's birth was legally ordained via the UN partition resolution of November 29, 1947. Two states – Jewish and Arab – were to be established between the Jordan River and the Mediterranean Sea. Jews cheered the patchy territorial crazy-quilt they were accorded, existentially untenable though it was, and proceeded to meet all UN prerequisites for independence. The Arabs vehemently rejected the offer of a Palestinian state and, in vituperative defiance of the UN, set out to destroy the embryonic Jewish state rather than construct one of their own.

On Israel's first day, Arab League Secretary-General Abdul-Rahman Azzam Pasha articulated Arab priorities. Sending forth seven Arab armies to slay the newborn "Zionist entity," he declared: "This will be a war of extermination and a momentous massacre which will be spoken of like the Mongolian massacres and the Crusades." The Arab agenda and intentions were unmistakable. New Israel's citizens harbored no misconceptions.

The Arabs had already violently opposed the Jewish community which existed in this country pre-WWII and which was ripe for statehood before the Holocaust. The "Great Arab Revolt" of 1936–39 – fomented by the still-revered Haj Amin al-Husseini and financed by Nazi Germany – merely delayed Jewish independence. The Arabs denied asylum here to desperate Jewish escapees from Hitler's hell (see "It's Not the Settlements, Stupid"). Thereby they doomed these refugees to death. The blood of numerous Holocaust victims indelibly stains Arab hands.

But that's not all. Husseini, in the role of pan-Arab prime minister, spent the war years in Berlin, where he hobnobbed with Hitler, Himmler, Eichmann, et al. He broadcast Nazi propaganda, recruited Muslims to the SS and actively foiled the rescue of any Jews, even children, during the Holocaust.

The Arabs of this country were avidly pro-Nazi, saluted each other with *"Heil Hitler,"* flaunted the swastika, hoarded arms, harbored German spies, blueprinted an extermination camp near Nablus and planned to heartily welcome Rommel's invading Afrika Korps.

The war that the entire Arab world launched against newborn Israel, three years post-Holocaust, was explicitly geared to complete Hitler's unfinished mission. Not only was there no attempt to camouflage this genocidal goal, but it was broadcast boastfully for all to hear and be intimidated. Clearly Israeli independence was fraught with the most extreme and tangible danger.

Hence no fanfare could conceivably accompany the official inauguration of the state, and with good reason. Acute security anxieties decreed that Israel's Independence would have to be declared almost furtively. If tipped off via advance publicity, the Egyptians were likely to disrupt the ceremony with deadly aerial bombardments.

Thus a veil of secrecy shrouded the intention to proceed with the declaration at 4:00 p.m. on the fifth of the Hebrew month of Iyar, which in 1948 fell on May 14. Tel Aviv had to be the venue because Jerusalem was besieged. The choice of Habima Theater for the purpose was nixed precisely because it would allow for a bigger bash, more honorary guests and more folks potentially prattling.

But fewer participants could be crammed into the undersized auditorium of the Tel Aviv Museum at 16 Rothschild Boulevard, once the home of the city's first mayor, Meir Dizengoff. The matchless historical honor was, therefore, conferred on this most unpretentious address. Mimeographed and unsigned invitations were sent out. Everything was clandestine (though confidentiality was soon breached anyhow). The declaration itself was protected in a basement bank vault lest it be destroyed in enemy air strikes. These indeed came, just hours afterward, at daybreak (of May 15, 1948).

As Israel's masses danced in the streets on the night that followed the declaration of independence, Abdullah I, king of Transjordan (this brainchild of British imperialism now parades under the moniker of the Hashemite Kingdom of Jordan), positioned himself dramatically at the center of Allenby Bridge over the Jordan River. At the stroke of midnight, he pulled his ornate gilded pistol from its holster, held it up in the air and fired to signal the start of the Arab invasion. Its aim was to ethnically cleanse the land – or as it was then phrased none-too-diplomatically, to "throw the Jews into the sea."

Israel's thwarting of the genocide plotted against its people is now presented as a premeditated Israeli-instigated ethnic cleansing of Arabs. The capacity of the human mind to tolerate falsification cannot apparently be underestimated.

The battle plans called for the Jordanian-led Arab Legion, the Iraqis, Syrians and Lebanese to converge on the Jezreel Valley and from there to move in a concerted offensive on Haifa. The Egyptians were assigned to take Tel Aviv from the south, with Yemeni and Saudi participation. But hubris caused deviations. Abdullah coveted Jerusalem and the Syrians focused on the Jordan Valley.

Still, the Arab generals who drew up the blueprints for neonatal Israel's annihilation figured it would take two weeks to complete the job, deviations notwithstanding. They had compelling reason for optimism.

The infant state, assaulted ferociously from every direction and furiously fighting for its very life, possessed no resources or military hardware. Its population of six hundred thousand also comprised the old, the infirm and the very young – all hardly combat worthy.

But these noncombatants nevertheless became the enemy's primary targets. For three days, from May 15, Tel Aviv was mercilessly bombed by the Egyptian Air Force.

Spitfires swooped down on the very section of Tel Aviv where the *Teti* was moored. The first aerial pounding lasted three days. Its worst came on May 18 when the Central Bus Terminal was bombarded, killing forty-one civilians in only that one incident, wounding hundreds of others, inflicting severe damage in the heart of town and even hitting Tel Aviv's beloved one double-decker bus.

The Egyptian planes were back two days later. They would hound

Tel Aviv well into late July. Fifty Tel Avivians were killed between July 13 and 16. Hadassah Hospital was among the targets, as were queues of shoppers – housewives and children. Even the Red Cross, never too friendly to Jews or to Israel, complained about "indiscriminate bombing of non-military targets."

Hot on the heels of independence, the makeshift Israel Air Force challenged Egyptian pilots for supremacy of the skies. This, despite the fact that the IAF was assembled from an improvised mishmash of light civilian aircraft requisitioned from or contributed by their owners and precariously adapted for military purposes.

A curious assortment of outmoded and surplus WWII planes – as well as prewar antiques – were additionally acquired, mostly from Czechoslovakia. Israel's air fleet was more than anything powered by ingenuity and sheer pluck – like the rest of the IDF.

Tel Aviv's attraction of the 1940s, a double-decker bus, destroyed by Egyptian bombers during an attack on the city's central bus terminal in which forty-one people were killed

Because its ragtag army stood its ground, despite the worst of odds, Israel is today accused of the crime of surviving and is portrayed as a menacing ogre for having dared to come into the world rather than surrender.

But it wasn't without a terrifying price. Besides the hundreds of Tel Aviv's casualties, the entire country bled profusely. The Old City of Jerusalem fell to Abdullah's legionnaires on May 29 (the 1967 Israeli reversal of the Jordanian conquest is now dubbed "occupation"). The attempts to open the bottleneck blockade on the road to Jerusalem at Latrun loomed as young Israel's most painful failure of the War of Independence.

The British had turned their hilltop Taggart Fort at that crucial junction over to the Arabs, who used it to besiege Jerusalem with an eye to emptying West Jerusalem too of its Jews.

When the War of Independence was finally over a year and a half later, Israel mourned six thousand dead, a full 1 percent of the fledgling state's population. But perhaps the most tragic sacrifice – alas, hardly atypical for that era – was epitomized by the *Teti*'s passengers. Many of them gave their lives for their country just one week after arriving on that fateful first day of independence.

The next morning they made their way to the encampment at Tel Aviv's Kiryat Meir (at the end of today's Zeitlin Street), where they enlisted in the IDF. Most – fresh off the boat, with Holocaust horrors still fresh in their minds – ended up in the Alexandroni Brigade and Division 7, which were dispatched to Latrun. The battlefield training they received consisted of a few instructions, generally incoherent to them, on the way to the front line.

What's That about Daughters?

Can the world offer a sympathetic hearing to a group that claims divine rights to annihilate an entire nation? Apparently so.

Hamas is increasingly indulged by self-acclaimed forward thinkers who might not relish being reminded that the Hamas Charter's first section opens with the blunt assertion that "Israel will rise and will remain erect until Islam eliminates it as it had eliminated its predecessors."

And lest anyone pooh-pooh this, Hamas anchors its Jew-revulsion in the Koran: "Ignominy shall be their [the Jews'] portion wheresoever they are found.... They have incurred anger from their Lord, and wretchedness is laid upon them.... They disbelieved the revelations of Allah, and slew the Prophets wrongfully.... They were rebellious and transgressed" (Surat al-Imran 3:109–11).

This is no trifling lip service which Western postmodernists so blithely belittle. Dissidence is deemed heresy in Muslim dominions and heresy exacts pitiless retribution, as the Hamas Charter indeed warns: "Whoever denigrates the Hamas movement's worth, or avoids supporting it, or is so blind as to dismiss its role, is challenging Fate itself. Whoever closes his eyes from seeing the facts, whether intentionally or not, will wake up to find himself overtaken by events, and will find no excuses to justify his position."

Hamas isn't about amicable accommodation. It "strives to raise the banner of Allah over *every inch of Palestine*." Moreover, calling itself a "humane movement," Hamas stipulates that "safety and security can only prevail under the shadow of Islam.... Members of other religions must desist from struggling against Islam...for if they were to gain the upper hand, fighting, torture and uprooting would follow."

Clearly it's Hamas's way or the highway. But few Obama administration stalwarts or EU pontificators will let Hamas's own covenant prevent them from making nice to Allah's fearsome warriors. It's the hottest trend sweeping through the West's chic "nonjudgmental" classes.

It's a pattern that replicates itself. The international community can't wait to whitewash, exonerate, find extenuating excuses for and otherwise legitimize Arab terrorists, lessen their culpability, conceal their ideology, make light of their record, explain away their sins and in general gloss over their proven malice.

It began with Fatah and has now, incredibly, moved on to Hamas. The process is similar. The terrorists' prime victim (Israel) is demonized to provide pretexts for targeting it and to create a pervasive premise whereby the victim deserves any and all misfortunes. Concomitantly, the terrorists begin to carry out some of their more repugnant operations under other names and covers.

This enables them to feign innocence, when it so suits them, and appear to all and sundry as nothing less than the actual moderating forces in the arena, as quasi-good guys, and as suitable interlocutors who are overall deserving of understanding.

Some of the worst Fatah atrocities were perpetrated over the years under mutating monikers that took the heat off the chief conspirators. These embedded in the popular mind surrogate nasties like Tanzim or al-Aqsa Martyrs' Brigades, to say nothing of associate PLO gangs that shared some of the dirty load and helped obfuscate the guilt.

Hamas has gained prodigious expertise in pulling off the same sort of brazen deception. It occasionally slaughters under different guises and on other occasions it merely allows associates to carry out hits.

These associates – like Islamic Jihad – are fully tolerated and allowed a free hand. When Hamas doesn't stomach any particular faction, there's no mistaking its terrifying animus. Gaza's ultra-extreme Salafists have tasted it on more than one occasion in ferocious raids and executions which didn't spare wives, children or elderly parents. Salafist mosques weren't accorded the status of sacrosanct sanctuaries, either.

Therefore, when Islamic Jihad barrages southern Israel for days on end with assorted missiles, mortars and whatnot, there's no escaping the conclusion that it has obtained Hamas's green light to do so.

The sham allows Hamas to parade as at least semi-reasonable. It allows assorted self-professed good souls the world over (along with their eager leftist echoes inside Israel) to agitate openly for a rethink on Hamas, for conferring respectability upon it, for treating it as a bona fide negotiating partner, for trying to cut deals with it, for seeking coexistence with Gaza's warlords.

Poignant hand-wringing about Gaza's fictitious humanitarian plight was from the outset geared to generate compassion for Hamastan. Hence Israel's defensive blockade to foil gunrunning to the Strip was censured as a brutal siege against helpless civilians trapped in a virtual concentration camp.

This falsehood is recycled as an axiomatic truth, and human rights advocates have become the staunchest defenders of fanatics who disdain the very sentimental broadmindedness they exploit to bamboozle polite Western society.

The address by a Hamas emissary at a function facilitated by the UN Human Rights Council in Geneva provides one example of creeping acceptance of Hamas internationally. The UNHRC, of course, embodies the cynical skewing of august values and the deliberate deformation of rights-based discourse. But penchants for sugarcoating Hamas extend beyond this discredited forum.

Chocolate-box Switzerland, where UNHRC is ensconced, is a cogent case in point. A Hamas delegation visited Geneva to attend a session of the Inter-Parliamentary Union, which purportedly fosters dialogue between parliaments in a bid to promote "peace and cooperation among peoples" and "the firm establishment of representative democracy."

Invoking its hallowed neutrality, Switzerland doesn't list Hamas as a terrorist organization and accordingly admitted its hotshots without any reservation.

Also on Hamas's Swiss itinerary was a university conference organized by the Geneva-based Droit Pour Tous (Right for All) NGO to mark Operation Cast Lead's third anniversary. Mushir al-Masri, who represented Hamas, insisted that "Hamas never attacks civilians." Thereafter al-Masri and his cohort Khamis al-Najjar chummily hobnobbed with Swiss politicians in the capital, Bern.

Al-Masri described his talks as geared to stress "the need for openness and positive engagement with Hamas by Switzerland and European countries, because Hamas is open to Europe."

His junket to Switzerland coincided with reports of contacts between Hamas chief Khaled Mashaal and Swiss Middle East envoy Jean-Daniel Ruch in the framework of efforts to "normalize relations with European governments."

"Switzerland has regular contacts with Hamas which stem from its traditional policy of dialogue, in particular over conflict resolution, respect for human rights and international humanitarian law," asserted Swiss Foreign Ministry spokeswoman Carole Wälti.

Such sanctimony raises two possibilities. Perhaps Switzerland (along with plenty of other European states, exhibiting varying degrees of disingenuousness) knows what Hamas is but just doesn't really give a hoot. A kinder alternative is that the Swiss don't quite know what Hamas preaches (or don't wish to burden their selective conscience with excess information – as per precedents from Third Reich days about other genocidal harangues).

That said, it's easy to gain enlightenment. Anyone who peruses Hamas's own charter won't encounter a conspicuous predisposition for compromise. Palestine, declares Hamas, "has been an Islamic Waqf throughout the generations and until the Day of Resurrection, no one can renounce it or part of it, or abandon it or part of it. No

Arab country nor the aggregate of all Arab countries, and no Arab King or President nor all of them in the aggregate, have that right."

There's more: "So-called peaceful solutions, and international conferences to resolve the Palestinian problem, are all contrary to the beliefs of the Islamic Resistance Movement. For renouncing any part of Palestine means renouncing part of the religion." The charter's unequivocal position is that "there is no solution to the Palestinian problem except by Jihad."

Anyone familiar with *Mein Kampf* will discover kindred insinuations about the insidious forces of "International Judaism." Jews, avers the Hamas Charter, citing the infamous fake *Protocols of the Elders of Zion* as proof, are the instigators of all strife on this planet: "There was no war that broke out anywhere without their fingerprints on it."

Get a load of Hamas historiography: Jews "stood behind the French and Communist Revolutions and behind most all revolutions.... They also used money to establish clandestine organizations...to destroy societies and carry out Zionist interests. Such organizations are: the Freemasons, Rotary Clubs, Lions Clubs, B'nai B'rith, etc. All of them are destructive spying organizations."

Nobody, contends the Hamas Charter, disputes that Jews "stood behind WWI, so as to wipe out the Islamic Caliphate.... Jews established the League of Nations in order to rule the world by means of that organization. They also stood behind WWII.... They inspired the establishment of the UN and the Security Council to replace the League of Nations, in order to rule the world by their intermediary."

Lavishing liberal love on Gaza won't do the trick because Hamas is leery of do-gooders who come with "publicity and movies, curricula of education and culture, using as their intermediaries their craftsmen who are part of the various Zionist Organizations which take on all sorts of names and shapes such as the Freemasons, Rotary Clubs, gangs of spies and the like. All of them are nests of saboteurs and sabotage."

Of more immediate concern is the charter's reminder to "every Muslim that when the Jews occupied Holy Jerusalem in 1967 and stood at the doorstep of the Blessed Aqsa Mosque, they shouted with joy: Muhammad is dead, he left daughters behind."

Sounds nuts? You didn't cheer Muhammad's demise in '67? You don't know anybody who did so at the Temple Mount? You can't imagine any Jew chanting such bizarre claptrap upon returning to the Jewish Holiest of Holies? You suspect this must be a loony gag?

And what's all this about daughters?

What strike us as demented ravings constitute calumny and incitement that tug hard at cultural chords deep inside Hamastan. But precisely because we're so utterly baffled by them, they underscore the gaping psychological and intellectual chasms which most likely cannot be bridged no matter how much we try to suck up to Gaza's Muslim Brotherhood offshoot.

The Hamas Charter's own bottom line for the above inscrutable gibberish about Muhammad's daughters leaves no room for doubt: "Israel, by virtue of its being Jewish and of having a Jewish population, defies Islam and the Muslims." Need any more be said?

The German "Robbed Cossack"

In 1903 Shalom Aleichem, the giant of Yiddish literature, wrote a letter to Leo Tolstoy, the giant of Russian literature. It was shortly after the gruesome Kishinev pogrom. Shalom Aleichem planned to publish a modest literary compilation whose proceeds would be earmarked to aid the dispossessed victims of the atrocity.

He asked Tolstoy to write a foreword in the shape of a brief message to "Russia's millions of distraught and disoriented Jews, who more than anything need a word of comfort." Tolstoy never so much as bothered to reply.

The famed novelist, fêted as the conscience of Russia, received dozens of such letters urging him to speak out against the slaughters, then a seminal trauma in Jewish annals. The Holocaust was decades away. Nobody over a century ago could imagine anything more bloodcurdling than the horrors of Kishinev. But not everyone was moved – not even a renowned humanitarian like Tolstoy. Not only did he not speak out, but he resented the entreaties.

He replied to one Jewish correspondent only, Emanuel Grigorievich Linietzky, to whom he caustically complained about being pestered. Tolstoy then blamed the czar's government, absolving the masses who bashed the skulls of babies, gouged children's eyes, raped their mothers and sisters, eviscerated them, beheaded men and boys, quartered and mutilated them and looted all they could carry.

We hear much the same throughout Europe at each memorial to the Holocaust. The upgraded, systemized, gargantuan-scale German sequel to Kishinev was by all accounts committed by unidentified extraterrestrials called Nazis. All the others, Germans included, were their victims.

But Tolstoy foreshadowed an even more sinister inclination that would fully and hideously burst upon our scene many decades after the Kishinev devastation. The great author and icon of compassion exhorted Russia's shaken Jews to behave better.

The implication was that the Jews were somehow guilty, needed to improve themselves and achieve higher virtue in order to merit better treatment.

And so wrote Tolstoy to Emanuel Grigorievich: "The Jews must, for their own good, conduct themselves by the universal principle of 'do unto others as you would have them do to you.' They must resist the government nonviolently...by living lives of grace, which precludes not only violence against others, but also the partaking in acts of violence."

Given the background of Eastern Europe's downtrodden Jewry, such "turn-the-other-cheek" sermons appear chillingly pitiless (to say the least) because all the Jews had been doing was turning the other cheek. Taken in a broader context, Tolstoy argued against Jewish self-defense before any self-defense was actually attempted. Jews, Tolstoy in effect said, share culpability for their tribulations, must suffer quietly and cannot rise to protect themselves.

Sounds familiar? It ought to. It's exactly what we keep hearing today from current preachers of goodwill, literary or otherwise. The more things change, the more they sickeningly stay the same.

Enter Günter Grass. Germany's Nobel laureate for literature has alerted the world to the danger which the Jewish state poses to global peace and warned that little Israel is out to no less than exterminate the Iranian people, all eighty million of them. It doesn't matter that we – including even the loopiest left-wingers on the outermost fringes of our political spectrum – know that this is utter drivel.

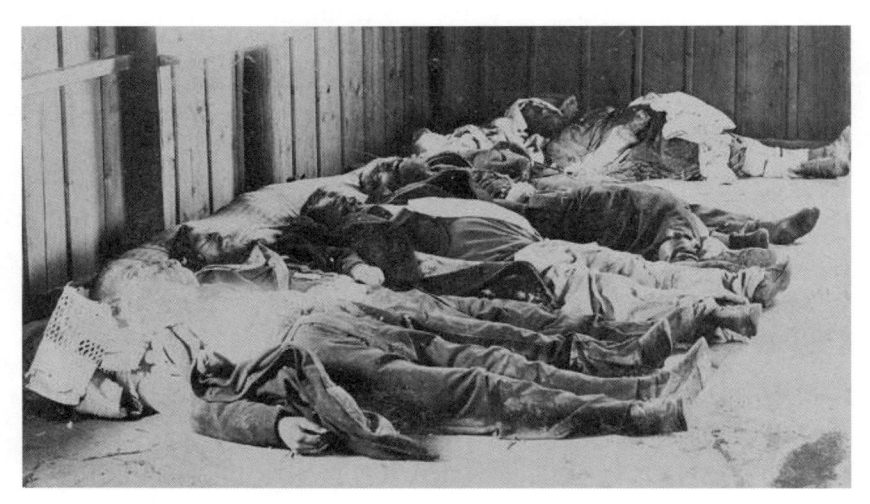

Victims of the Kishinev pogrom

The last thing on any Israeli's mind is annihilating Iranians. We only want to make sure that they don't nuke our tiny über-vulnerable national home. Too much to ask? When it comes to Jews, anything is apparently too much.

This is particularly pertinent for us in the springtime of the year, when we collectively remember the six million who perished in the very Holocaust in which Grass, by his own candid admission, was an enthusiastic accomplice – as distinct from a coerced conscript, not to mention a conscientious objector. But his stained personal history clearly constitutes no incentive to discreet reticence on his part. Like many Europeans, Grass has lost all shame and the disappearance of shame is the new bon ton among like-minded genteel Jew-haters.

It's politically incorrect to even accuse Grass of thinly disguised anti-Semitism. That instantly turns him into the muzzled good guy and us into loathsome Jews seeking to silence yet another legitimate critic of Israel with their doomsday weapon: charges of anti-Semitism. Moreover, any remote reference to the Holocaust is sure to elicit howls of derision.

This diabolical yet prevalent deformation of perceptions confers on all anti-Semites the freedom to slander, while denying Jews the right to call a spade a spade.

It's a foolproof arrangement. Jew-revulsion now masquerades behind acutely inflammatory anti-Israel and pro-Arab propaganda, whose disseminators inevitably deny anti-Semitic motives. Their favorite ploy is to present Israel-bashing as just deserts for the Jewish state's policies.

Post-Holocaust circumspection has bred cleverly camouflaged anti-Semitism – not less dangerous or less in-your-face but more cunning and deceptive. Most contemporary anti-Semites are remarkably practiced in accompanying their invective with instant disclaimers, by now an expected part of the pattern.

Grass is extraordinarily true to form.

Indeed, he already gets star billing on a host of Judeophobic websites, which celebrate him as yet another upstanding and righteous critic of Israel, an honorable observer pilloried as an anti-Semite in order to suppress his heartfelt outcry.

Thus Grass becomes the ultimate robbed Cossack in a rationalized German adaptation of the infamous Russian tradition. Anti-Semites – whether they specialized in mere pogroms or outright Holocausts – habitually portrayed themselves as the aggrieved side.

Robbed Cossack Grass actually volunteered for the barbarous Waffen-SS (branded a "criminal organization" at the Nuremberg Trials). But what of it? He has put it all behind him, wiped his own slate clean and now feels empowered to launch anti-Jewish diatribes at will. Professing to have propelled himself to a loftier leftist plane, he can reproach the Jews and, like Tolstoy before him, demand they do nothing to defend themselves.

If they do intransigently opt for self-defense, they become, in Grass's idiom, "the greatest danger to the world." It's Israel that threatens Iran and not vice versa. By his criteria, our forebears threatened Egypt's pharaohs, the Amalekites, the Assyrians, the Babylonians, Haman's Persians, Greeks, Romans, Crusader marauders, Muslim conquistadors, Spanish inquisitors, Chmielnicki's Ukrainian mass murderers, Russian pogromchiks, to say nothing of the Germans, whose führer always screamed hysterically about the danger posed to the world by "the forces of International Judaism," compelling him to formulate a "final solution" to their problem.

Fallacies of the sort which spawned the worst tragedies that befell our nation are still promulgated passionately today. An unbroken chain of lies links the hounding of Jews throughout the ages, rendering flagrant fabrications, like Grass's, ever pertinent.

With mounting disbelief we witness world callousness toward the Jewish state that arose against all odds from the ashes of that great Holocaust conflagration. It's beyond our grasp that we are vilified while supposed advocates of justice and seekers of peace cosset Arab/Muslim torchbearers of Nazi genocide.

We can't comprehend the hypocrisy. We can't understand how assorted glitterati and literati perennially postulate that those who strive to continue what the Nazis failed to finish are actually the "victims' victims." Europe loves to regard Israelis as victimizers and sympathize with "victimized" Arabs/Iranians/Muslims.

A German friend, Josef H., notes that official reactions in his country to Grass's diatribe "were 99 percent negative." Nevertheless, he writes, "I admit that I very rarely meet people who feel that they have to stand up for Israel when Israeli-Palestinian problems are mentioned. So I normally abstain from using the word 'Israel' in any conversation in order not to set fire to explosive material."

Josef asked a member of his own extended family what he thought of the Grass imbroglio. The relative, Josef relates, "a really decent, reliable, honest man, generally following Christian principles… answered, without thinking twice about it: 'Grass is right.'"

Such is the climate of opinion around him that Josef requested I not reveal his surname. Significantly, to his mind, Grass echoes his fervent Nazi past, deeply rooted in his psyche.

Grass isn't the only Nobel literature laureate of such a mindset. Some, like Britain's Rudyard Kipling, didn't even wax indignant pro forma when accused of anti-Semitism. Kipling unflinchingly blamed the 1917 Bolshevik Revolution on an "international Jewish plot." In 1919 he backed the publication in the UK of *The Protocols of the Elders of Zion*.

In 1920 Kipling agreed only conditionally to read proofs of the memoirs of T. E. Lawrence (Lawrence of Arabia) prepublication, vowing to return them if he finds them "pro-Yid."

Kipling dismissed Einstein's general theory of relativity as a component of a comprehensive Jewish conspiracy to destabilize world order.

It didn't matter that it wasn't so. It doesn't matter that every Jew knows there's no Jewish world-domination conspiracy. What matters is that the Kiplings and their ilk expressed the zeitgeist of their day, just as Grass now does – regardless of whether his country's establishment sanctions his opinion.

The fashionable, respectable anti-Semitism of European intellectual salons in the early twentieth century made the Nazi persecutions of Jews palatable. The fashionable, respectable anti-Israelism of European intellectual salons in the early twenty-first century makes Ahmadinejad's calls for our extinction palatable.

And above all hovers Tolstoy's sanctimonious spirit, which hints that our misconduct is the root cause of our misfortune.

Obama of the Open Mic

"The tongue weighs practically nothing," notes the anonymous aged adage, "but so few folks can hold it."

Some supercilious sorts don't even seem to try too hard – like American president Barack Obama, given to remarkable and repetitive chattiness when he's precariously near open microphones. He is so accident-prone, in fact, that we're forced to deduce that he personifies that most rare of hybrids – the *schlemiel* and *schlimazel* rolled into one.

Yiddish clearly distinguishes between the two categories of klutziness. The schlimazel is the one on whom soup is spilled, while the schlemiel is the one who spills it. The uncommon confluence of bad luck and clumsiness leaves one and the same character suffering embarrassment while serving as the instrument of his own embarrassment.

It's bad enough that Obama chooses to make nice to foreign headliners and disclose to them defeatist strategies – the sort he cultivates secretly and most certainly shouldn't want exposed to all and sundry. However, if the penchant to resort to such manipulative candor cannot be overcome, it should – one would think – be best practiced behind closed doors.

Obama's predilection to prattle in the vicinity of plugged-in sound equipment either denotes extraordinary overconfidence and a smug presumption of invulnerability or is indicative of exceptional foolhardiness.

Whatever it is, Obama is serially careless.

He once chitchatted chummily with French then president Nicolas Sarkozy during the G20 summit in Cannes. "I can't stand him. He's a liar," a chagrined Sarkozy blurted in reference to the man both of them love to loathe – Israel's own prime minister, Binyamin Netanyahu. Word is that Sarkozy's feathers were ruffled because Bibi didn't credit him with Gilad Schalit's release.

Pointedly, Obama not only failed to defend Netanyahu but actually expressed unreserved agreement with his cantankerous interlocutor. "You're fed up with him, but I have to deal with him even more often than you," Obama bellyached.

The trouble was that this frank articulation of unambiguous aversion toward Israel's democratically elected head of government – a staunch ally of America – was inadvertently broadcast to journalists covering the event.

One would imagine that after his on-mic misadventure, Obama would be unable to again pull off the pretense of impartiality. Nonetheless, he audaciously did just that and proceeded to welcome Netanyahu to Washington as his forever bosom buddy. Campaign seasons soften animus – or seem to. Accordingly, Obama spared no effort to convince his Jewish electorate that he's not halfway as sinister as some say.

But when a politician loses fear of amplifiers and visible recording paraphernalia, all sorts of things are bound to spill out. And so at another international conference (the Seoul Nuclear Security Summit) Obama hobnobbed with another leader (outgoing Russian president Dmitri Medvedev) when that darn mic was (unbeknownst to him) switched on.

Thus unawares, Obama exhorted not only the Russian honchos but also the whole listening world not to fall for his electioneering blarney. His subtext was that he's obliged to say one thing pre-election to hustle votes, but that afterwards, if he secures his second term, he'll do another thing entirely.

This is how it went:

> Obama: "On all these issues, but particularly missile defense, this can be solved but it's important for him [Vladimir Putin] to give me space."
> Medvedev: "Yeah, I understand. I understand your message about space. Space for you..."
> Obama: "This is my last election. After my election I have more flexibility."
> Medvedev: "I understand. I will transmit this information to Vladimir."

The Obama-Medvedev banter wasn't Israel-centered. It revolved around America's planned anti-ballistic shield for Europe (mostly against Iranian attack). But Obama's predilection for deception should disconcert us too because likely the same sort of double-dealing is now practiced in regard to Israel's life-and-death perils.

Obama unabashedly establishes that what he promises now isn't how he'd conduct himself in his final term, when the dread of the electorate is lifted from his shoulders. It's not like we didn't infer this, but Obama's admission must intensify our intuitive insights. He indisputably plots his course exactly as we suspect.

Privately – with all the calculated conniving that implies – Obama relayed a message to Medvedev's patron, Russia's once-and-future boss Vladimir Putin, that greater "flexibility" vis-à-vis Kremlin opposition to American missile defenses will follow Obama's reinstatement in the White House. Post-election (when Obama has nothing to lose) he'd be free to cut a deal with the Russians that would have been deadly to his pre-election interests.

Once he's impervious to voter-backlash, Obama in effect suggests to his Muscovite counterpart, he'd be prepared to please the Russians even if he thereby displeases the American people. But he needs a period of grace because the Americans he undertakes to bamboozle are also the very ones whom he'll have to persuade to reelect him.

The purported leader of the Free World no less than offers the most powerful first-hand corroboration of his fecklessness to his prime geopolitical adversaries. Mind you, ex-KGB hotshot Putin wasn't born yesterday. In 2009 Obama terminated the missile defense system for the Poles and Czechs. Obama-esque goodwill, though, went unrequited. Russia helped build Iran's nuclear reactor at Bushehr, stymies anti-Iran sanctions and underpins Syria's Bashar al-Assad.

That said, Obama's latest cozying up to Medvedev represents a whole new twist on appeasement. There's no getting away from the fact that Obama appealed for Putin's forbearance in order to help him win reelection. Putin's payoff would come when second-term President Obama accedes to his demands.

What Medvedev was asked to tip Putin about wasn't supposed to be shared with American voters or overseas allies.

From Obama's words it emerges that he considered it essential that his capitulation to Russian pressure against missile defense development be kept under wraps – for now. Voters, hence, have every right to ask whether there are other surprises Obama might spring if reelected.

In that vein, Jewish voters (those who still care) need to ask whether Obama is being straight with them in his palaver on the Middle East, both as regards Iranian nuke ambitions and Palestinian cynical stonewalling. Obama's pro-Arab/pro-Muslim predilections mustn't escape the scrutiny of American Jews, no matter how knee-jerk liberal most of them invariably are.

If Obama – as the latest flap in Seoul signaled – isn't shooting straight with the American public in general, odds are that he deliberately deludes his Jewish supporters.

Worse than the incredible recklessness of making risky (if not altogether unethical) pitches while wearing a microphone is the blithe manner in which Obama strove to brush the slip-up aside. His flippancy all but screams out that he holds his plebeian voters in thinly disguised contempt.

Even more disconcerting is the fact that he appears to have succeeded in laughing away the incident, as if it constituted no more than an actually endearing indiscretion involving pesky electronic gadgetry. He somehow managed to paper over the shocking content of his overheard conversation – conspiring with an inimical foreign rival behind the backs of his own voters, with an eye to duping these voters.

Hardly much can be more serious than that and potentially more politically disastrous. Still, Obama comes off as immune to what would quash the prospects of other incumbents. Lack of honesty with the voting public – especially when so glaringly exposed – should by logic be catastrophic to his reelection cause. And yet the fallout is barely perceptible, as if Americans refrain from dwelling on the ramifications of clandestine "flexibility" with Russian autocrats.

It's no joke when the leader of the world's sole remaining superpower proposes to placate a hardnosed, pushy competitor who aspires to regain his country's erstwhile superpower status. It's worse when electoral advantage is linked to playing fast and loose with basic security. And it's worst when the president himself is unmistakably heard peddling this shady transaction.

These aren't tendentious leaks from unnamed sources. What was unintentionally imparted to us is as credible as can be, precisely because it wasn't intended for our ears. Truth surfaces when arrogant jabberers let their guard down, feeling free to expound on hidden agendas – expediently hidden for very ulterior motives.

Without much ado, Putin was told that his irresponsible record will be rewarded by more gratuitous pliability from Obama. America's allies everywhere must now be wary in the utmost extreme – and principally so Israel, which is the most threatened and loyal of the allies and in the vanguard of them all. Should Obama win his "last election," we will all have lots to worry about.

No amount of post-gaffe lightheartedness on Obama's part should be allowed to downscale our alarm about his possible reelection.

Jews have every reason to be leery of a second Obama term, after he'll have waged his last campaign, as he himself stressed. Obama's lack of candor regarding Israel has been demonstrated all too often. The above-quoted badmouthing of Netanyahu at Cannes is only one of numerous examples.

And we must always bear in mind that what we overhear by coincidence is surely a negligible fragment of worse utterances to which we never become privy. What the open mic divulges is but an infinitesimal indication of what's said out of our earshot. But that fortuitous tiny tidbit is a fortunate omen because forewarned is forearmed.

We'd better hope this omen robs us of peace of mind – for the sake of our own self-preservation. All bets should now be off because Obama plainly doesn't deserve the benefit of our doubt. Indeed, considering shenanigans such as those he broached to Medvedev, doubt becomes nothing less than mandatory.

Medvedev assured Obama: "I stand with you." His endorsement, though, must elicit the precise opposite from us. In the wise words of playwright Tennessee Williams, "We have to distrust.... It is our only defense against betrayal."

Sabina's Misrepresented Murder

By August 11, 1942, pioneer psychoanalyst Sabina Spielrein must have ditched all illusions about German civility. On that day, she and her daughters – accomplished cellist Renate, twenty-eight, and promising violinist Eva, eighteen – were, like thousands of other horrified Jews, force-marched through the central streets of the Russian city of Rostov-on-Don. They were herded toward Zmievskaya Balka (Snake Gully), where they were soon shot, together with Red Army POWs.

Thus – ignominiously and brutally – ended the tempestuous fifty-seven-year-old life of a strong-willed woman, exceptionally independent and nonconformist for her time. In Western cultural enclaves she's sporadically remembered (in books, plays and films) for her affair with one of the fathers of psychoanalysis, Carl Jung.

It was a big deal back in the early years of the twentieth century, when she lived in Germany, Switzerland and Austria. It was a case of opposites attracting. Jung, an unabashed anti-Semite, was both enticed by the spirited petite and repelled by her Jewishness. She was mesmerized by his Aryan looks and fantasized about a love child in whom the best of the Jewish and Aryan would splendidly combine.

Sigmund Freud, whose great break with Jung was – among

other causes – sparked by this liaison, wrote to Sabina: "You must learn to discern the difference between friends and enemies (I mean Jung)."

In 1911, Sabina had settled down and married a Jewish physician from Russia, Pavel Scheftel. She returned with him to Moscow in 1923 and then moved back to her native Rostov. In 1936 the regime outlawed psychoanalysis, closed down her psychiatric clinic and seized the family's property. Pavel died in 1937 during Stalin's "Great Terror" and Sabina's three brothers, all noted academicians, also perished in those purges.

Sabina Spielrein

When invading Nazi forces occupied Rostov, Sabina said, "I know Germans, they are a civilized nation. They are not capable of evil deeds."

Today astonishingly little is known in her native land about Freud's disciple and the founder of psychoanalysis in Russia. It's as if she never existed. But her elimination from Russian collective memory only underscores Sabina's Jewish lot.

After the Soviet Union's fall, the Russian Jewish Congress put up a plaque commemorating Jewish victims at the Zmievskaya Balka mass grave of twenty-seven thousand – known as Russia's Babi Yar. That plaque was recently removed and arbitrarily replaced with a new marker, which, in the style of the defunct USSR, identifies the dead only as "peaceful citizens of Rostov-on-Don and Soviet prisoners of war."

No rationale is given for why certain Soviet citizens were targeted by the Nazis. Moreover, no mention is made of slain Jewish refugees from Poland, who were decidedly not Soviet citizens. It's as if Jews were never there and none were annihilated because of their Jewishness.

This isn't an instance of localized hardheartedness. It's commonplace throughout the former USSR, and not only in Russia. Its roots reach deep and explain as much about today's Russia as about past Soviet idiosyncrasies and why they still persist.

The Soviets spawned their own singular version of Holocaust denial. They didn't deny the carnage; they merely obfuscated the identity of whom Hitler singled out for systematic extermination.

Thus according to the official Soviet version, there never was specific anti-Jewish butchery in Nazi-ruled Soviet territory. There was heroic resistance against German occupiers, in which Soviet citizens were callously massacred. The distinct Jewish tragedy is obscured by submerging it in the overall wartime narrative (which fails to dwell on the Ribbentrop-Molotov Pact).

Little wonder then that Mahmoud Abbas (Abu Mazen) authored his Holocaust-denial treatise at Moscow's Communist-era Russian University for Friendship between People (aka the People's Friendship University of Russia, aka the Patrice Lumumba Friendship University).

The mendacity lives on. Abbas personally and the Palestinian Authority media he controls consistently glorify terrorist atrocity perpetrators, who with Nazi-like zeal lust after Jewish blood. Palestinian Media Watch, for example, revealed that Abbas's PATV broadcast greetings and praise to the Fogel family's slaughterers, tried and imprisoned in Israel.

Hakim Awad's mother sent "greetings to dear Hakim, the apple of my eye, who carried out the operation in Itamar." His aunt extolled "Hakim Awad, the hero, the legend." The TV host effusively concurred.

On March 11, 2011, Hakim and Amjad Awad invaded the Fogel home in Itamar and knifed to death a father, mother and three youngsters (aged eleven, four and three months). At the time Russian-educated Abbas insisted Arabs were incapable of such bestiality. Yet now Abbas's media turns convicted baby killers into national heroes and role models.

But not only does Soviet-like duplicity endure and thrive in Abbas's latifundia; it takes on sinister incarnations in Russia.

It was convenient at the height of the Cold War to ascribe Moscow's malevolence solely to Communist machinations. But Communism is purportedly gone while Russia tenaciously clings to the wrong side of history, as in its obdurate defense of Damascus despot Bashar Assad and its outright assistance in constructing Iran's nuclear facilities, to say nothing of its ongoing opposition to stringent sanctions against Tehran's ayatollahs.

This calls to mind the USSR's strategy before the June 22, 1941, monstrous German betrayal. Until then, the Russians ensconced themselves firmly on history's wrong side.

Foreign Minister Vyacheslav Molotov applauded the Third Reich's conquest of Warsaw. The German invasions of Denmark and Norway caused him to "wish Germany complete success in these defensive measures." Upon receiving news of the French collapse, Molotov conveyed "the warmest congratulations of the Soviet Government on the splendid success of the German Wehrmacht."

Putin's Russia, despite its quasi-democratic façade, seems to harbor the same wrongheaded great-power aspirations as its Soviet predecessor. These had less to do with exporting communist ideology than with Russian nationalist ambitions.

The plain fact of the matter is that Russia still offers succor to the Jewish people's worst enemies. It emits exceedingly troublesome vibes. It reverts to type – be it in critical geopolitical maneuverings or in just expunging the unique Jewish Holocaust from its chronicles. It's in this inimical ambience that the mass murder of Jews at Zmievskaya Balka can be misrepresented.

Russian parliamentarian Tamara Pletneva condescendingly advises Jews to "forget the bitterness and live in peace.... The memorial should commemorate all the war victims.... So why single out Jews?"

Perhaps because the Nazis singled them out. Despite rampant Plenteva-type portrayals of yesteryear's Jews as incidental victims and of present-day Jews as obsessively parochial, the only reason that

Sabina and millions of fellow ill-fated Jews were put to death was because they were Jews.

In 1913, when Sabina was expecting her first child, Freud wrote her, expressing the hope that the baby "will develop into a stalwart Zionist." He added: "We are and remain Jews. The others will only exploit us and will never understand or respect us."

There is a message here for the Jewish state almost a century later.

With Intent to Deceive

Appearing in Ramallah on the Palestinian Authority's *Shahid* (martyr) Day, Knesset Member Ahmed Tibi proclaimed that "nobody is more admirable than the *shahid*...the ultimate source of pride...the symbol of the homeland...who blazes the trail for us and paves the path to liberty with his blood."

To preempt Israeli backlash, Tibi feigned innocence. The word *shahid*, he averred, means a person "killed by the occupation."

Yet in everyday Arabic, suicide bombers and perpetrators of any bloodcurdling atrocity in Allah's name are popularly dubbed *shahid*s. The Palestinian Authority's media, schools and mosques – all under professed moderate Mahmoud Abbas's control – glorify *shahid*s as models of emulation for all, from pint-sized preschoolers onward.

No Arab harbors doubt about what *shahid* means. Thus Tibi winks to his Arab listeners, who understand him perfectly, while he disingenuously pretends otherwise to us.

Tibi isn't alone. Jerusalem-based Muhammad Hussein, the PA's mufti (appointed by none other than the aforementioned Abbas, aka

Abu Mazen), declared at Abbas's own Fatah faction's forty-seventh anniversary rally in Jerusalem that religious salvation is impossible without first eliminating the Jews. His diatribe, citing the Hadith (sayings attributed to Islam's progenitor Muhammad), was aired January 9 on PATV (controlled by Abbas).

"The Hour [of Resurrection] will not come until you fight the Jews," Hussein railed. "The Jew will hide behind stones or trees. Then the stones or trees will call: 'O Muslim, servant of Allah, there is a Jew behind me, come and kill him.'"

But Hussein, who frequently refers to Jews as "Allah's foes" and as "decedents of monkeys and pigs," subsequently feigned innocence, insisting he was just quoting holy texts, which alas, "cannot be changed as they're sacrosanct, noble and oblige every Muslim."

The logical conclusion is that killing Jews is a hallowed religious commandment. As inveterate democrats, therefore, we cannot interfere with Hussein's freedom of worship and assorted democratic rights.

Ditto for a whole host of Arab MKs, who enjoy all the Jewish state's parliamentary perks, especially the freedom to thumb their noses at us in ways that wouldn't be tolerated anywhere – certainly not in post–Arab spring Muslim strongholds, nor even in any Western democracy, never mind one embattled and struggling for survival.

Foremost among these MKs is Haneen Zoabi. She hobnobbed with Hamas leaders, praised them to the hilt, participated in the *Mavi Marmara* provocation of 2010, partied with terrorists released in the Schalit swap and authored an inflammatory foreword to vehement Israel basher Ben White's latest book, *Palestinians in Israel: Segregation, Discrimination and Democracy*. There she castigates Israel as a "colonialist racist project." She explicitly applauds exploiting "the power inherent in democracy to undermine the moral and political legitimacy of Israel."

Her previous pearls of wisdom include: "A Jewish state leads to the end of democracy"; "The largest threat to Zionism is democracy"; and "to demand full civic and national equality is actually to demand the end of Zionism. So we don't hate Zionism. Zionism hates democracy."

Zoabi feigns innocence as a promoter of democracy. Her bottom line is that the disappearance of Israel as a Jewish state is democracy's praiseworthy, progressive objective. To oppose said objective is undemocratic.

Thus democracy is successfully assaulted by using the democratic idiom against it. Democrats fear raising a ruckus lest they be admonished for not being as self-destructively democratic as cynical anti-democrats oblige them to be. Willy-nilly, democrats turn into timid accomplices in their own destruction.

In 1946 George Orwell wrote an essay, "Politics and the English Language," in which he highlighted the abuse of political terminology.

"The word *Fascism* has now no meaning," he noted, "except in so far as it signifies 'something not desirable.' The words *democracy, socialism, freedom, patriotic, realistic, justice* have each of them several different meanings which cannot be reconciled with one another.... Statements like 'Marshal Pétain was a true patriot', 'The Soviet press is the freest in the world', 'The Catholic Church is opposed to persecution', are almost always made with intent to deceive."

Zoabi, Tibi, Hussein and other fellow upholders of their democratic rights to bay for our blood indeed all make ostensibly innocuous noises "with intent to deceive."

More than it attests to our devotion to democracy, the fact that we keep tolerating Tibi and crew for so long attests to angst about being judged by our enemies as not suicidally democratic enough. Needless to stress, this aberration undermines Israel's survival prospects – physical as well as democratic.

The incitement we stomach drives a dynamic. It radicalizes the Arab street within Israel proper. Radical anti-Zionism begets more radical anti-Zionism. Radical candidates radicalize their electorate,

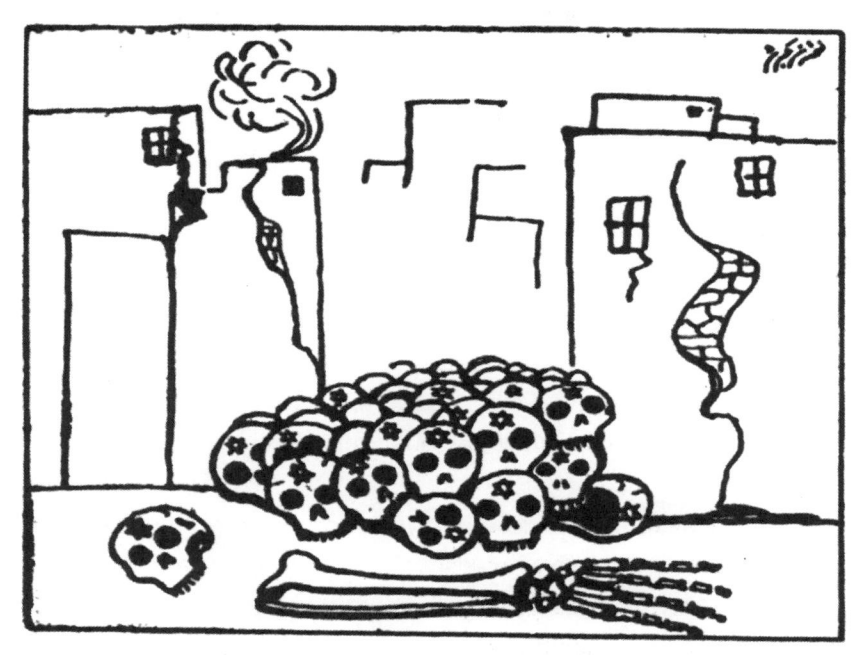

Genocidal sentiments inspired ghoulish political cartoons rampant in Arab journals on the Six-Day War's eve – this one from Syria is captioned "The Barricades of Tel Aviv."

which in turn makes radical rhetoric an indispensable vote-getter in the Arab sector. This vicious cycle hinges on our broadmindedness.

While we effuse self-congratulation for our exceptionally enlightened liberalism, a momentum that exploits our liberality agitates for our extinction. Our forbearance confers legitimacy upon it.

The mufti who merely quoted his prophet's exhortation to slay us won't be indicted. He won't be pilloried as was once-obscure rabbi Yitzhak Shapira, whose esoteric booklet on rules of warfare, *Torat Hamelech*, catapulted him to notoriety. Only Jews are censured.

Consistently, we play along with our worst enemies by abetting their slander merely to look liberal. This makes Jew-revulsion the badge of open-mindedness, justly deserving of protection under the right of free expression.

Conversely, Jewish resentment of anti-Jewish hate becomes uncool fascist muzzling of honorable opponents of fascism. The very term *anti-Semitic* is no longer politically correct because no one is quicker than anti-Semites to deny anti-Semitic motives.

They bristle with righteous indignation at the very suggestion that hating us might imply anti-Semitism. Heaven forefend we foolhardily stray into that semantic minefield. Equally rash is to dare bring up the Holocaust. That invariably occasions Judeophobic jeers which discomfit us.

Also to be avoided is reference to any of the ghastly massacres perpetrated by Arabs against Jews throughout the twentieth century. Numerous horrific episodes occurred before there even was Jewish sovereignty to fulminate against, to say nothing of the "occupation" that resulted from the 1967 war.

The Arabs instigated that war in order, as they said (back then without sly verbal artifice), to eradicate us, throw us into the sea, pulverize us to dust, incinerate us to ashes, reduce us to skeletal remains that would litter the *judenrein* streets of Tel Aviv.

Genocidal sentiments inspired ghoulish political cartoons rampant in Arab journals on the Six-Day War's eve. That, however, was when our would-be annihilators fully expected victory, before they were thwarted and thereupon pronounced themselves pitiable, hapless victims without an unkind thought among them.

But such reminiscences are so yesterday, uncool and politically incorrect. The prevailing bon ton behooves us to erase from mind any memory of Arabs plotting genocide in 1967.

It's patently indecorous in polite society to mention that the Arabs – far from being victims – were the aggressors, that they still are, that they feign innocence, that they pose as democracy's champions with intent to deceive.

Good Manners and High Morals

There sat Palestinian Authority chieftain Mahmoud Abbas in the front pew of the Church of the Nativity, reverently observing the Christmas midnight mass. He appeared so meek – the model of admirable moderation, good manners and high morals.

TV anchors and scribblers worldwide fell for his consummate act and expressed solemn appreciation for the affectation. Critical appraisal was conspicuously absent.

Abbas – the on-and-off and now on-again political ally of Hamas and Islamic Jihad – took great pains to quasi-usurp Christmas from Christendom and impart the impression that Christmas is intrinsically also a Muslim celebration, "a Palestinian holiday" from which bogeymen Jews alone deserve exclusion.

Significantly, this aroused no protests – the subjugation of Christians in Muslim societies and foremost in Bethlehem notwithstanding.

This supposed Christian-Muslim front comprised the gist of the homily delivered by the Middle East's most senior Roman Catholic, patriarch of Jerusalem Fuad al-Tuwal, a Jordanian Arab.

He effusively welcomed Abbas, congratulating him for "his unfaltering efforts to achieve a just peace in the Middle East, a main thrust of which is the creation of a Palestinian state." The patriarch commiserated with the Palestinians, who "turned to the UN in the hope of finding a just solution." According to his monologue, "they were asked to reengage in a failed peace process," which "has left a bitter taste of broken promises and of mistrust."

And guess who embittered the pitiable Palestinians? Guess who cast a dark, sinister shadow over their Muslim Christmas? Those Jews, of course. Who else?

Living up to the ecclesiastical hype, Abbas wished the worshippers "love and peace" and, presumably in that spirit, proceeded to slam

Jewish settlements as "immoral and indefensible.... I wish for the Palestinian people that next year will be the year that peace will be implemented in the occupied Palestinian lands," he said. "We, my brothers, believe in peace and are working to implement peace."

Had any further elucidation been needed about his concept of peace, Abbas furnished it pre-Christmas, when traveling to Ankara to shower affection upon the convicted terrorists deported to Turkey as part of the Gilad Schalit swap.

Outstanding among them was Amna Muna – tangible proof that evil can come in attractive guises. Abbas hugged her warmly and sat down for a chummy chat, not to mention his hefty financial reward.

Muna was actually supposed to be released into Gaza, but refused, citing her secularism as problematic in the Hamas fiefdom. In actual fact, though, she feared retribution.

This insolently unrepentant and most aggressive despot of the women's prison security wing tortured noncompliant fellow inmates, by, among other means, pouring boiling oil and wax on them.

Muna and Abbas (PATV)

Turkey was understandably her preferred destination. She now plies the school lecture circuit there, vowing to return to active "combat against the Zionists" and exhorting pupils to become *shahid*s (martyrs).

Muna – for those who forgot – is the fetching Fatah operative who via Internet contact lured sixteen-year-old Ophir Rahum to a cruel death on January 17, 2001. In a way, her atrocity is even more gruesome than the more common forms of Arab-inspired carnage. She might not have claimed as many lives as some of her compatriots, but what she did was spine-chillingly upfront and personal.

She schemed to get her hands on a Jewish kid, chose her victim with coldblooded deliberation, falsely befriended him and lured him in a premeditated hunting expedition that began long before twenty AK-47 bullets riddled Ophir's young body.

The homicide was meticulously and maliciously plotted and executed painstakingly, over months, in scrupulously calculated phases, to wrest an unsuspecting boy from his protective environment and trick him to a rendezvous with a hail of bullets.

Ophir yearned to make love, not war. He embodied the shared Israeli dream of peace and bliss. With stars in his eyes, he was enticed. He wanted to believe the pretty decoy who flirted with him, the sly impostor who posed as "Sally."

The striking seductress arranged to meet the smitten schoolboy. He traveled from Ashkelon to Jerusalem; she picked him up at the bus stop and drove him away. Eventually, her accomplices shot his kneecaps and she, as per her own crowing account, stood there, taunting him and cackling mirthfully as he screamed in pain before being put to death. She still often derisively mimics his last cries.

One would expect that Abbas, fêted abroad as the prince of moderation, would at least wash his hands of murderous Muna and condemn her unequivocally. Instead, this supposed man of peace has made Muna his Ramallah regime's poster child – the object of reverence and compassion, the model for emulation.

That speaks volumes because the lionized icon's underlying moral code inevitably characterizes the collective which sponsors and supports her.

The Turkish get-together wasn't Abbas's first public embrace for Muna. It wasn't inadvertent, nor an isolated, inconsequential political gesture. It was preceded by accolades aplenty.

In 2008, for instance, Abbas handpicked five female recipients for the PLO's highest medal of heroism, the al-Quds Mark of Honor. All the women he named were then behind Israeli bars. This was touted as "a humanitarian gesture," geared to highlight their "sacrifice and suffering as Israel's captives, to raise their morale and pay tribute to them."

The five included Ahlam Tamimi, pivotal in the August 9, 2001, atrocity at Jerusalem's Sbarro pizzeria. She escorted the suicide bomber to the eatery where he killed fifteen persons, including seven children and five members of a single family. Muna too starred among Abbas's designated heroines.

Predictably, the international community made no fuss about Abbas's choices. Neither did Israel's own left wing.

Apparently, when chronic peaceniks have nobody to appoint as their interlocutor, they pretend that the hypothetical lesser evil is humanity's great hope for the greater good.

Yet by paying lavish homage to child slayers, Abbas endorses terror and escalates Palestinian psychological warfare, which – in order to manipulatively tug at the heartstrings of progressive do-gooders – camouflages mass murderers as prisoners of conscience, persecuted altruists and vindictively incarcerated political philosophers.

Abbas cunningly postures as Israel's hapless victim, as a saint on the side of the angels, indeed as a victim of terrorism rather than its devious promoter. His heart is artlessly in the right place. He seeks to do the right thing – which he would sincerely do, were it not for those obstructionist Israelis.

Doesn't Abbas, after all, respectfully promise on every occasion to quell incitement within his latifundia?

Seemingly in the enlightened vanguard of the global good-guy brigade, Abbas convinces willingly gullible saps of what they're anyway predisposed to imbibe. The watching world voluntarily laps up Abbas's fabrications and encouragingly promotes the PA figurehead's deception.

However, the inescapable subtext of glorifying Muna is that her crime is Abbas's true ideal – his prescription for all Israelis. In a better world this truth wouldn't be eclipsed by the sanctimonious chatter of the charming charlatan, seemingly spellbound by Christmas in the Church of the Nativity.

Muna is the benchmark of popular Palestinian intentions toward all Israelis. That's why Abbas acclaims her malevolence instead of denouncing it, instead of beating his own breast for sanctioning and commissioning her bloodlust.

Banana Noses and Freckles

Back in junior high I had a classmate called Patty Christie, better known to her peers as Cookie. She was big, plumpish and her ruddy baby face was often conspicuously plastered with makeup, to the strident displeasure of our homeroom teacher.

One day Cookie announced assertively that "all Jews have banana noses." Uninitiated in the irrationalism of stereotyping, I rose to the defense of our tribe: "Oh, yeah? How come my nose isn't like that?" Cookie shot back without hesitation: "'Coz you're not Jewish."

"Yes, I am," I replied defiantly.

"No, you're not," she insisted. "You got freckles."

I was stumped and all I could come up with was, "Huh, what's that got to do with anything?"

I found myself asking that very same question, with as much bewilderment, after the current White House resident informed the whole world about his daughter Malia's busy schedule on the bar/bat mitzvah circuit. That was somehow supposed to prove that Obama is the most pro-Israel president ever, endear him to American-Jewish hearts and win him political support, campaign contributions and crucial votes.

But, as with Cookie's kooky argumentation, I couldn't find the connection.

Malia's dad pulled out all the stops when appearing at the Union for Reform Judaism Biennial in Maryland. His cliché-ridden routine wouldn't have shamed any campy Borsht Belt comedian in the intensely embarrassing era of Catskill overkill.

Nonetheless, Obama's performance, demeaning and hackneyed though it was, went over big. It earned him no fewer than seventy rounds of rapturous applause. It dripped with schmaltz, served up liberally by Jewish speechwriters charged with dishing up smarmy tastelessness.

After effusive "Shabbat shalom" wishes, Obama chitchatted chummily: "My daughter Malia has reached the age where it seems like there's always a bar or bat mitzvah – every weekend – and there is quite a bit of negotiations around the skirts that she wears at these bat mitzvahs. Do you guys have these conversations as well? All right. I just wanted to be clear it wasn't just me. As a consequence, she's become the family expert on Jewish tradition. And if there's one thing I've learned from her, it's that it never hurts to begin a speech by discussing the Torah portion. It doesn't hurt," Obama beamed, with a feigned Yiddish intonation.

Taking his daughter's informed advice, he launched on a *d'var Tora* (Torah-based lecture), homing in on Joseph (as per that week's Torah portion) and repeating the word *hineni* (here I am) over and over and over, as if casting some cloying spell.

Other Hebrew words, like *tikkun olam* (repairing the world), followed. That too went over big. Too much is never enough.

Then it got greasier yet: "When my Jewish friends tell me about their ancestors, I feel a connection. I know what it's like to think, 'Only in America is my story even possible.'"

Finally, Obama reached the wearisome issue of Israel: "As President, I have never wavered in pursuit of a just and lasting peace: two states for two peoples; an independent Palestine alongside a secure Jewish State of Israel. I have not wavered and will not waver. That is our shared vision."

Doesn't it sound nice? Obama self-servingly set out to make nice and since the "two-state solution" has been elevated to the status of an unassailable sacred dogma, commitment to it is hardly likely to antagonize his faithful followers.

To their ears it's heresy to suggest that the last thing Palestinians want is a Palestinian state dwelling in idyllic coexistence alongside a secure, accepted and recognized Israel. Honchos in both Ramallah and Gaza may expediently exploit the two-state slogan, but they never truly espoused the cause of two-state harmony. Still, no unpleasant truth can spoil smug pageants far away from the real nastiness.

So Obama went on: "I know that many of you share my frustration sometimes, in terms of the state of the peace process. There's so much work to do. But here's what I know: there's no question about how lasting peace will be achieved. Peace can't be imposed from the outside. Ultimately, the Israelis and the Palestinians must reach agreement on the issues that divide them."

Music to our ears, except that pressure can be exerted while being denied. The relentless pursuit of deals can mean relentlessly coercing Israel. It can mean sending Defense Secretary Leon Panetta to blame Israel for any impasse and bully it to "just get to the damn table" (as he said at a Brookings Institution conference in December 2011). It can mean Obama's secretary of state trashing our democratic credentials (as Hilary Clinton did on the same occasion when she likened voluntary gender segregation on a limited number of bus lines serving Jerusalem's most ultra-Orthodox and secluded communities to Jim Crow and implied Israel was beginning to look like Iran).

But nothing like the above was mentioned – not a word on equating settlements with terrorist atrocities, on the equivocation vis-à-vis Iran, on Obama's pro-Muslim predilections (beginning with his sycophantic 2009 Cairo speech and all the way to having NASA "reach out to dominantly Muslim countries"). Likewise omitted was the animus toward Israel's elected government.

This near-loathing wasn't a negligible lapse of good manners and it wasn't miraculously replaced overnight by a magnificent meeting of the minds. Everything remains as it was, but Obama's aim is to make it seem that the rift never existed or, alternatively, that he healed it phenomenally.

The operative verb is "seem." No real change had to take place, only to appear that it did.

American Jews (those who still care) need to ask themselves whether they aren't falling for a false façade yet again when they applaud Obama's bald-faced claim that "no US administration has done more in support of Israel's security than ours. None. Don't let anybody else tell you otherwise. It is a fact."

Even Jewish liberals mesmerized by Obama's apparent radicalism need ask themselves if it's moral to judge us Israelis – to pretend to know better than we what's best for us and to tell us to take existential risks. When all is said and done, it's our lives on the line and no skin off American-Jewish noses.

That's what ultimately matters and it has nothing to do with whether the Obama family's "expert on Jewish tradition" is invited to bar mitzvahs and prattles about quoting pertinent Torah portions. Malia's best friends may be Jewish but this doesn't make her father our best bud. He may enunciate *"hineni,"* but this doesn't attest to his goodwill toward the Jewish state.

Malia's bat mitzvah fashion statements are about as relevant to Israel's ongoing struggle for survival as my freckles were to Cookie's contentions. The Jewish answer to Obama's kitschy Catskill skit should be: "Huh, what's that got to do with anything?"

The Nudnik's Oft-Kibitzed Refrain

Indubitably the worst kind of nudnik is a kibitzer and the worst kibitzer is the incorrigible chronic sort who just won't let go, who is so full of himself that he utterly fails to realize what a tiresome, preposterous broken record he has become.

Bill Clinton, the United States' ex-president and darling of all too many of his country's inveterate Jewish liberals, doubtless knows that the Yiddish-derived *nudnik* denotes a nag, a pest and an all-around nuisance. At about the same time as *nudnik* became entrenched in American colloquialism, the Yiddish verb *kibitz* likewise entered the lexicon and its current dictionary definition is "to intrusively offer unwanted, meddlesome advice to others."

Nudnik Clinton kibitzes with habitual relish, as if his assertions were valid and as if his judgmental pronouncements still counted.

No matter how hard we try to consign him to the hindmost recesses of our memory, he keeps popping up with another exasperating rerun of the irksome old routine. In his latest kibitz-fest he lashed out at Prime Minister Binyamin Netanyahu, insisting that the reason no Israeli-Palestinian peace had yet blossomed was the fact that obdurate Israelis had voted for Netanyahu.

Never mind that we weren't blessed with bliss pre-Netanyahu. Clinton himself failed miserably to garner glory by brokering agreement over a decade ago. He had summoned then PM Ehud Barak and then PA honcho Yasser Arafat to Camp David in 2000 in an imperious bid to impose his solution upon them. He twisted Barak's arm to agree to cede everything, including Jerusalem's Jewish Holy of Holies (save – no kidding – for subterranean strata of the Temple Mount).

But, despite the egregious largesse, Arafat refused and launched another intifada – a bloodbath that cost over a thousand Israeli lives about whom Clinton never had much to say. He still avoids dwelling on the human toll of his officiousness.

During a recent roundtable with bloggers on the sidelines of the Clinton Global Initiative, he unabashedly blamed Netanyahu for not subscribing now to the terms of that monumental Camp David flop of all those years ago.

In stark contrast, the PA's knuckles aren't rapped. It's even praised as "the finest Palestinian government they've ever had in the West Bank." Curiously Clinton avoided noting that in 2008 Netanyahu's predecessor, Ehud Olmert, improved on Barak's offer but got no peace either.

To be fair, Netanyahu wasn't the only culprit named by the unreconstructed Clinton. The former White House tenant even takes God to task for allowing Yitzhak Rabin to be assassinated and Ariel Sharon to suffer a debilitating stroke. Presumably, had it not been for divine sabotage, Clinton might have trumped the Almighty.

But the core impediment to Clinton's ambitions is the Israeli collective. The troublesome makeup of our population facilitated the formation of Netanyahu's government in the first place. Most contrary among Israelis are "all these immigrants coming in from the former Soviet Union, and they have no history in Israel proper, so the traditional claims of the Palestinians have less weight with them."

But, hey, haven't we heard it all before? Isn't this the nudnik's oft-kibitzed refrain? For a number of years already Clinton has been letting us know that his problem is the composition of Israel's population. It's who we are that gets his goat.

According to Slick Willy's astute analysis circa 2010, immigrants constitute "the hardest-core people against a division of the land. This presents a staggering problem. It's a different Israel. Sixteen percent of Israelis speak Russian."

Arab potentates probably agree and would like to be rid of "Israel's Russians" as much as of any trace of Jewish presence in this land. Yet their genocidal hate and terror-mongering aren't censured by Clinton as obstacles to peace.

Among the foremost obstacles cited in his previous kibitz was the fact that "an increasing number of the young people in the IDF are the children of Russians and settlers." Moreover, it's not that he's pleased with the "non-Russians" either.

Native-born Ashkenazim somehow rate grudging approval, racist overtones notwithstanding. But the Jewish state's non-Jews earn Clinton's top marks: "the most pro-peace Israelis are the Arabs." Given Clintonite definitions of "pro-peace," Jews of Middle Eastern extraction don't make the grade.

"Moroccans," he yammered, are too "right-of-center," even if not quite as disruptive an element as Russians. The Moroccans' desire for "normal lives" (presumably as distinct from Russians), he pontificated in 2010, can turn them into "swing voters," who might support the Israeli party of Clinton's choice.

Clinton's unconcealed overbearing intrusion into a fellow

democracy's internal processes is of course nothing new. He was always unabashedly partial to Israel's Left – our sole tolerable political component, to judge by Clinton's non-too-objective past rhetoric and record.

Back in 1999 Barak was his outright favorite and Clinton spared no effort to help him defeat Netanyahu. Indeed Clinton did for Barak what few American presidents ever dared openly do even for their most promising foreign protégés.

Clinton pulled out all the stops in his barefaced intervention in Israel's domestic politics – in a fashion unseen since the CIA's blatant interference in Italy's post-WWII election. Brashly, Clinton didn't even bother to cover up his tracks but dispatched his own spin doctors, private pollsters and campaign strategists to boost Barak.

Clinton could hardly contain his glee after Barak's 1999 win. On the eve of Barak's first Washington visit as prime minister, the eager American host quipped that he's "as excited as a kid awaiting a new toy." It was pretty demeaning to look upon the leader of an allied independent state as a plaything but, with incomparable chutzpah and outrageous meddling, Clinton made Barak's battle his own.

Now Clinton echoes assorted self-promoted experts (generally with axes to grind) who rationalize that it's not the Israeli Left's policies which were its downfall, but the electorate's composition. Clinton blames Israel's objectionable voters for frustrating his wishes. It may be childish, churlish and petulant but it's essentially the familiar psychological phenomenon of transference.

Had he not been raised high on the pedestal of statesmanship and omniscience, Clinton's bizarre gibberish might all be chalked up to personal hang-ups. However, as in Jimmy Carter's case, asinine humbug gains inordinate currency when spouted by exalted, supposedly super-savvy senior luminaries. It therefore sways more impressionable minds and is exploited to greater effect by unscrupulous propagandists than would otherwise be the case.

Clinton's careless prattle might, albeit unintentionally, delegitimize aliya just as much as Jewish settlement has already been delegitimized. Since the advent of Zionism, the Arab subtext had been that whatever betokens Jewish life and vitality in this land perforce undermines justice and harmony. Bottom-line priority: weaken Jewish interests in the Jewish homeland.

In the existential contest forced upon Israel, the stakes are literally our lives. Compulsive kibitzers who insist on periodically impressing our imperiled citizenry with their peerless perception are more than an infuriating distraction.

The nudnik kibitzer's most exasperating habit is throwing players off their game with cock-and-bull chatter precisely at the most crucial moment of greatest concentration. Kibitzers aren't always comical, especially not in a danger-fraught fight for survival.

Optimism Was Compulsory

Basic combat training

Israeli babies born when the concocted-in-Norway peace was first announced are now old enough for the draft. Indeed most of them are already in uniform. They were born under the Oslo sign. It seemed a great time to come into the world.

They took their first breaths as the Oslo accords were inaugurated with whoops of rapture. Niggling doubt was politically incorrect and accordingly drowned out with heaps of scorn and wrath in the name of goodwill and broadminded tolerance. Optimism was compulsory.

But, looking back, was optimism vindicated?

Had the Oslo dreams panned out and even partially justified the hype, there would be no more need to train any more adolescents in the arts of war – especially this very symbolic batch of 1993-vintage recruits.

But alas, OC Home Front Command has recently imparted to us the glad tidings that "the possibility for a multi-front war has increased including the potential use of weapons of mass destruction." As Major General Eyal Eisenberg assesses our situation, our perils are acute, if not unprecedented.

Expounding on the dangers, he noted that during the latest confrontations on the Gaza front, "We discovered a new weapon. We therefore instructed the public to take extra precautions and seek cover under two roofs and not just one."

Whoa, hold on! What's that? We won't get into the defense-tactic technicalities of recommending a double-roof protection. Suffice it to point out that Oslo was supposed to make us secure, luxuriant in blissful peace. No one was supposed to fire on us from anywhere in proto-Palestine. Oslo was to usher in a rosy new dawn in the image of the *New Middle East*, as scripted by its visionary starry-eyed author Shimon Peres.

The glowing sales pitch on the White House lawn by Oslo's first sucker, Yitzhak Rabin, comes to mind: "In the alleys of Khan Yunis and the streets of Ramat Gan, in Gaza, Hadera, Rafah and Afula, a new reality is born. The hundred-year-old Palestinian-Israeli conflict is ending."

How Peres's dupes roared with derision when warned that their concessions would result in Katyushas raining down on Ashkelon.

Those prescient Israelis who dared warn were pronounced unadulterated anathema and denigrated as Hamas collaborators.

"Where are those Katyushas?" Rabin sardonically teased. As more and more political fortunes were sunk into the Osloite pit and as more and more intoxicating fumes were inhaled by more and more gullible and/or opportunistic junkies, so it became harder to kick the addiction. How unremitting were their efforts to hook others. No ploy was too objectionable.

To be fair, we need to stress that pro forma, Rabin is still – strictly speaking – right. Not a single Katyusha has shattered Ashkelon's calm. Adept at Newspeak linguistic manipulation to a degree that would floor George Orwell, our media resorts to the improved Katyusha's alternative nickname: Grad. Same thing. Nevertheless, a different moniker facilitates deception and denial.

For the sake of restraint we won't even dwell on the fact that dire predictions that Ashkelon would come under fire were painted as unbelievably insane and outright malicious scaremongering in 1993. Yet reality has proven yesteryear's worst worrywarts as not pessimistic enough. Even they didn't dare conjure up scenarios of Ashdod, Kiryat Gat and Beersheba being in Gaza's rocket range.

It shouldn't take a mastermind to work out that something in the grand Oslo design didn't quite go to plan – not that this would be remotely admitted by Peres, his agenda-pushing sidekicks and the whole weird gamut of farsighted creative omniscients who gravitate to the left wing of our political arena.

Even less than a confession of egregious error would do in lieu of an apology. Mild soul-searching and an acknowledgement that Oslo is dead would suffice. But it's unrealistic – even now – to expect moral stocktaking and intellectual honesty from the bumbling bamboozlers who inflicted Oslo upon us.

The Oslo high rollers imported Arafat from Tunis, along with his lieutenants and forty thousand henchmen, whom they armed. They imparted to the citizenry a sense of a nothing-to-lose emergency. Peres waived no opportunity to remind Israelis that time works against them. "What's the alternative?" he ceaselessly inquired whenever challenged, insisting repeatedly that at worst Oslo is the least of the evils menacing us.

That was patent misrepresentation, not only in the light of hindsight wisdom. Israel wasn't beset by mortal existential perils in 1993. Nothing mandated surrender. The PLO leadership resided sumptuously abroad and world opinion grew accustomed to the fact. Tampering with all this was incomprehensibly rash.

We're still paying for Peres's devil-may-care adventurism. His "peace" harmed Israel incalculably more than the so-called occupation he bemoans with European sanctimoniousness, as if he had become a visiting stranger himself, a bit distant from our reality.

Oslo kick-started Israel's historic delegitimization and grotesque demonization. It has been a steep downward slide ever since. Numerous Israeli lives were sacrificed to the Oslo Moloch ("victims of peace" or "offerings of peace," in unconscionable Osloite parlance). The international community's pariah, we were never as vulnerable since 1948. Peres opened the gates of hell.

In the 1950s prominent social psychologist Leon Festinger, progenitor of the cognitive dissonance theory, focused on the obsessive rejection of tangible reality by fanatic followers of fantasy. He studied a small cult that awaited the imminent arrival of aliens from another galaxy. They calculated dates and prepared meticulously for the great event – which never materialized. Yet members of the flying saucer cult didn't relinquish their faith in "Guardians" from outer space and their promises for a new universe.

This led Festinger to observe in his groundbreaking 1956 book *When Prophecy Fails* that the collapse of prophecies disseminated by cults "often has the opposite effect from what the average person might expect. The cult following gets stronger and the members even more convinced of the truth of their actions and beliefs."

Israel's homegrown peace cult is proof positive. Not only don't Oslo's progenitors beat their own breasts in contrition for what they wrought, but they beat the breasts of their political opponents. Rather than regret all the giveaways by Israel, they aver that everything would have been hunky-dory had we only given more and divested ourselves of additional strategic assets with greater cheer rather than sourpuss grudging.

The operative premise here is that even if today's government won't accept this wisdom, tomorrow's might. Osloites keep formulating the starting point for future bargaining and setting the stage for the next disaster. Harbingers of the New Middle East refuse to be dissuaded.

As Festinger noted:

> A man with a conviction is a hard man to change. Tell him you disagree and he turns away. Show him facts or figures and he questions your sources. Appeal to logic and he fails to see your point.... [P]resented with evidence, unequivocal and undeniable evidence, that his belief is wrong…[he] will frequently emerge, not only unshaken, but even more convinced of the truth of his beliefs than ever before. Indeed, he may even show a new fervor about convincing and converting other people to his view.

Boycott Is Beautiful

Only Sigmund Freud could probably account for why strains of "Suicide Is Painless" (the *M*A*S*H* theme song – both in the 1970 movie and subsequent TV series) pulsated persistently inside my cranium each time Israel's anti-boycott bill (proposed to outlaw the blackballing of targeted segments of our population) was being rehashed for the umpteenth time on our airwaves.

Whatever the subconscious trigger was, the lyrics (written by director Robert Altman's fourteen-year-old son) evolved as they reverberated in my mind's ear. The refrain "suicide is painless" soon morphed into "boycott is beautiful."

Resorting to amateur psychoanalysis, I could vaguely work out what led me to regard boycotts as beautiful. I must have subliminally succumbed to all that high-minded leftist palaver about boycotts constituting a legitimate form of free speech. As such, boycotts become a positive expression of human rights, which is desirable and hence an object of our unstinting appreciation.

My own appreciation, hardly superficial and faddish, was thoroughly grounded in historic precedent. The benefits of boycotts are undeniable.

For example, in the 1870s the Anti-Coolies Association and the Supreme Order of the Caucasians initiated boycotts of Chinese businesses and laborers across America's West. Many immigrants sailed back to China. Others fled to San Francisco, home to the largest US Chinatown.

The northern California burg of Truckee offers instructive insight into how a successful boycott functions. Members of the White Labor Club and the Caucasian League exercised their constitutional right to free speech when they declared a boycott under the banner of "The Chinese Must Go." The Truckee Chinese Boycotting Committee adopted the following resolution: "We recognize the Chinese as an unmitigated curse to the Pacific Coast and a direct threat to the bread and butter of the working class."

It's sort of reminiscent of the terminology adopted by Israel's renowned champions of democracy against "settlers," including

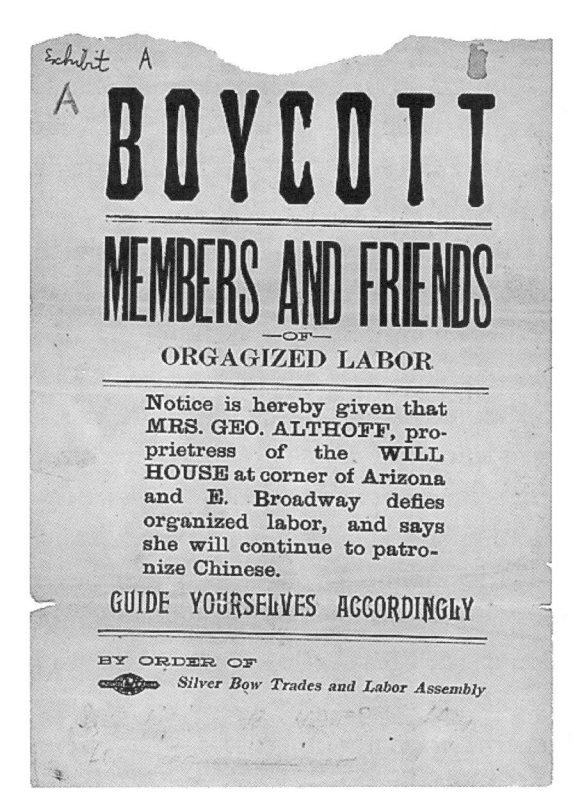

> **BOYCOTT**
>
> **MEMBERS AND FRIENDS**
> —OF—
> ORGAGIZED LABOR
>
> Notice is hereby given that MRS. GEO. ALTHOFF, proprietress of the WILL HOUSE at corner of Arizona and E. Broadway defies organized labor, and says she will continue to patronize Chinese.
>
> **GUIDE YOURSELVES ACCORDINGLY**
>
> BY ORDER OF
> *Silver Bow Trades and Labor Assembly*

An American poster announcing one of the many anti-Chinese boycotts that proliferated throughout the West in the late nineteenth century

residents and employees in Jerusalem neighborhoods beyond the Green Line. Do our peaceniks attempt to end all Jewish presence outside the 1949 armistice demarcations, along the lines of what took place in Truckee? Most likely.

The upshot of the democratically declared Truckee boycott was that all its Chinese laborers were fired and Chinese businesses withered when customers stayed demonstratively away. Every non-Chinese emporium in town refused to sell anything to the Chinese. It was their democratic right, wasn't it?

Eventually, all this forward thinking culminated in America's 1882 Chinese Exclusion Act, which barred Chinese entry into the US for ten years, forced already-resident Chinese to reapply for visas and permanently denied American citizenship to all Chinese. This boycott-born bounty was extended until finally repealed in 1943.

Meanwhile back in Europe, much the same sentiment raged against very veteran Jewish communities. The 1882 International Anti-Jewish Congress in Dresden strove to boycott Jewish merchants and professionals. Freedom of speech, however, didn't fare as well in Austria, whose authorities banned the slogan "Don't buy from Jews." But freedom's clever defenders soon modified their motto to "Buy from Christians only."

Poland managed virulent Judeophobia even before it gained independence in 1918. Its endemic anti-Jewish boycotts were always hatched in democracy's name, many spearheaded by the National Democratic Party – notorious as Endek, its Polish acronym.

In newly independent Poland, the Endeks zealously blamed Jews – a full eighth of the population – for the country's economic woes. This spilled over to America, where in 1919 Polish-Americans and assorted Slavic sympathizers declared a boycott of all Jewish enterprises in the US. They petitioned the US government, charging Jews with "importing racial conflicts" to the States and "condemning the insincere tactics of the Jewish imperialists."

These boycotters, upholding their rights as Americans, emulated the old-country's innate penchants. Strangulating elementary Jewish subsistence was Poland's time-tried recipe for ridding itself of poverty and backwardness.

Polish boycotts received official sanction in 1920 when Endek leader Wladyslaw Grabski took over as prime minister. He made Jewish life miserable via a variety of nasty measures. Unobtrusive among them was the boycott-enhancing edict obliging all store owners to display prominent oversized signs bearing their surnames over shop windows. This expedited the identification of Jewish establishments, which could then be singled out to facilitate the implementation of a legitimate democratic boycott.

It's intrinsically akin to the demand that all goods manufactured over the Green Line be clearly labeled. Blacklists of brands to boycott serve a similar purpose against latter-day "Jewish imperialists."

For reasons of political correctness we won't enter the minefield of Nazi boycotts. Analogies with Hitler's Germany are the exclusive preserve of the enlightened Left. Suffice it to say that the Third Reich's prototype inspired escalation elsewhere – including in Poland, where picketers asserted their rights to free speech by harassing Jewish vendors and their non-Jewish customers.

In 1937, Poland's last prewar premier, Felicjan Sławoj Składkowski, quipped in the noblest democratic tradition (so unlike our own Binyamin Netanyahu): "Economic boycott? Please!"

Poland's anti-Jewish boycott was eventually dubbed the "cold pogrom." Shortly before the Holocaust, multitudes of anyhow mostly poor Jews, with nowhere to go, were bereft of their residual livelihood.

Anti-Semites habitually recommend "hitting Jews in the pocketbook." Which is probably why the Arab League has adopted this ploy against the Jewish state and why the Palestinian Authority last year instituted its own boycott. PA premier Salam Fayyad had personally tossed "settlement products" into huge bonfires to the approving whoops of onlookers.

With such venerable role models, how could our own leftist sophisticates resist doing the same? Israeli professors, authors, filmmakers and artistes relish whipping up anti-Israel passions abroad and directly inciting to boycotts. It's not purely ideological. Such activity is lucrative. It assures academics a hearty welcome in the most prestigious campuses – if they only vilify Israel vehemently enough. It helps sell books and movies, stage shows and mount exhibitions.

Advantageous for their advocates, boycotts are indeed beautiful.

If our Left insists on the legitimacy of boycotts, we should all cheerfully concur. Were it not for the detailed blacklists peaceniks compile, we might not figure out which pickles and pretzels were produced on Jerusalem's out-of-bounds outskirts and which fine wines are verboten. But now we can use the boycott database to buy precisely what they seek to ban.

Moreover, the beauty of boycotts doesn't end here. We can instigate counter-boycotts. Once the Left has given us the green light to boycott targeted segments of Israeli society, we might, theoretically, boycott Israeli-Arab businesses and workers. That would obviously be the quickest scheme to delegitimize boycotts. They will suddenly lose their attractiveness and democratic sheen.

What's acceptable against some Jews would be decried as rank racism if employed against non-Jews. This is the immutable postulate of asymmetry.

That said, nothing prevents us from inconsiderately turning any adversity into a double-edged sword. Boycotts cut both ways. Herein reside the potential benefits of miscellaneous prohibitions, the fonts of their latent beauty – or, paraphrasing the words of young Mike Altman's schoolboy angst:

> …Boycott is beautiful
> it brings on many changes
> and I can take or leave it if I so feel.
> …and you can do the same thing if you will.

Remember the Tsunami of 1949

Fearmongering is largely the forte of the fringes. When it infects the mainstream, however, we ought to get seriously worried. This denotes a successful scare job by forces who, in the words of America's immortal satirist H. L. Mencken, aim "to keep the populace alarmed – and hence clamorous to be led to safety – by menacing it with an endless series of hobgoblins, all of them imaginary."

There's therefore more than ample cause for concern when assorted Osloites conjure up tsunami images to warn us that we're about to be inundated if we don't heed them. It's even more disconcerting that they infects others, who then wail, panic-stricken, about the imperative to stem the tide with yet more conciliatory concessions.

This doesn't auger well. Appeasement never solves problems. It doesn't even facelift tarnished reputations. It inevitably makes bad situations immeasurably worse.

To be sure, what we serially face in the UN is unpleasant. No joy will be instilled in our hearts when the General Assembly's automatic Israel-bashing majority eventually votes in favor of Palestinian statehood within the 1967 lines – in flagrant disregard of what led up to 1967 and what later followed.

Yet we needn't quake and shiver in our sandals. We've been through worse.

If we survived the seismic surge of 1947–49, then whatever lurks in the offing should be a walk in the park. Even before and immediately after Israel's birth, our political landscape abounded with proto-Osloite sorts. They too were prone to getting cold feet.

If it were up to them, Israeli independence wouldn't have been declared when it was. History's one-off opportunity was seized only thanks to David Ben-Gurion's pluck and outright bossiness. Without him, this singular chance might well have been missed.

Likewise, if it weren't for Ben-Gurion, Jerusalem wouldn't have become the Jewish state's capital. The 1947 UN Partition Plan earmarked a status of *corpus separatum* (separate entity) for Jerusalem, to be overseen by international administrators.

Since the Arabs had already violently rejected the partition resolution – besieged Jerusalem, conquered and occupied parts of it, expelled all Jews from the Old City and demolished sacred Jewish sites – Ben-Gurion saw no logic in unilateral Israeli adherence to impotent UN proclamations.

On December 5, 1949, five days before the UN General Assembly was to reiterate the internationalization of Jerusalem (and kick off preparations to take control), Ben-Gurion defiantly declared Jerusalem as Israel's capital.

Without trepidation he told the Knesset: "We consider it inconceivable that the UN would attempt to sever Jerusalem from the State of Israel or infringe upon Israel's sovereignty in its eternal capital.... Jewish Jerusalem will never accept alien rule after thousands of its youths liberated their historic homeland for the third time, redeeming Jerusalem from destruction and vandalism.

"We do not judge the UN, which did nothing when member nations of the UN declared war on its resolution of 29 November 1947, trying to prevent the establishment of Israel by force, to annihilate the Jewish population in the Holy Land and to destroy Jerusalem, the holiest city of the Jewish people.

"Had we not been able to withstand the aggressors who rebelled against the UN, Jewish Jerusalem would have been wiped off the face of the earth, the Jewish population would have been eradicated and the State of Israel would not have arisen. Thus, we are no longer morally bound by the UN resolution of November 29, since the UN was unable to implement it....

"The attempt to sever Jewish Jerusalem from the State of Israel will not advance the cause of peace in the Middle East or in Jerusalem itself. Israelis will give their lives to hold onto Jerusalem, just as the British would for London, the Russians for Moscow and the Americans for Washington."

The UN remained impervious. On December 10, 1949, its General Assembly voted by a whopping majority (38–14, with 7 abstentions) to uphold its 1947 resolution and place Jerusalem under the auspices

BG visiting troops, 1949 (to the left of BG is Yigael Yadin, who would become the IDF's second chief of general staff)

of a UN Trusteeship Council, to be governed by the council's own appointees.

That was the tsunami of 1949.

It threatened to engulf fledgling Israel. But Ben-Gurion didn't lose his cool. Instead of bowing to pressure, he mounted the Knesset podium yet again to repeat what he had enunciated a mere few days earlier: "We cannot assist in the forcible separation of Jerusalem, which would unnecessarily and unjustifiably violate the historical and natural rights of the Jewish people."

He assertively stressed that "the State of Israel has had, and will always have, only one capital – eternal Jerusalem. This was so three thousand years ago and so it will be, we believe, to the end of time." Ben-Gurion then put to the plenum's vote his proposal to transfer the Knesset and the government from Tel Aviv to Jerusalem. It was approved.

The tsunami of 1949 didn't swallow little Israel up. The resolution remained as another testament to the UN's self-accentuated irrelevance. Most foreign embassies remained in Tel Aviv but no foreign overlords were installed in Jerusalem.

We were far more vulnerable then. There literally wasn't enough food to feed the population. We weren't the world's darlings even when we fought for our very lives three years post-Holocaust.

During their entire long UN-flouting invasion of newborn Israel, the Arabs were actively aided and abetted by the Brits, while the Americans slapped an arms embargo on us. The UN, which didn't stop the concerted multi-state Arab assault, found nothing better to do than send observers to keep tabs on "illegal" Israeli moves.

Yet little embattled Israel didn't cower.

This is something for successful strong Israel to remember. Current tsunami alarms are being raised by obsessive Osloites with political axes to grind, who anyhow chronically advocate Israeli retreats under all circumstances and pretexts.

The tempests these Osloites forecast are more akin to extortion threats than to horrific cataclysms. It's quite likely that the UN will adopt another in a dishonorable list of declarative anti-Israel resolutions. But that won't necessarily make it a tsunami (just as the November 10, 1975, Zionism-is-racism resolution didn't). Not all tsunami predictions unavoidably result in deadly deluges.

If our knees don't buckle, we won't fall and won't be swept away.

Remember: the last person who wants the IDF out of Judea and Samaria is Mahmoud Abbas. He knows that the immediate upshot would be his brutal ouster and a Hamas takeover. Besides, Abbas doesn't control the entire area the UN purports to sign over to him. He already has no power over the Gaza Strip. Nevertheless, hardly exuding liberal pluralism, Abbas repeatedly stipulates that the territories must be absolutely *judenrein*. Will the UN help him evict 660,000 Israelis from parts of Jerusalem and beyond?

The UN didn't the last time the Palestinians declared independence (November 15, 1988). On December 15, 1988, another tsunami-like UN majority (104–36) recognized that Palestinian state. Palestinian embassies mushroomed everywhere. We weren't swept away.

Don Abbas Makes an Offer

On behalf of the godfather himself, his consigliere Saeb Erekat was dispatched to slyly put forth a seemingly new offer, seemingly sensible, seemingly conciliatory but still an offer that cannot be refused – an ultimatum geared to guarantee the Syndicate the same gains as previous ploys. By one contrivance or another, Don Mahmoud Abbas (Abu-Mazen) comes out ahead.

Abbas, intoned the consigliere in his role as chief Palestinian negotiator, might forgo unilateral action at the UN General Assembly in September and restart peace talks, "but only if Netanyahu accepts the basis of the 1967 border, and declares it publicly, in addition to agreeing to freeze construction in the settlements."

Predictably, word is that Judge B. Obama (the mob's favorite mediator) actively backs the scam, which helps Abbas look good while ceding nothing. The Don might let us off without punishment, return to the bargaining table and palaver as befits his honorable statesman reputation.

Abbas has lots invested in that image. Appearing honorable is his stock in trade, much as it was for Mario Puzo's Don Vito Corleone. The quintessential Godfather did his darndest to lend the impression of a legitimate, respectable businessman – an olive oil importer. To all and sundry he was known as a reasonable man, a negotiator.

Indeed if his negotiating partners "showed respect" and paid up, peace blossomed.

Above all, Corleone desired tranquility. If he got his way, not a hair on any endangered head would be harmed. However, were his interlocutors unwilling to oblige and capitulate to his eminently reasonable demands, "warehouses were burned, truckloads of olive-green oil were dumped to form lakes in the cobbled waterfront streets."

Then came stiffer penalties, like that meted out to the rash wholesaler who "disappeared, never to be seen again, leaving behind, deserted, his devoted wife and three children, who, God be thanked, were fully grown and capable of taking over his business and coming to terms with the Genco Pura oil company."

That's precisely how business is done in our region. Don Abbas is outwardly a respectable statesman, bespectacled, clean-shaven and with better fashion savvy than Mustachio-Yasser, his sophistication-deficient predecessor Mafioso. Abbas purports to be levelheaded, a negotiator, a man of peace – on his terms, of course.

And as long as the "mark" – Israel – acquiesces to those terms and makes the required concessions to buy limited cessations of savagery, the Godfather will restrain his hoods.

So far, Don Abbas has gained much goodwill thereby. But the façade should fool nobody. The Godfather pays hefty monthly wages to all goons doing time behind bars, including the Itamar butchers, who took the lives of Ehud and Ruth Fogel, their two young sons and baby daughter.

Don Abbas shells out generous outlays to the murderers' families too. He glorifies his killers on every occasion. He names local streets and facilities in their honor. He turns them into acclaimed role models. He agitates for the release of each and every imprisoned hit man – among them also the slayers of the Fogel children.

Don Abbas keeps his thugs sweet and at the ready for the next phase of what in gangland parlance is called a shakedown. You pay mobsters not to torch your business, break your legs or take your life. If you fork over what they dictate, they protect you – from their own arsonists, bone crushers and contract assassins. If at any point you can no longer afford ever-exorbitant protection racket fees, they'll let you have it, Corleone-style.

But for now Don Abbas prefers to keep his threat latent and instead bully Israel with the terrifying prospect of being hauled, shaking and shivering, before the Mafia Families' general assembly – their kangaroo court. There, at the UN, Abbas is always assured an automatic majority.

The General Assembly will, after its own fashion, offer us the classic Godfather choice – either accept Abbas as your self-styled executioner or have your death sentence pronounced by the crime conglomerate.

The outcome will be identical.

Abbas's abiding aim is to dismantle the Zionist entity. That mandates disposing of the Jewish majority of the only democracy in the Middle East. Israel is destined for de-Judaization by cynical exploitation of the democratic idiom to undermine its democracy.

On the ideological plane this means denying that Jews possess the right to self-determination. At the very most Israel may be temporarily stomached as "a state for all its citizens." The next step is to supplant the Jewish majority with an Arab one.

The practical prerequisite is shrinking anathema Israel to its untenable 1949-to-1967 dimensions. That would leave it cripplingly weakened and vulnerably squeezed at its midpoint into a nine-mile waistline. These are what ultra-dove Abba Eban once dubbed the "Auschwitz lines."

All this would be achieved without renouncing the "right of return," i.e., the right to overrun Israel by millions of hostile Arabs.

Once Israel is suitably shriveled, its indefensible boundaries would be assailed daily via stage-managed mass demonstrations by combative pseudo-noncombatants clamoring for their "right of return." The recent elaborate *nakba* and *naksa* extravaganzas (Arabic terms meaning respectively "calamity" and "setback," referring to Israel's creation in 1948 and victory in the 1967 war) were mere foretastes of what Don Abbas plots.

Amnesty International, Human Rights Watch, UN agencies and assorted do-gooder NGOs would all respond to the humanitarian imperative of inundating Israel with its implacable enemies.

Eventually, Abbas reckons, Israel will lose the willpower to withstand international pressure or its actual ability to continually barricade itself. After its defenses are breached, the final and fatal process of deconstruction will begin – replete with clashes, "legitimate Arab resistance" and blood in the streets.

In rare unison, the Arab states will roar support for their battling brethren – the very states who mass murder their own citizens.

With Arabs callously massacring each other, it takes minimal imagination to envisage what they'll do to the Jews whom they were brainwashed from birth to revile as Satan incarnate. The butchering of the Fogels in Itamar was just a grisly preview of coming attractions. So is the failure of the world to be shocked by that atrocity – not that it's unexpected.

There never are even muffled murmurs of outrage when Israeli towns are rocketed and when Israeli civilians are targeted. However, a deafening cacophony of rebuke arises as soon as Israel dares react. Israeli self-defense is inherently delegitimized and axiomatically equated with war crimes. Adding insult to injury is the pretense that denial of the right of self-defense to Jews – and to them alone – isn't anti-Semitic.

This is the irredeemably biased tribunal of world opinion with which Don Abbas browbeats us. If we submit to his diktat, he'll magnanimously leave up to us the mechanism by which we'll be compressed into the Auschwitz lines. It's either the kangaroo court's preordained verdict or the Godfather's preconditions as per the latest offer we can't refuse – if we play by his rules.

Don Abbas and his consigliere mean their offer to be as fair as the one Don Corleone made the Hollywood mogul who denied the Godfather's "godson" a movie role. The powerful producer awoke to find the head of his most prized racehorse in his bed. Just the head.

Roger Waters' Jarring Music

Was Binyamin Netanyahu in his salad days a Pink Floyd freak? Possibly not, but that's no reason not to lend an ear to the band's erstwhile lead singer Roger Waters.

It's not that the aging rocker's opinions should remotely constitute any yardstick for what's decent and honorable. If anything, they most definitely shouldn't. Waters has consistently, almost robotically, espoused every wrongheaded doctrinaire leftist cause since his star first twinkled in the frenzied firmament of psychedelic and "progressive" music.

No modicum of evenhandedness should be expected from this self-important and predictable propagandist for radical politics which a priori demonize Israel. But it may be useful for us, by way of a reality check, to hear what he says to justify his antagonism toward us.

Expounding to al-Jazeera on why he supports anti-Israel boycotts, Waters claimed that Israelis only "pay lip service to the idea that they want to make peace with the Palestinians, and they sort of talk around the possibility of a two-state solution." In other words, Israeli peace overtures, proposals and plans are insincere.

It matters diddly that Waters doesn't even begin to grasp the rudiments of the actual roots of this dispute (Arab genocidal attacks against the Jews from 1920 all the way to these days) or the complexity of our situation (an Arab Palestinian state already exists on four-fifths of original Palestine, even if it was renamed Jordan).

It doesn't even matter that he counts the Negev as one of the areas from which Israel allegedly evicts Palestinians to preempt the two-state solution. A quick glance at the map might indicate to Waters that the Negev is inside Israel proper, within what he purports to set aside as a rightful reservation for the Jews of the Middle East – assuming this isn't only "lip service to the idea" on his part.

In any case, facts are inconsequential minor bothers in his ever-trendy postmodern outlook. Yet Waters's assertion that a successive variety of extravagant (and eminently foolhardy) Israeli sacrifices are all two-faced, and not to be believed, isn't his private idiosyncrasy. Indeed, this is the prevalent perception not only among Waters's obsessive ideological clones but across most of respectable polite society in Europe especially. This has become the axiomatic premise.

Therefore, whatever we offer in our hysterical search for good-guy credentials is likely to be discredited and to paradoxically deepen our isolation.

A brief mini-reprieve could only be attained by our outright capitulation, contrition and self-condemnation. In short, by abnegation of our very struggle to survive. Our suicide might be acknowledged, temporarily at least, as laudable.

Since wholesale self-destruction isn't what Netanyahu could consciously opt for, anything less wouldn't only be a waste of time but would do actual harm. Consequently the notion of wowing world opinion with yet another compromise is a dud. It cannot but end in a diplomatic debacle, domestic demoralization and a defense flop to boot.

The suggestion that yet another supposedly new peace initiative might mitigate our plight boggles the mind. It's bound to be a washout, just as Netanyahu's June 2009 Bar-Ilan speech generated nothing even marginally beneficial but wrought us lots of damage.

In his effort to alleviate excruciating external pressure – especially from the inimical Barack Obama – Netanyahu for the first time proclaimed newfound devotion to the two-state scheme.

Exasperatingly, however, his popularity abroad wasn't thereby enhanced. Quite the contrary, as yesteryear's Pink Floyd soloist intones, Netanyahu – and with him Israel collectively – remains suspected, portrayed at best as an agent of delay, if not altogether an intransigent holdout. This only intensifies the enticement to crush Israel's perceived noncompliance.

For ten months Netanyahu froze all Jewish construction in Judea, Samaria and parts of Jerusalem to deny Abbas pretexts for not talking. Yet while all eyes were accusingly fixated on scoundrel Israel, nobody paid attention to how Ramallah figurehead Mahmoud Abbas undermined the very two-state solution concocted to appease him.

Abbas handily managed to scuttle all mediation while ingeniously succeeding in painting Israel as obstructionist. Now his insistence on a categorical construction freeze is regarded around the globe as a nonnegotiable prerequisite.

There's an inescapable dynamic here. Incremental concessions are inevitably rejected by the emboldened Arab side, and hence are judged as insufficient if not meaningless by the international community. The more piecemeal goodwill gestures Israel makes, the more these are devalued and taken for granted.

Each such concession becomes a self-evident right for the Palestinian side and a conceded loss for Israel. Previous concessions – even if rebuffed at the time – form the new square one from which to demand more of Israel during the next push for renewed "negotiations."

The upshot is that we aren't mistrusted because we're not forthcoming enough but because we're too forthcoming. By default Netanyahu accepts Abbas's rules of bargaining: no Palestinian budging but "painful concessions" from Israel. Netanyahu has repeatedly pledged his readiness for the latter.

His only caveat is that giving Abbas what he wants must be accompanied by security arrangements geared to keep as many Israelis as possible from being slaughtered by the Palestinians who'll take control of the hilltops overlooking Israel's densest population center on the coastal plain, where we would all be sitting ducks.

While Netanyahu stresses Israeli security, Abbas postures as the determined resistance leader who demands due justice for the downtrodden. Abbas impresses shallow listeners as a liberator aiming to redress profound wrongs. In the topsy-turvy narrative espoused by a voluntarily gullible world, Israel is automatically at fault while its would-be annihilators are desperate insurgents against injustice.

By not challenging Abbas's pose as the champion of overthrowing oppression, Netanyahu allows him to paint Israelis as oppressors.

Bibi should go back to basics, play hardball and holler from the rooftops that there is justice in the Zionist revival and an inborn tie to Eretz Yisrael, that we aren't foreign interlopers and vile occupiers in our own homeland, that we were attacked both in 1948 and 1967, that we fought for our very lives and not for the glory of conquest.

Talking about Jewish rights is uncool, which perhaps is why most of us prefer pragmatic security-oriented parlance. Yet worthy and cogent though it may be, exclusive reliance on security concerns implies that we only seek means to further entrench ourselves in usurped property. Such insidious subtexts are underscored when we indicate inclination to cede territory. This doesn't really radiate apparent moderation; it weakens Israel's case.

Whereas aggrieved "native" Abbas fights to regain the "legacy of his forebears," we carp about the minutiae of border arrangements. We appear like mediocre bureaucrats clinging to as much of our ill-gotten gains as we can. This is Roger Waters' jarring music. Why should we dance to his tune?

Ibrahim and Ibn-Rabah

Quite incredibly, representatives of Western democracies on UNESCO's executive delivered a self-destructive blow to their own heritage when demanding that Rachel's Tomb in Bethlehem and the Cave of the Patriarchs in Hebron be removed from the inventory of Jewish heritage sites. UNESCO's resolution redefined them as mosques – as if they had been Muslim from time immemorial. It sought to detach seminal biblical place-names from any Jewish connections.

It's one thing to willfully subscribe to mind-blowing colossal deception; it's quite another to shake the foundations beneath one's own civilization. Politically incorrect as it may be in our postmodern multicultural existence, Europe's and America's democracies are constructed on Christian foundations. By accepting Muslim deconstructionist diktats, the West not only injures the Jews. It foremost injures its own legacy.

To be fair, the world's current most inveterate revisers of the past – the Muslims – are relative newcomers to the fanciful world of fabricated historiography. Long before Islam at all existed, Christians were obsessed with their own retrospective rewriting and they were preceded by pagans. Perhaps it was all already foretold by the biblical Balaam, who prophesied (Numbers 23:9) that Israel shall be "a people who dwells alone and shall not be counted among the nations."

Consequently Christianity could expend so much effort on cleansing the historic Jesus of his Jewishness. But telltale vestiges remain in the New Testament attesting to the truth which volumes of convoluted rationalizations and distortions couldn't quite erase. Just turn to Mark 12:28–30, where Jesus is asked which is the most important commandment of all. He replies without equivocation: "Hear O Israel, the Lord our God is one; and you shall love the Lord your God with all your heart, with all your soul and all your might."

Any Jew would instantaneously recognize this as the primary article of Jewish faith, a direct quotation from Deuteronomy 6:4–9. For observant Jews it is an obligatory prayer each morning and evening. It's the Jewish bedtime prayer. It's the prayer inscribed within the *mezuza* on every Jewish doorpost. It's the final prayer uttered by the faithful before death. It is the prayer with which Jewish martyrs perished at the hands of their executioners – whether from the ranks of the Catholic Inquisition, Muslim jihadists or Hitler's henchmen. It is what Jesus valued most.

He surely would unreservedly identify Hebron and Bethlehem as incontestably Jewish and the tombs therein as unquestionably sacred to Jews like him. Thus when Westerners voted to call the Cave of the Patriarchs the al-Ibhrahimi Mosque and Rachel's Tomb the Bilal ibn-Rabah Mosque, they thereby also belied and betrayed Christianity. The Christian narrative cannot stand apart from Jewish history.

Since Islam's debut on the world stage, however, Muslims have made it their routine custom to expropriate the holy sites of others. When Muslim conquistadors first invaded Jerusalem, they called it Bayt al-Maqdis, their adaptation of the Hebrew Beit Hamikdash – the Holy Temple. Al-Quds – the present-day Arabic contraction of the original – continues to resonate with the very Jewish heritage which Islam now takes inordinate pains to obliterate.

The latest Arab claim is that the very inclusion of the Hebron and Bethlehem tombs among Jewish heritage sites will somehow compromise Muslim freedom of worship.

The irony is that Arab notions of freedom don't extend to others. A century ago Yitzhak Ben-Zvi (in time Israel's second president) and his wife Rachel Yana'it Ben-Zvi hiked to Hebron. Each described, in separate books, how they were barred from the cave. It was decades before Israel's birth.

Ben-Zvi wrote: "The entrance to the Patriarchs' Cave was prohibited to non-Muslims. Jews were allowed to climb no higher than the seventh step in the courtyard. Only brave-hearted Jewish women dared enter, masquerading in Arab garb and their faces veiled according to Arab custom."

Rachel recalled: "Hebron's Jewish women would sometimes

A vintage Jewish postcard featuring a photo of Rachel's Tomb back in 1900

infiltrate the cave veiled and costumed like Arabs. Only by stealth could they pray at our forefathers' tombs. When Hebron's Arab fanaticism escalated, Jews were forbidden even to glance into the cave. Hate spewed from the Arab guards' eyes and from Arab worshippers who brushed against us on their way in. We arrived at the steps and stood silent. I refused to climb the seven permitted stairs. The insult was too searing."

So much for Arab pluralism and tolerance. Actually, the Arabs don't demand liberal equality of us, which we anyway grant. They want it all and they want us out, as they did when their forebears descended in 1929 on peaceful homes in Hebron's ancient Jewish community and gruesomely put their innocent inhabitants to death to glorify Allah.

Were Israelis to unconditionally submit to ever-mutating Arab historiography, then all attachments to the Western Wall and Mount of Olives would have to be abjectly relinquished. By the wisdom of redrafted Arab chronicles and UNESCO, it behooves us to obey. Hence Jerusalem isn't one whit different from Hebron or Bethlehem.

Bethlehem's case is the most enlightening. Until 1996 Bethlehem Arabs themselves spoke of Rachel's Tomb. Only then, at the height of their terror offensive, did they switch to calling it the Bilal ibn-Rabah Tomb. Ibn-Rabah was an African slave and Muhammad's muezzin, reputed to have fallen in battle in Syria. Indeed Damascus's Bab Saghir Cemetery has dibs on what's said to be Bilal's grave.

On July 2000 Yasser Arafat insisted to Bill Clinton at Camp David that no Jewish temple ever existed. This is now official PA mantra. PA officially installed headliner cleric Sheikh Taissir Tamimi proclaims repeatedly that "Jerusalem had always only been Arab and Islamic." The Cave of the Patriarchs, he declared, "is a pure mosque, which Jewish presence defiles. Jews have no right to pray there, much less claim any bond to Hebron – an Arab city for 5000 years.... All Palestine is holy Muslim soil. Jews are foreign interlopers."

Back in 1950 poet Natan Alterman penned a tongue-in-cheek reply to a near-identical proclamation ("Palestine is an Arab country and always was. Foreigners have no part in it"). Entitled "An Arab Land," Alterman's verses appeared on the Labor daily *Davar*'s front page. By replacing biblical Hebrew names with Arabic adaptations, Alterman appeared to amplify the spirit of progressive Arab scholarship. I translated it long ago:

> A clear night. Treetops shiver,
> Vibrating the view with an airy whisper.
> From above, Arab evening stars
> Sparkle over an Arab land.
>
> The stars wink and flicker
> And bestow their quivering glitter

Upon the tranquil city al-Quds
In which once reigned King Daoud.

And from there they gaze and witness
The city of El Halil in the distance.
The city of Father Ibrahim's tomb,
Ibrahim who begat Is'hak.

And then the clever rays so fast
Rush the golden glow to cast
Where the waters of the river El Urdun flow,
Where Ya'acub once did go.

A clear night. With an airy wink
The stars legitimately blink
Over the mountains of an Arab land
Which Mussa from afar beheld.

Memo to Kibitzers and Kvetchers

Israel's ambassador to Washington is the guest at a prestigious nationally televised interview series but is soon set upon by his particularly pugnacious host. The strikingly prosecutorial interviewer homes in on "the charge that Israel threatens world peace with a policy of territorial expansion."

He quotes "a major Arab spokesman" who asserts that "the area of the territories held by Israel today exceeds by about 40 percent the area of the territories given Israel by the United Nations. Most of this added area…was taken by force and should therefore be relinquished by Israel."

Oh hum. So what's the big deal? Aren't we habitually painted as insatiable gobblers of Arab land and aren't we just as routinely required to cede our ill-gotten gains?

True, this could all have been a colossal bore, were it not for the date of the above face-off. It took place on April 12, 1958, shortly before Israel's tenth birthday. And that makes Abba Eban's appearance on the *Mike Wallace Interview* program supremely important.

Almost every demonizing and delegitimizing canard we have by now grown so inured to already manifested itself back then. It's almost as if nothing changed except incidental names of protagonists and the fact that Eban's suave wit and unflappable poise are no more. Otherwise, what was thrown at Eban by Wallace (born Myron Leon Wallechinsky to Jewish parents) sounds garden-variety familiar over fifty-three years later.

But most of our opinion-molders prefer we not develop a sense of historical continuity. They have vested interests in keeping us from recognizing our travails as a single ongoing saga. Chopping our past into small disconnected segments helps distort the big picture and warp it to fit political agendas. This can work because we're a peculiar folk.

We're a nation of inveterate kibitzers (meddlesome dispensers of unsolicited and often irrelevant advice). We're a nation doggedly hankering after indistinct, idealized times-that-were. We're a nation of chronic bellyachers, forever bemoaning the present and bullyragging whomever we ourselves put in charge (who obviously has less sense than the least among us does).

We're experts at being argumentative and contrary, which is perhaps why we already gave our first liberator – Moses – such a hard time, and why we could never (thankfully) kowtow to a dictator or even unite behind a cohesive religious authority. Any scholarly rabbinical viewpoint invariably sparks raging debate.

Given our idiosyncratic predilections, it's no wonder our national pastime is kvetching about how much better things used to be.

For Israel's left wing, the good times ended on June 4, 1967, before we won the Six-Day War. Israel's angst-filled peaceniks yearn for that tiny, imperiled, hemmed-in Israel, which they tell us was universally loved and admired. Why? Because we were diminutive, not an ogre empire, not an interloping conquistador, not an oppressive occupier. Nobody could resist our untainted wholesome charms.

This is seductive. We all wax nostalgic, which is why we can all fall for the fable. Hence it's imperative that we consider whether we ever were – even as a renascent pioneering people – the darlings of the civilized world.

Once we make allowance for cumulative historical processes and the propaganda-amplifying potential of new technologies (like the World Wide Web), it becomes obvious that the differences we perceive are mostly in detail rather than substance. The bare essence was uncannily the same back in the day.

Just get a load of Wallace's opening salvo: "In its ten years as a state, Israel has been involved in repeated violence, major border incidents and two open wars." The subtext is that there's something unsavory and belligerent about Israel, that it's a troublemaker.

But then Wallace pulled out bigger guns – the Arab refugees: "Such men as historian Arnold Toynbee have said this: 'The evil deeds committed by the Zionist Jews against the Arabs are comparable to crimes committed against the Jews by the Nazis.'"

Are we shocked? What can be more perversely prevalent in our existence than Nazi epithets hurled at the country that resisted annihilation merely three years after the Holocaust?

But perhaps we should all memorize Eban's timeless retort. He accused Toynbee of

> monstrous blasphemy. Here he takes the massacre of millions of our men, women and children, and compares it to the plight of Arab refugees alive, on their kindred soil, suffering certain anguish, but of course possessed of the supreme gift of life. The refugee problem is the result of an Arab policy which created the problem by the invasion of Israel, which perpetuates it… and which refuses to solve the problem which they have the full capacity to solve.

Just as worthy of recall is Eban's comment about Israel's alleged expansionism. He advised everyone

> not to lose any sleep at night worrying about whether the State of Israel is too big. Really there is nothing more grotesque or eccentric in the international life of our times than the doctrine that little Israel, eight thousand square miles in area, should become even smaller in order that the vast Arab Empire should still further expand.

Wallace escalated his provocation: "Mr. Ambassador, do you… foresee further territorial expansion by Israel?" In gentlemanly tones Eban objected: "I don't like the word 'further,' Mr. Wallace…. I wonder whether the issue isn't one of *Arab* expansion."

Wallace wouldn't let go: "Israel benefited territorially from a war, from armed violence."

Eban was unfazed: "Yes, I'm glad to say that I hope that whenever countries wage a war of aggression, as the Arab States did, they should be the losers."

Unswayed, Wallace pressed on: "As a member of the Judaic faith, which

Abba Eban as he appeared in the 1958 Mike Wallace interview

cherishes social justice and morality, do you believe that any country should profit territorially from violence?"

The entire exchange reveals the pervasiveness of anti-Israel mainstream-media bias long before the Six-Day War. Although the Arabs controlled all the territories which Palestinians currently claim for their state, Israel was portrayed, already then, as an occupier – because it successfully fended off a concerted attack by seven Arab armies on the day of its birth.

Eban, it needs stressing, was an out-and-out dove. Yet it was he who on November 5, 1969, told *Der Spiegel*:

> We have openly said that the map will never again be the same as on June 4, 1967. For us, this is a matter of security and of principles. The June map is for us equivalent to insecurity and danger. I do not exaggerate when I say that it has for us something of a memory of Auschwitz. We shudder when we think of what would have awaited us in the circumstances of June 1967, if we had been defeated.... This is a situation which will never be repeated in history.

What was true then remains true still.

Isolation I – How Not to Be *Ill*

There was a rapturous turkey trot in old Turkey the other day. Led by their president Abdullah Gul, the Turks and their guests jumped for joy and did their springy one-step to celebrate Israel's obvious ostracism.

"This is a clear manifestation of how Israel isolated itself," Gul, who chaired the summit of the Conference on Interaction and Confidence Building Measures in Asia (CICA), exulted. Twenty-one of CICA's member-states (with the single exception of Israel) "deeply deplored" Israel's interception of the Gaza-bound *Mavi Marmara*.

In unwavering unison, such gracious paradigms of international fair-mindedness and evenhandedness as Mahmoud Ahmadinejad of Iran, Bashar al-Assad of Syria and Hamid Karzai of Afghanistan – as well as Russian PM Vladimir Putin and PA figurehead Mahmud Abbas – all "expressed their grave concern and condemnation for the actions undertaken by Israel" and denounced its "blatant violation" of international law.

Reveling in ostensible rectitude, Putin warned: "We can't allow a new flame to flare up in the Middle East." Gul laid righteous indignation on thick by announcing: "It is impossible for us to forgive the bloodshed."

Similar spectacles are reenacted on some scale or another almost around the globe. No self-respecting city, campus or festival can resist garnering glory by whacking Israel. It's a grand batter-Israel bash and a hit show wherever it's staged. The plotline uncannily resembles that of Swiss playwright Friedrich Dürrenmatt's now-classic 1956 tragicomedy *The Visit of the Old Lady*.

The allegorical setting is the hard-luck town of Guellen (*guelle* in German means soggy excrement), to which much-married native daughter Claire Zachanassian returns, now an elderly bizarre multi-billionaire. Guellen sorely needs a cash transfusion, but Claire quickly clarifies that her generosity has strings attached. She'll bestow great affluence on Guellen's denizens if they only put to death the lover she claims jilted her in her youth. At first the townsfolk refuse to kill Alfred Ill, now the respected general-store proprietor. But Claire knows – precisely as do the real world's cynical oil-rich Arab/Muslim master manipulators – that everything is for sale, supposed virtue foremost.

Claire's predictions are soon borne out. One by one Ill's neighbors abandon him in a grotesque display of hypocrisy. Despite their alacrity to appease and profit, they continue to posture as morally upright – like members of the international community vis-à-vis Israel – and blame the victim for a monstrously magnified set of "unforgivable" sins.

In no time Ill becomes the object of intense revulsion, regarded as the source of all that ails Guellen. The townspeople refuse to forgive Ill for the collective suffering he "caused" them. There are no bounds to the lengths they'll go to rationalize and justify their greed.

Sounds familiar to us defamed and demonized Israelis?

Guellen's initially principled mayor is the very one who swings public opinion against Ill and in the end offers him a gun so that he may spare everyone angst and end it all "peacefully." When Ill seeks succor from the priest, he discovers that the "man of God" too has sold his soul.

The policeman – akin perhaps to international peacekeepers in our own mind-blowing saga – refuses to protect Ill, denying that he is at all in any jeopardy. He hurls invective at him and traps Ill in the auditorium, there to be slaughtered.

The town's doctor, one of Guellen's better sorts, eventually collaborates in the murder and, in his professional capacity, determines that Ill died of a "heart attack."

Perhaps the most stinging betrayal is that of the "humanitarian" schoolmaster, the archetypal well-intentioned intellectual, who holds on to his values longer than the others – a bit like America in our case. He had attempted to intercede with Claire and then to expose her villainy. Eventually he tells Ill that his neighbors all turned into predators, who cannot be opposed personally by one educator.

Presumably poor hounded Ill could at least rely on his own family, like we Israelis assume we can rely on our Jewish brethren out there in the world's big real-life Guellens. But both Israelis and Alfred discover otherwise.

Among the ranks of our brethren abroad are indifferent, well-off Jews who don't want to be bothered with our niggling, never-ending travails. Worse yet are trendy, sophisticated ultra-liberals for whom Israel has become an embarrassing burden. Apathy and/or antipathy toward Israel can accrue assorted potential rewards for estranged Jewish types overseas. So it was for Ill's kin. His son Karl and daughter Ottilie, both originally unemployed, attain inexplicable prosperity.

Bottom line: Israel is indeed isolated but that's only because it's cast as the Alfred Ill of the worldwide farcical extravaganza. We're alone only because Arab/Muslim clout and wealth successfully bribe, corrupt and brainwash bona fide democracies and apparently free-thinking journalists into voluntary, even avid complicity in the attempted delegitimization of Israel. Longer-term genocidal plots needn't be explicitly admitted and proclaimed, but the groundwork for mass murder is being methodically prepared.

That said, we needn't consider ourselves as heading deterministically for Ill's bitter end. Nothing is preordained. Our self-preservation hinges on not obscuring the realization that our detractors are the duplicitous, self-serving equivalents of Guellen's avaricious inhabitants. It's crucial that we understand that we are vilified and targeted as part of a scheme as sinister as that which led to Ill's premeditated slaying.

We can prevent our own tragic demise by deviating consciously from Ill's path. Although his nice-guy demeanor went unappreciated by the voracious chorus that bayed for his blood, Ill accepted his fate. He forgave his family and submitted meekly to the death sentence maliciously meted out to him.

We mustn't submit to slander by outright enemies like Ahmadinejad or Erdogan, but neither must we respectfully bow down to the judgments of the Obamas, Merkels, or Putins who undercut our survival prospects. It's up to us not to be Ill. The antidote to the Ill-effect is remaining convinced of our inner truth.

In our case, a dose of Dürrenmatt ought to be followed up by a morsel from our own poet Natan Alterman. A founder of the Land of Israel Movement, Alterman was acutely pained by the fact that (already in his day) doubts began to be cast on the legitimacy of Israel's existential struggle, portraying it as the aggressor and dismissing Jewish claims to the Jewish homeland. To him these were dark omens portending a Jewish mental aberration that could precipitate Israel's downfall.

After his death in 1970 several unpublished works were discovered in his literary estate. The most evocative of these poems, "Then Satan Said" (which I translated), became his heavy-hearted, somber last legacy.

There Alterman conjured an allegorical evil stratagem in which

>...Satan then said:
>How do I overcome
>This besieged one?
>He has courage
>And talent,
>And implements of war
>And resourcefulness.
>...Only this shall I do,
>I'll dull his mind
>And cause him to forget
>The justice of his cause.

Isolation II – My American Cousins

When one of the world's more influential economists, Nobel laureate Paul Krugman, took pains on his visit here to dissociate himself personally from Israel's obvious odiousness, I was hardly surprised. I couldn't quite put my finger on what in Israeli statecraft incurred Krugman's displeasure, but his annoyance seemed de rigueur.

Why? Because Krugman sounded so much like my own blood relations in Obamaland. It was from them that I gained incipient insight into Israel's isolation – even within the Jewish context.

It began to dawn on me during the worst years of the Second Intifada, when buses here blew up, supermarkets were dangerous places, fast food eateries became frequent targets and just going out meant you might be putting your life on the line. Most of my American family – comfortable, self-satisfied, assimilated and resplendent in impeccable liberal credentials – didn't appear much perturbed about our well-being. Concerned inquiries usually came from non-Jewish friends.

But the very same kin were aghast to discover before the 2008 American presidential election that we didn't share their ebullient enthusiasm for Barack Obama. Indeed I quickly concluded that, even when severely goaded, it's best not to exercise my freedom of speech. We, the uncool and benightedly reactionary Israeli branch of the clan, were anyhow already frowned upon, disapproved of and exceedingly close to familial excommunication.

I kept uncharacteristically mum when a once-favorite cousin fulminated in unambiguous rebuke: "*You* people liked Nixon. He was good for *you* but he was awful for *us*." I couldn't decide whether she only addressed her provincial Israeli relatives or perhaps all Israelis collectively, but I was reminded of the Passover Haggadah's emblematic Wicked Son.

He's the one who intones: "What is this service to *you*?" In other words, he detaches himself from the Jewish collective, relishing the role of an objective observer, who standoffishly passes judgment on fellow Jews rather than identifying with them.

A younger cousin of mine glories in this role. He got into Facebook fisticuffs with my daughter over his support for the *Mavi Marmara* thugs. My daughter retorted that not living here, in our shoes, and hardly knowing what he's talking about, he mustn't dispense unsolicited advice whose consequences he won't have to bear. But the cousin immodestly insisted that he bases his opinions on "a good upbringing, years of education and a natural high level of judgment" (all of which presumably we lack).

Not living in Israel, he added, "is a conscious choice I make so as not to fall in line with the national psychosis Israelis suffer from, the psychosis that prevents many Israelis from rationally engaging in the world." After advising us to read and heed the *New York Times*, he went on to wish Israelis "liberation from oppression, both foreign and domestic, and from internal bonds created by historically justified but fundamentally self-destructive fears."

Evincing the same smugness as my various cousins, Krugman probably agrees, though as a very fussed-over guest in our insular little land he would think it a tad impolite to say so. Still, it's inevitable that, having patted us on the back (for our economic resilience), he'd follow it up with a kick in the pants.

To maintain his reputation in the radical halls of American academe and left-leaning media (he is a *New York Times* columnist) Krugman must cleanse himself of anything which might hint at sympathy for a state that the more successful and affluent American Jews tend to consider a bothersome burden.

This isn't calculatingly cynical. It's almost knee-jerk.

Hence Krugman had to stress that his presence in Israel shouldn't be taken as "an uncritical endorsement of everything the Israeli government does" and that "there is a lot that troubles" him about Israel's "policy, both domestic and in the region." His Jewishness evidently entitles him to give us a piece of his mind because, like "many American Jews," he's troubled "in the way you are troubled when someone you love is behaving in a self-destructive way."

Krugman then warned us against "a lot of people on the other side of the US spectrum who have a vision of the real America that does not include people like me and therefore does not ultimately include people like you either.... They may for tactical reasons endorse whatever the current Israeli government does but in the end they are not on your side and in the end sometimes critical friends are."

This is where it does get disingenuous. Jews, who haughtily disdain Jewish interests, resort to shared Jewish genes to caution us against conservative non-Jews, who support us warmly. Those who like my cousin lament Israel's "fundamentally self-destructive fears," play the anti-Semitic card when it suits them. Krugman intimated that the unidentified "people on the other side of the US spectrum" hate him and us for who we are.

Nevertheless, I'd rather take my chances with "the other side" than with Krugman and many of my ultra-"progressive" cousins. During most of Zionism's history, it must be admitted, Zionists (and later Israelis) weren't by-and-large American Jewry's bon ton.

Save for an extraordinary honeymoon following the Six-Day War, we impeded the American dream of certain Jews. If a terrible fate befalls us, "Jewish-Americans" will recall Krugman's admonition that we "trouble" them. They'd congratulate themselves for not having, in my cousin's words, succumbed to our "psychosis." They'd perhaps shed compulsory tears, as they did for Europe's butchered Jews post-Holocaust, but we mustn't count on a massive portion of America's Jewish mass – no more than Europe's Jews could before and during WWII.

The Jewish-owned *New York Times*, by which my cousins swear and where Krugman publishes op-eds, typifies that segment of US Jewry. During all of WWII it saw fit to publish only two lead editorials on Jewish issues. One, on January 22, 1942, was an acerbic attack on demands for all-Jewish military units under British auspices (which were eventually created as the Jewish Brigade). While the extermination of Jews continued unabated, the *Times*'s indignation was spent on preventing the formation of "a Zionist army."

In February 1942 the rickety illegal immigrant ship *Struma* sank after the British refused to let refugees from Hitler's hell enter this country. All but one of its 768 passengers perished. The *Times* accorded it four bland paragraphs on an inside page. The *New York Post* and the *Washington Post* judged that the horror deserved editorial condemnation.

Contrast that with the *Times*'s earlier front-page treatment for the capsizing of another "illegal" vessel, the *Patria*, whose tragedy was caused by a miscalculated Hagana attempt to disable the ship's engines so the British couldn't remove it from Haifa port.

The *Times*'s scale of values was unmistakable – a story that embarrassed the Zionists won pride of place; the one that highlighted Jewish misfortune and embarrassed Zionism's foes was downplayed.

It's still oppressively so nowadays.

Musings on Skillful Salami Slicers

Salami slicing, a familiar if infamous ploy, has long been a favorite of assorted shysters whether in business, party politics or geopolitical machinations. It wasn't invented by the Arabs in their tactically mutating but strategically consistent war against the Jewish state. That said, the Arabs are matchless masters at deploying the deceit, whereas delusional broadminded Jews voluntarily cast themselves as the ultimate dupes.

I once wrote that "while Israel serially drew back from its positions…Arab orientations during all that time hadn't budged a fraction of a millimeter. Their only modifications were tactical. Instead of eradicating Israel in one fell swoop (which they didn't do only because they couldn't), they settled on slicing Israel's salami bit by bit to deprive it of strategic depth, render it more vulnerable to predations and erode it by demonization and demoralization. The basic premise remains that at most the existence of the unwanted 'Zionist entity' is admitted temporarily de facto, that this entity must shrink and that Arabs have a right to deluge it."

I was surprised – taken aback, more accurately – by the reams of mail this one paragraph generated. What seems obvious to folks with even a modest measure of historical memory cannot clearly be taken for granted in our postmodern times. Various readers vehemently demanded corroborative information. For some in this day and age the terminology itself appeared esoteric.

It therefore becomes necessary to explain that the essence of salami slicing in the figurative sense is small, seemingly innocuous and disconnected actions which, taken in isolation from each other, look inconsequential. Embezzlers, thieves and con artists, for instance, are adept at shaving off apparently paltry amounts in regularly repeated transactions. Initially nobody notices the minor losses. Over time, however, these accumulate to considerable sums.

In politics the salami technique was nefariously used by the Soviets to install Communist regimes in post-WWII Eastern Europe. The new overlords started dominating the politics of countries under their control slice by slice, until the entire sausage was devoured. The salami indeed entered our political lexicon courtesy of Hungary's Stalinist puppet Matyas Rakosi, who referred to the means employed by his party in the late 1940s as *szalámitaktika* – salami tactics. Rakosi maneuvered his opposition to slice off its rightist flank and then its center. Soon only Communist collaborators remained.

It's therefore particularly enlightening to realize that it was none other than the Soviets, in this case via their Romanian proxies, who intensively instructed Yasser Arafat and his henchmen throughout the seventies in the indisputable benefits of calculated salami slicing.

In his 1987 book *Red Horizons*, ex-chief of Romania's Securitate (secret services) Ion Mihai Pacepa exposes in detail the Moscow-sponsored conspiracy to ingratiate Arafat with the West and "promote him from terrorist to statesman." Pacepa was personally instrumental in reinventing Arafat and the so-called Palestinian struggle as a de rigueur revolution.

In 1978 Pacepa became the highest-ranking Soviet-bloc defector ever. The Americans spent three years debriefing him, so plentiful and valuable was his data. Inter alia Pacepa revealed that Romanian despot Nicolae Ceausescu was entrusted by the Kremlin with face-lifting Arafat's image and inculcating

Ion Pacepa

in him "more palatable tactics." Ceausescu also arranged a monthly stipend of $200,000 for Arafat, helping him amass over $300 million (when the dollar was incomparably mightier) in Swiss stashes.

Page after intriguing *Red Horizons* page is crammed with Ceausescu's exhortations to his protégé to "[pretend] to break with terrorism. The West would love it.... Pretending over and over.... It's like cocaine.... The West may even become addicted to you and your PLO."

How prophetic.

Ceausescu offered Arafat respectability "to erase with one stroke all American pretexts for isolating you,...Brother.... That's what I want from you, Brother Yasser. Help me to show that I'm the only one who has any influence over you." By manipulating Arafat, Ceausescu sought to bolster his own image as an indispensable mediator. He aimed to earn himself favored status in Europe and America, and even a Nobel Prize.

Not that Arafat was easy to convince. Even perceived moderation could tarnish his patriotic credentials. Ceausescu reassured him: "You can keep as many operational groups as you want, so long as they are not publicly connected with your name. They could mount endless operations all around the world, while your name and your 'government' would remain pristine and unspoiled, ready for negotiations and further recognition."

Pacepa carefully uncovers the elaborate deception honed in Bucharest and executed with meticulous malice. What makes it credible is that it's not postfactum disclosure, padded with hindsight wisdom. His tip-offs about the premeditated perfidy saw print six years *pre*-Oslo.

Pacepa recounts Arafat's earliest successes in marketing his supposedly reformed persona. First Bruno Kreisky and Willy Brandt were conned. Arafat learned to slice the salami expertly by the time Shimon Peres shoved Israel under the PLO blade at Oslo, crowning Arafat's sinister pose with success beyond his dreams.

Most astounding of all is the fact that Arafat took little trouble to disguise his aims. Already in his May 10, 1994, address to Muslims in South Africa, Arafat proudly crowed that Oslo was a ruse, like the fraudulent seventh-century Kureish truce to lull the defiant Jewish tribe into complacency until the opportunity for attack presented itself and the insubordinate Jews were slaughtered.

If that wasn't an obvious enough salami-slicing recipe, things were more unmistakably spelled out on January 30, 1996 (well into the Oslo fiasco), when the much-lamented "prince of peace" addressed Arab diplomats in Stockholm. The Nobel Peace laureate judged that the "peace process" must inevitably result in Israel's downfall.

"We Palestinians will take over everything, including all of Jerusalem," Arafat exulted. "Peres and Beilin," he emphasized, "already promised us half of Jerusalem."

According to Arafat, Israel's collapse hinged on "PLO efforts to split Israel psychologically into two camps.... We plan to eliminate the State of Israel and establish a pure Palestinian State. We'll make life unbearable for Jews by psychological warfare and a massive influx of Arabs."

In other words, Arafat promised to slice the salami. His cultivated assistant/understudy was Mahmoud Abbas (Abu Mazen), who now dons Arafat's mantle in Ramallah and like him dishes up salami slices to a ravenous world, while posturing simultaneously as the pitiable underdog and the valiant altruist.

There was never much resonance to Pacepa's revelations about the origins of the Palestinian stratagem. Even pre-Obama the international community didn't care to know. In the ultra-radicalized Obama era, salami slicing is elevated to a sanctioned sacrament.

It's therefore more important than ever for the shrinking ranks of individuals with still-healthy suspicions of overly skillful salami slicers to recall that Pacepa – who dealt with more than one man's share of unsavory characters – considered Arafat the dirtiest rogue he encountered, "lying in every sentence and denying what he promised the day before."

In time, Pacepa stressed, he "felt a compulsion to take a shower whenever I had been kissed by Arafat, or even just shaken his hand."

Edgardo and the Quarterbacks

Fate inserts assorted unexpected subplots into our lives. A reader from Germany responded to a column of mine in so insightful a manner that I thought it merits acknowledgement. From there sprang forth a friendship-by-email that still thrives. This non-Jewish German quickly explained that his unwavering support for Israel is by no means the bon ton of his Bavarian milieu and that his outspokenness on Israel's behalf hardly enhances his popularity.

A relative of his, a philosophy professor who currently teaches in China, won't hear of visiting Israel due to its "flagrant human rights violations."

But aren't Beijing's abuses, pressed my internet interlocutor, far more off-putting?

China, retorted the professor, "clearly imposes capital punishment according to the law. Hence any reasonable person must arrive at the conclusion that China is a *Rechtsstaat*" – a state of justice. Not so Israel, judges the professor. "What law anywhere permits bombardment of Hamas training camps? Israel therefore is a *Räuberland*" – robbers' land. The professor stresses that he wouldn't even dignify Israel with the title of "state."

It didn't end there. My friend wondered whether double standards, demonization and delegitimization of Israel don't attest to anti-Semitism (as per Natan Sharansky's three-D test). The professor stood his ground: "If you want to know why anti-Semitism is resurfacing, ask all those people who had lost money and whose living standards were lowered. You will then hear names like Goldman-Sachs and Lehman Brothers and you will know why."

The Jewish collective is clearly held liable for the conduct of individuals. It matters nothing that publicly traded companies like Lehman's and Goldman's haven't been necessarily or exclusively

Jewish-run for years. Non-Jewish names like Bear Stearns, Merrill Lynch or Morgan Stanley obviously trigger no hostility.

My friend recently attended a family birthday party where one of the guests, a retired German judge, opined that "you can't make peace with a Jew." Plain and simple with no reservations or elucidations. His flat-out ruling went unchallenged by any of the celebrants. It was axiomatic.

Those among us who still strive to pretend that Jew-revulsion isn't a formative factor out there may dismiss these as irrelevant anecdotes. But they aren't. They are crucial facts of life which many Israelis and Jews prefer to repress.

It's more comforting to make believe that we don't face bottomless blind hate which we cannot mitigate. It's distressing to recognize that underlying animus (even when camouflaged and rationalized) poisons minds and tilts the scales forcefully against Israel in the kangaroo court of world opinion.

It's disagreeable to realize that de rigueur Israel-bashing has unleashed latent predilections which, despite their transitory apparent abeyance, festered beneath the floorboards of human decency. They aren't really suppressed even in a country like Germany, where minimal introspection and circumspection (not just on the official level) may be expected.

Admitting that the cards are stacked against us, that there's little we can do to make ourselves better liked, goes against the ancient Jewish instinct to ingratiate ourselves. We want the world to appreciate the *real* us – virtuous, liberal and altruistic to a fault.

It's reassuring to assume, even if misguidedly, that everything hinges on our improving our behavior. That imparts a semblance of control. The reverse awareness, even though eminently accurate, is agonizing. It implies lack of control.

It tells us that even our best conduct can't change the way we're perceived. We cannot facelift our image. We can explain ourselves till we're hoarse and employ the most ostensibly effective and sophisticated PR but it won't make an iota of a difference. We'll end up convincing ourselves, preaching to the choir and not getting so much as a polite hearing abroad.

That's what happened in the Gaza-bound flotilla's case. We couldn't emerge smelling sweet no matter how things were handled. Our hankering after good press is essentially what emboldened *Mavi Marmara* terrorists to resort to homicidal violence against Israeli sailors. We willingly fell for the illusory façade of "aid ships" ferrying pacifist Kumbaya-crooning philanthropists.

We fell for their mendacious mantras because we desired to show restraint and to regard the *Marmara*'s Hamas/Muslim Brotherhood passengers in the same amiable light that their propaganda radiated throughout Europe and in America's "progressive" enclaves. We wanted to be just as loved in those same quarters. We declined to delve into why terror mongers are endeared and why we, who seek to defend ourselves, are so vilified.

Refusing to look unpleasant truth squarely in the face, we sent naval units to a violent encounter armed with paintball guns. The shipboard Hamas-boosters promised nothing but passive noncompliance and we chose not to remember that even when Arabs blow up fast food eateries and lob rockets into a sleepy outlying town they manipulatively resort to "human rights" and "resistance" terminology.

If anything, we were guilty only of wishful thinking. It's therefore especially galling that Israel's most ardent promoters of such wishful thinking and self-deception are our loudest Monday-morning quarterbacks, the ones who most vehemently let us know (in retrospect, of course) which moves the government should have made. Their hindsight vision, as always, is remarkably flawless.

But Israeli self-flagellation is fundamentally futile. There is no way Israel could have won or could win the world's sympathy. In the recesses of too many minds within the supposedly enlightened international community dwells the notion that Jews are inherently to blame for whatever befalls them. It's nothing new. It's unrelated to any policy practiced by any Israeli government. It predates Israel.

It can be monstrous.

In 1858 Bologna the papal police burst into the Mortara home and abducted the Jewish family's six-year-old son Edgardo. The pretext was that sometime during his infancy, Edgardo's nanny surreptitiously baptized him. The Vatican remained impervious to the widespread outcry and the distraught family's entreaties. Pope Pius IX "adopted" the child and kept him cloistered in a monastery. Edgardo was never returned. In time he was ordained a priest and dispatched to proselytize Jews.

Edgardo Mortara

Yet Pius IX managed to blame the Jews for the outrage. He maintained the parents could have Edgardo back instantly, if only they would convert. When they refused, Pius cleansed his hands: obstinate Jews inflict pain on themselves. All the Mortaras had to do was give in.

The identical message resonates today. Obstinate Israel inflicts pain. All Israel needs do is voluntarily capitulate. Otherwise, it will be pilloried.

My late father used to say, "We will be condemned whatever we do, but to be condemned for nothing is stupid. We ought to at least earn the inevitable censure, deserve it just a bit."

The sooner we come to grips with this reality – unlovely as it is – the better for our national psyche. We have to do what's good for us and not view ourselves through lenses tinted by the prevalent likes of the above-mentioned professor and judge.

Symptom of Craziness

The Egyptian blockbuster movie *Cousins* (*Welad Ela'am*), ostensibly set in Tel Aviv (actually filmed in far-off Cape Town), unabashedly demonizes Israelis as Nazis. In one scene, as drivers halt their vehicles for Holocaust Day's memorial siren, the Arab hero of the plot provocatively asks an old man standing at solemn attention, "And what about the Holocaust you perpetrated against the Palestinians?"

Dwarfing and distorting the Holocaust serves our enemies – from Iran's Mahmoud Ahmadinejad to Ramallah figurehead Mahmoud Abbas.

This is the common Arab warp of history. It goes entirely unchallenged in the Arab/Muslim milieu and is fast becoming axiomatic in Europe and among the so-called progressives who proliferate in America's media and campuses.

Their assorted misrepresentations omit to mention that the very word *genocide* was coined post-Holocaust specifically to describe what was plotted against the Jewish people. Eventually the term was devalued and used in reference to any bloody combat, though Europe's Jews were never a combatant side and instigated no aggression against Germany. Not even the remotest casus belli existed against them.

The Nazi-era annals of those with only tenuous Jewish links – such as the once-great Wittgenstein clan of Austria – paradoxically illustrate how unparalleled the Holocaust was, how distinct from even the worst massacres of recent history which are fallaciously compared to it and used to diminish its terrifying uniqueness.

This is particularly odd given the fact that the Wittgensteins weren't Jewish according to any Jewish criteria, that none perished in any of Germany's industrialized death facilities and that some Wittgenstein scions fought with distinction in the Wehrmacht. Unlike the struggling Jewish masses, the Wittgensteins were among the wealthiest members of the prewar European upper crust. They were intellectually brilliant and exceptionally eccentric by any yardstick. They could plainly afford to be.

The powerful and prominent Viennese Wittgensteins are today perhaps most renowned for their youngest son Ludwig, considered one of the greatest twentieth-century philosophers, and for his brother Paul, who gained international fame as a concert pianist despite having lost his right arm fighting for Austria in WWI.

Yet precisely because they were so atypical and so far removed from the Jewish experience, the upheaval that was visited upon them by the Third Reich serves to demonstrate what set the genocide against the Jews apart from atrocities like the slaughter of Armenians in 1915, Cambodia's Khmer Rouge purges or Rwanda's tribal carnage.

All the above were episodes of grisly mass murder but they were, first and foremost, the product of sporadic unleashed barbarism, rather than of methodical and meticulous premeditation, kick-started by systematically executed designs to deprive its victims of their dignity. WWII's great bloodletting was ushered in years earlier via preliminary bureaucratic strictures. It was hardly a sudden spurt of violent passion. It wasn't an unpredictable war crime. It wasn't vengeance on a belligerent adversary. Neither the Jews in general nor the Wittgensteins in particular were by any stretch of the imagination Germany's foes.

Yet the Wittgensteins, practicing Christians for three generations, were reduced post-*Anschluss* to frantic attempts – chronicled grippingly in Alexander Waugh's *The House of Wittgenstein* – to secure for themselves at least the dubious *Mischling* (half-breed) status, in the hope that they would be thus entitled to reduced oppression.

For that status only two Jewish grandparents were tolerated. The Wittgensteins' maternal grandmother was incontrovertibly of non-Jewish extraction but not so their three other grandparents. The only way out was to assert that their paternal grandfather, Hermann

Paul Wittgenstein in concert

Christian Wittgenstein (born Hirsch Moses Meyer), was sired in an illicit affair his mother supposedly had with a scoundrel German aristocrat. Better a German bastard than a respectable Jew.

The desperate Wittgensteins had to appeal to the Reich Agency for Genealogical Research, which raked profits from processing thousands of "Aryanization" requests from distraught quasi-Jews. Waugh calls it "a symptom of craziness…that in June 1938 the future security of one man, his daughters, siblings, his nephews, nieces and cousins all hung in the balance, all dependent upon who had slept with whom way back in January 1802."

In the end the Wittgensteins were pronounced *Volljuden* (full Jews). The absurdity was compounded in the case of Paul's two little daughters by the same Catholic mother. The offspring of an extramarital relationship between a Jew and an Aryan born after July 31, 1936, was automatically classified a full Jew. That applied to Paul's younger child Johanna, born in 1937. Her sister Elizabeth, however, less than two years older, was listed as a half-breed.

As *Volljuden*, the Wittgensteins were ripe for robbery. Paul was hounded in intricate plots to surrender the fortune he had secreted in Switzerland or harm would come to his two fatuous elderly sisters who stayed in Vienna and became hostages. The Nazis pursued Paul all the way to his ultimate refuge in New York.

The convoluted details constitute a thriller in themselves but more than all else they show how painstakingly the road to Auschwitz was paved, how the Final Solution targeted all Jews trapped in the Nazi net – steadily stripping them first of their self-respect, accomplishments, livelihood and possessions, and then of the breath of life itself.

This was done to no other group – not even to gypsies, some of whom were persecuted but others left alone. It was haphazard. Much depended on way of life, even on place of residence. But ancestry wasn't an instant, irreversible death sentence. Only with Jews it was.

Only presumed Jews could be marked for annihilation because of "tainted" lineage. Only with suspected Jews could a toddler's birth date offer a potential stay of execution or mandate execution – for the crime of having been born. In the end reprieve was denied even to those initially considered fortunate enough to achieve half-breed status or boast the more advantageous birthday.

For Jews their life's choices were irrelevant. Even social climbers who betrayed the Jewish collective, who turned their backs on Jewish heritage and haughtily despised fellow Jews, weren't spared thereby. Nothing could save anyone deemed too Jewish to live.

Most appalling of all: this wasn't merely officialdom's ruthless edict. The population cheered. Waugh describes the gloating attendant to discoveries that certain socialites were, alas, half-*Juden*.

That was the true measure of the horror – there was nothing an individual could do about undesirable ancestors. Jewish impurities in the family tree destined one for destruction. That was decisive for any Jew – even for the last hidden baby and even for the Wittgensteins, who strove their mightiest to deny that mortifying Jewish connection.

There are no equivalents for this, not that the producers of *Cousins* would be swayed by any of the above. Historic accuracy hardly concerns hatemongers or lesser Holocaust-banalizers. Truth is strictly verboten where today's symptom of craziness is endemic.

Putty in His Hands

Lonely, vulnerable, affection-craving Israel always yearned for friends. It always also liked to kid itself that it has friends. Hence, at a ceremony some half a century ago, standing alongside Charles de Gaulle, David Ben-Gurion extolled French friendship for little renascent, plucky Israel. With no compunctions, haughty de Gaulle doused Ben-Gurion's warm sentiments. "In international affairs," he intoned superciliously, "there are no friends, only interests."

Though unpleasant and untactful, de Gaulle was at least honest – which is more than can be said for Barack Obama.

It doesn't take a paranoid conspiracy-theory promoter to speculate that the pressure brought to bear by the US president on Israel has little to do with furthering the peace process. Obama's pressure in fact contradicts the cause of peace. It's no conjecture to argue that it has everything to do with attempting to diminish Israel, shoving it into a corner, intensifying the ostracism to which it's subjected and making it more of an international pariah than it already is.

Ben-Gurion and de Gaule in Paris during Ben-Gurion's official visit on June 14, 1960

Why?

Because that would weaken and demoralize Israel to such an extent that it would become putty in Obama's hands. He could then appease the Arab world at Israel's expense.

Along that line too we may conclude that Obama, having wasted years of invaluable time, doesn't really intend to prevent Iran from obtaining nuclear weapons. He certainly doesn't want Israel to preempt that probability either. He prefers Israel helpless, threatened and frightened.

Why?

Because then Israel would be putty in his hands and he'd presumably earn the undying gratitude of the Arab/Muslim world.

That's why, rather than engage in dialogue with Israel, Obama spoils for a confrontation – all the while professing to be our best friend. And we credulously repeat his assurance and use it as a cogent rationalization for why we mustn't displease him. Who can afford to upset a devoted friend? Especially when friends are so rare.

It all calls to mind an old Plains Indian admonition that "what looks true by the glow of the campfire isn't always true in sunlight." Native Americans, after all, learned from bitter experience to mistrust the compassionate posture of the Great Father in Washington and his treaty promises.

Our own tribal myth, often repeated around our proverbial campfire, persistently portrays various White House residents as our trusted friends, who presume to know better than we what's best for us. Thus Obama presses for benevolent eugenics – needless to say for our own good – when insisting we forthwith freeze all construction and effectively end natural growth in what he calls settlements, including significant swaths of Jerusalem. No greater problems plague the world than Jewish babies.

Obama's radical ideologues are obsessed with the nitty-gritty of Jerusalem's daily metropolitan minutiae. They even looked exceeding askance on blueprints for a new hotel and shopping center near the Old City. They know the devil is in the details and no detail, no matter how outwardly trivial, escapes their scrupulous attention. They'll relentlessly breathe down our supposedly sovereign neck and show us who's boss – friendly-like.

But who are we to quibble and second-guess? Our best friends may indeed be shrewd beyond our inferior comprehension. Or it might be that what looks like friendship isn't what it seems.

If we examine the history of Israeli-American relations in the non-distorting sunlight we may conclude that the US consistently deprived Israel of victory, indirectly encouraged Arab attacks, instigated terrorism and incentivized Arab intransigence. What's euphemistically labeled a "peace process" was always the process to divest Israel of vital strategic assets. Israeli governments in effect never negotiated with Arab interlocutors without intervention by America.

Way back in 1948, despite Harry Truman's hesitant de facto recognition of newborn Israel, America's arms embargo emboldened Arab invaders. When Dwight Eisenhower forced Israel out of the Sinai in 1957, he promised to keep the Tiran Straits open. Nasser blockaded them a decade later, but America reneged on its assurances, signaling Egypt that its aggression will be tolerated. Had the US honored its undertaking, there would have been no Six-Day War and no "occupation" for Washington to urgently seek to end.

The US-brokered 1970 Israeli-Egyptian truce hinged on American guarantees that no heavy weaponry would be advanced. On the ceasefire's *first* night, however, the Egyptians moved dozens of anti-aircraft missiles to the Suez Canal's bank, facilitating the eventual launch of the Yom Kippur War. American silence was deafening. At the end of the 1973 war, the US saved the surrounded Egyptian Third Army from surrender, thereby robbing Israel of incontestable triumph.

Recurrently imposed cease-fires – whenever Israel begins inflicting pain on its enemies – fit the above pattern.

Ronald Reagan frequently noted that without Israel, the Soviets would have occupied the Saudi oilfields. This, though, never prevented Washington from trying to squeeze Israel back into the precarious June 4, 1967, lines.

But what about American assistance? Contrary to popular lore, the equivalent of what Israel contributed to the US immeasurably surpasses, even in monetary terms, the sum total of what America gave Israel from the 1970s on (prior to that we got nothing, yet miraculously managed to thrive nevertheless). America enjoyed access to Israeli intelligence, including information on Soviet weaponry; battlefield tryouts for American military hardware; their innovative improvement, etc.

Moreover, American aid costs us big time and 75 percent of it must be spent stateside. It coerces Israel to consume American-manufactured goods, from arms to uniforms. These can be produced locally. The fact that they aren't contributes to unemployment here and stunts research and development. America's new-generation fighter planes are so exorbitantly priced that it's no longer prudent to buy them. Yet what's the alternative? Our reduction to vassal-state status was completed when the US vetoed the Israeli-made Lavi combat jet and exports by Israel's defense and aviation industries.

Then the Pentagon nixed Israel Aerospace Industries' participation in a tender to supply military aircraft to India. Israel is essentially ordered to withdraw from whichever tender US firms also compete in or face the consequences of jeopardizing the "special bond." Israel was forced to prefer Boeing to Airbus and to retract higher import tariffs on large cars.

Obama's secretary of state, Hillary Clinton, even badgered Bibi to allow seven containers of American carp into Israel customs free. Our gefilte fish is Washington's business.

America has its own interests, however misguided, and Obama takes to extremes the underlying premise that Israel is a sore in the backside. When Israeli leaders obsequiously suck up, they allow dim and flaring campfire illumination to obstruct this reality. They duplicate their predecessors' flagrant fundamental misconceptions to Israel's detriment.

It's not that we have better friends than America. We don't. In fact, we have *no* friends. De Gaulle's harsh truth should guide our policymakers and be enunciated loudly and fearlessly. Pseudo-friends can be comforting and useful occasionally, on condition that we maintain suspicious vigilance, as another bit of Native American folk wisdom advises: "Beware the friend who covers you with his wings, only to injure you with his beak."

The Good Cop Goes to Auschwitz

Arab-Muslim attitudes to the Holocaust are manifold, cunningly complex and often ostensibly contradictory. But these apparent incongruities are predominantly tactical. The endgame is how to best combat the remnants of Europe's destroyed Jewry and their descendants in Israel.

The common denominator for the diverse ploys is an underlying hypocrisy that allows Holocaust justification, Holocaust denial and cynical Holocaust exploitation to thrive simultaneously in Arab discourse.

MK Ahmad Tibi (Ra'am-Ta'al), whose parliamentary salary is paid by you and me, not infrequently invokes the old canard that the Holocaust's true victims were Palestinian Arabs, whom a guilt-ridden West saddled with the unwanted Jewish state. In other words, hapless

Arabs paid Europe's penalty despite their self-proclaimed innocence.

Tibi, incidentally, who loses no opportunity to undermine anything of potential advantage to the Jewish state (even acceptance to the OECD), was voted the most popular politician in Israel's Arab sector. This was the uniform finding of the three leading Israeli-Arab papers: *Panorama*, *Kul al-Arab* and *a-Sinara*.

The second most popular Israeli-Arab politician, according to all three polls, is Hadash MK Mohammad Barakeh, who created a stir with his decision to join the Knesset delegation to the Auschwitz liberation memorial ceremony.

Tibi and Barakeh often play bad cop and good cop respectively. Both, as a preliminary measure to dismantling Israel, wish to replace the Jewish state with "a state-for-all-its-citizens." Both hotly reject Israel's national anthem, flag, emblem and Declaration of Independence.

Tibi is generally rowdier. When he was Yasser Arafat's sidekick, he once headed a delegation of hundreds of Israeli Arabs to Ramallah, where they shrilly chanted "a million *shahid*s (martyrs) will march on Jerusalem," and "we will open al-Aqsa's gates with the *shahids*' blood."

Barakeh prefers the politically correct context. His most recent antic, on the eve of the Auschwitz journey, was to walk out of a Yad Vashem symposium because he objected to a lecturer who noted that today Arab and Muslim societies – along with leftist movements and hard-line Communists in the erstwhile Soviet bloc – are tainted with Judeophobia. Out to impress us with his care and compassion, Barakeh pulled his stunt in the name of "opposition to Holocaust trivialization." The solicitous good cop seeks to silence the truth for unadulterated memory's sake.

His fellow Arabs spent decades mightily striving to obfuscate the truth and curry favor with whoever may find harangues about genocide unsavory. They present themselves not as heirs of Nazism's virulent collaborators but as resistance fighters. Concomitantly they manage to tarnish Jews as Nazis. It's a massive undertaking, Satanic and successful.

As Goebbels' devout disciples, they implement his big-lie theory and find the world all too receptive, if not altogether keen to imbibe the perfidy.

Barakeh is hardly original. Back in 1983 Arafat proposed to lay a wreath at the Warsaw Ghetto monument. We may quite safely assume that Arafat never intended to pay homage to the ghetto's desperate and passionately Zionist heroes, who fought a hopeless fight because they had no safe haven, state or army of their own.

Arafat was out to score PR points, while mocking the Jewish tragedy and national resurgence. Arafat strove to dissociate the Jew from Zion and portray himself as the spiritual successor to the ghetto heroes, doing battle with latter-day Nazis. The Holocaust's survivors and their descendants, obviously, were cast in the role of evil incarnate.

It was the most diabolical contrivance since the UN equated Zionism with racism.

The same twisted logic that could condemn the national liberation of the most downtrodden people on earth could cynically confer the title of "freedom fighters" on those who aim to destroy the national home of those who endured the Holocaust and of their children.

Barakeh merely follows in his mentor's footsteps. By appearing to identify with Auschwitz's victims, he implies an analogy between them and Palestinians. He schemes to usurp the most enormous Jewish loss to advance its anti-Jewish sequel.

For this purpose Barakeh must dodge the question of why the Arab world sheltered so many Nazi war criminals, including the infamous Alois Brunner. He must avoid the fact that Arab hostility to embryonic Israel predated WWII. He is motivated to obscure the inextricable link between Arab aspirations then and now.

Fraudulent narratives facilitate the cover-up of the direct connection between undying Arab enmity to the Jewish national renaissance and Hitler's Final Solution to the Jewish problem.

Barakeh cannot admit that the Arabs were among the first to latch on to Nazi ideology. Undisguised fascist parties proliferated prewar among them – from Syria's Nationalist Socialists headed by Anton Sa'ada to Ahmed Hussein's Young Egypt. They were anything but blameless bystanders, which is why their Holocaust record remains ever-relevant.

Local Arabs eagerly awaited Rommel's conquest of this country. They hoarded arms, openly rehearsed maneuvers to assist the Afrika Korps, harbored German paratroopers, spied, and greeted each other with "Heil Hitler" and Nazi salutes. Palestinian newborns were given names like Hitler, Eichmann or Rommel.

Their still-revered leader Haj-Amin el-Husseini was a fervent Nazi. His 1936–39 terrorist bloodletting, then unprecedented, was financed by Hitler. Husseini spent the war years in Berlin convening with the führer as his personal guest; the two reached a perfect meeting of the minds on the Jewish question.

The Mufti with Muslim SS recruits in Bosnia

Husseini – as "prime minister" of a pan-Arab government formed in the German capital – was lodged in a confiscated Zionist Hebrew school on Klopstockstrasse and awarded the equivalent of $20,000 a month (when the dollar was almighty) by the German foreign ministry. The sum was more than matched by the SS from its *Sonderfund* (funds robbed from Jews).

Husseini was put in charge of Nazi propaganda to Arabs and Muslims and recruited Bosnians to torture, brutalize and concentrate Balkan Jews for death transports, much as Ukrainians did such dirty work elsewhere.

Himmler organized guided tours for Husseini in Auschwitz and Husseini plotted a Middle Eastern extermination camp near Nablus. Himmler introduced Husseini to Eichmann and the two got along famously. This is backed by ample documentation from both the Nuremberg and Eichmann trials.

At the end of 1942 Eichmann ordered ten thousand Jewish children sent from Poland to Theresienstadt. The Red Cross offered to trade German civilians for them. Husseini got wind of the plan and protested vehemently to Himmler, warning that "little Jews grow to become big Jews." The deal was scuttled.

Husseini personally foiled any deal on the Holocaust's last-minute victims. His direct intervention was felt in every attempted negotiation on Hungary's Jews in 1944. He sealed their fate. They perished at the very end of WWII, in the very Auschwitz where Barakeh sanctimoniously chose to playact and thereby mask his confrères' still-unaltered propensities and purposes.

His tack is exceedingly more effective and sophisticated than his predecessors' fiery oratory about finishing what Hitler began. Yet Arab objectives haven't changed. The rhetoric has merely become more refined and conducive to winning friends and influencing people.

If Ahmadinejad Attended Harvard

You can hardly blame Obama. Most folks are prisoners of their upbringing. They cannot escape the mindset that took shape in their youth. Breaking through the bonds of early instruction/indoctrination requires a plucky character. Even then intellectual integrity doesn't always overcome the expediency of exploiting superficial truisms and old associations for ulterior motives and political ends.

It's hard to judge precisely into which sub-category Obama fits. Does he simply lack the knack to unfetter himself from what was inculcated into him or does he by now merely use platitudes and affiliations to further personal vested interests? But whether it's conformity or cynicism (or a convenient combination of both), the bottom line is that Obama seems to expect all global arena players to abide by Harvard conventions – to broadmindedly tolerate adversarial viewpoints, to submit a priori that no cause is unavoidably more just than any other and to effectively prefer ostensible third-world underdogs with a peeve.

My country, Obama was taught at Harvard, isn't necessarily more right; democracy isn't necessarily democratic or superior and belligerents can be soothed with sufficient sympathy, flattery and concessions. Obama's tour de force at Cairo University epitomized the ethos of post-Hippie-era Harvard.

Every bit as crucially formative was the enlightenment gained by Neville Chamberlain's foreign secretary Lord Halifax (Edward Frederick Lindley Wood) at aristocratic Christ Church, Oxford. Halifax would go on to become one of the prime architects of appeasement. After hobnobbing with Hitler, Göring and Goebbels in 1937, Halifax noted in his diary: "Although there was much in the Nazi system that profoundly offended British opinion, I was not blind to what he, Hitler, had done for Germany, and to the achievement from his point of view of keeping Communism out of his country." Hitler's feat involved banning the Communist Party and banishing its leaders and accused members to concentration camps.

Halifax signaled Hitler that German designs on Austria, chunks of Czechoslovakia and Poland weren't altogether illegitimate in British eyes, so long as German territorial expansion was "peaceful." And Halifax of course proclaimed unwavering faith in Hitler's professions of peace. Old attitudes die hard. Once reputations are staked on policies, no matter how misconstrued, it's not easy to acknowledge error.

Only after the Axis bully began misbehaving with particular impudence following 1938's Munich pact did Halifax finally figure out that this wasn't quite cricket. But to his credit Halifax did agonize, even if belatedly, and he did draw some extremely cogent conclusions. "I often think how much easier the world would have been to manage," he mused, "if Herr Hitler and Signor Mussolini had been at Oxford." Indubitably.

We've no way of telling if Obama has already reached the stage in which he laments the fact that Mahmoud Ahmadinejad wasn't like himself imbued with the liberal spirit at Harvard Law. However, our hope isn't lost. Obama may yet in future rant, in Halifax's immortal idiom, that the world would have been so much easier to manage had Ahmadinejad not enrolled in Iran's University

Lord Halifax (left), Neville Chamberlain (middle) with Mussolini (right)

of Science (where he led the "students" who in 1979 attacked the US embassy in Tehran and held fifty-two Americans hostage for 444 days).

In the fullness of time Obama may likely deduce that the Palestinian state he so fervently yearns for would have been a snap to establish had Mahmoud Abbas and Ismail Haniyeh imbibed progressive values at Harvard too. Had that been the case, dealing with them would then have been jolly straightforward and unproblematic.

But as inconsiderate fate would have it, Abbas's alma mater was the Patrice Lumumba People's Friendship University in then Communist Moscow (where he wrote a PhD dissertation denying the Holocaust, a fact which political correctness prohibits discussion of nowadays but one that creates a tangible ideological bond between Ramallah and Tehran).

Haniyeh's jihadist zeal was forged at that great repository of humanism, the Islamic University of Gaza.

One might expect that Obama's hypotheses would evaporate into their thin-air principal component in view of Abbas's incompatibility with notions of democratic accountability, rudimentary responsibility and credible reliability. Likewise, one might expect that Obama's schemes to reward Haniyeh's terrorist ardor with gratuitous gifts would be stymied by the proven catastrophic consequences of emboldening fanatic hatemongers.

But multipurpose delusions endure. So far Obama won't admit that he practices appeasement, yet he seems to assert that there just isn't enough of it.

The entire international coterie of baddies is delighted. Nothing suits it better than a leader of the free world who so dutifully complies with Harvard rules. So what if he assumes that they would too. Let him. They'll do as they please, undeterred because he's Harvard-bound to consider their perspective.

Israel, though, is ineligible for similar indulgent thoughtfulness (perhaps because its PM graduated from MIT). In other words, Israel is slated to pay the price of Obama's bigheartedness toward our region's Muslim warlords. The basic premise is that Israel gives and the PA gets, that Israel makes conciliatory concessions and the PA reluctantly consents to accept the proceeds, that the onus for quelling the chaos isn't on the merchants of mass murder but on Israel.

The fundamental doctrine of appeasement is the axiomatic given. Obama's Harvard-honed conviction is that Israel is somehow morally culpable for Arab bloodlust and is therefore charged with decreasing Arab displeasure. The conception of rogue regimes as harboring reasonable grievances that can be mitigated or redressed remains as integral to appeasement's rationale as does the good guys' reluctance to fight.

Reasonable grievances then and now – i.e., Sudeten and Palestinian "occupation" canards – are indistinguishable. Obama clearly has swallowed the claim that the Middle East conflict isn't about Arab aspirations to eradicate the Jewish state but about creating a Palestinian state. Never mind that before 1967, when "Palestinian" territories in question were under Arab rule, Palestinian self-determination remarkably wasn't an issue. It was subsequently raised as an irredentist ruse to wrest land from Jewish control. Same as German irredentism in Czechoslovakia.

Hitler successfully convinced enlightened Europe that the Czechs were cruel occupiers of the Sudetenland and ruthless subjugators of its ethnic Germans. Vulnerable Czechoslovakia, struggling for survival, was portrayed as the intransigent troublemaker.

Nothing substantive changed from the grotesque pre-WWII defeatism of decent democracies. On September 27, 1938, Halifax's boss, Chamberlain, opined, "How horrible, fantastic, incredible it is that we should be digging trenches and trying on gas masks here because of a quarrel in a faraway country between people of whom we know nothing."

Near death Chamberlain still insisted that the fault wasn't with appeasement: "Everything would have worked out OK if Hitler hadn't lied to me" – which presumably he wouldn't have, had Hitler operated by Oxfordian fair-play codes. Ahmadinejad, Allah forefend, is likewise every bit as unbothered by Harvard precepts.

Fond Jane and Mr. Braun

We're all familiar with holier-than-thou anti-Semites whose much-touted "best friends" invariably are Jews. Well, the good news is that Jane Fonda is awfully fond of us. She says so in her blog.

Given all that fondness, Fonda feels persecuted for no fault of her own. She cannot fathom why she must "wake up in the morning to a barrage of emails" about "a petition protesting the Toronto International Film Festival's decision to feature a celebratory 'spotlight' on Tel Aviv.... By doing this the festival has become, whether knowingly or not, a participant in a cynical PR campaign to improve Israel's image, make her appear less war-like."

Fonda is so fond of us that she insists our face remain as dirty, demonic and denigrated as she and her avidly mud-slinging chums (like Danny Glover, presumably our friend by association) deem appropriate for us. Truth may be detrimental to their ends, which obviously justify any and all means.

For these ends Israel need remain besmirched and blackened. And that was why fond Fonda, comrade Glover and over fifty other signatories (among them various indispensable useful-fool Israelis) had such a bone to pick with the Toronto festival, itself hardly a Lovers-of-Zion shindig by any measure.

It featured a bunch of films about Tel Aviv, many of which conform to the popular Israeli genre of self-deprecating pro-Arab flicks scripted for the explicit purpose of winning acceptance and accolades from Fonda and her ideological likes overseas.

Sucking up to the Fondas of this world, it's widely believed in our provincial backwoods, is the only way for an ambitious Israeli academic/artiste/author/moviemaker to carve out a career and bask in the ambience of moneyed Israel-bashing liberal patrons.

How deliciously ironic then that Fonda – albeit indirectly and inadvertently – punishes precisely those Israeli producers who obsequiously fawn to please just her sorts. Their radicalism and/or brownnosing make no difference. This effectively parallels two millennia of Jewish experience with assorted Judeophobes – including those who had cut no slack for urbane "Germans-of-the-Mosaic-persuasion."

Toronto's festival, according to the Jane-brand of spurious historiography, omitted to stress that "Tel Aviv is built on destroyed Palestinian villages, and that the city of Jaffa, Palestine's main cultural hub until 1948, was annexed to Tel Aviv after the mass exiling of the Palestinian population. This program ignores the suffering of thousands of former residents and descendants of the Tel Aviv/Jaffa area who currently live in refugee camps."

Uncool as it may be, according to George Orwell "speaking the truth in times of universal deceit is a revolutionary act." Fonda should appreciate revolutionary acts. In her younger years, when she bombastically boosted Huey Newton and the Black Panthers, she insisted that "revolution is an act of love. We are the children of revolution, born to be rebels. It runs in our blood."

So let's get on with the revolutionary act of telling the truth. Habitual knee-jerk detractors, who disdain historical references, please note that Fonda and crew were those who launched us on this foray into that past.

Recently I wrote of almost forgotten Tel Aviv founder Yosef Eliyahu Chelouche, a native of Jaffa, scion of a Jewish family from North Africa (kosher presumably for Third-World ennoblers) and a notable political dove till Arab bloodlust disillusioned him. In his 1931 memoires, long before Tel Aviv became the vast Zionist empire's icon, Yosef Eliyahu described those twelve deserted inhospitable acres purchased for a hefty sum in 1909 for Ahuzat Bayit (as the embryonic city was called). They were hardly occupied by Arab villages as Fonda-and-friends aver.

Yosef Eliyahu recalled them as "a sea of sand, a barren desert with powdery yellow mountains and hills, where jackals howled." Beyond Jaffa's crumbling, constricted alleyways stretched a surging sun-bleached wilderness. It was a daunting, almost impenetrable and seemingly endless expanse, without any visible points of reference or signs of human occupancy.

From its inception Ahuzat Bayit was traversed by a boulevard – not because it was a landscape design centerpiece. Tel Aviv would rise on rolling dusty dunes with unstable continuously shifting surfaces. These were pronounced unfit to sustain any structures. Sand was, therefore, removed by wheelbarrows from the knolls and dumped in lower-lying terrains. The deepest gully sliced through Ahuzat Bayit just where Sderot Rothschild now stretches. Gorged with so much soft sand, it was considered not firm enough for construction. Instead it was topped with fertile soil and bedecked with trees. If anything, Tel Aviv was reclaimed from an empty strip of desert.

Elementary intellectual integrity should oblige Fonda and her retinue of our "best friends" to recall that Jaffa was also a pivotal early twentieth-century Jewish hub. If anyone was forcibly dislodged therefrom, Jaffa's Jews were. The bloodletting of 1921 – the unprovoked five-day Jaffa-generated Arab riots in which forty-nine Jews were massacred (among them leading Jewish literati including left-winger Yosef Haim Brenner) and over 150 wounded – effectively brought down the curtain on Jaffa's Jewish community and boosted adjacent Tel Aviv as a separate, independent, viable, modern and thriving alternative entity.

The carnage filled twelve-year-old Tel Aviv with tents and makeshift sheds to shelter Jewish refugees fleeing the Jaffan bloodbath before even self-proclaimed anti-imperialists of the Fonda mold could conjure up supposed Jewish provocation for Arab butchery.

Pnina, Sarah's mother, in Little Tel Aviv of yesteryear

As to the 1948 escapades of Jaffans on the eve of Israeli independence, I will summon my own mother's testimony. The minaret of Jaffa's Turkish-constructed Hassan Bek Mosque, for instance, was used by Arab snipers to take frequent potshots at passersby on the adjacent streets of Tel Aviv. For Jane's attention, that was before we could conceivably be accused of becoming conquistador ogres.

My mother often recalled the mortal risk entailed in crossing the street to the corner grocery. She was nearly shot on her way to the dentist. One afternoon, her landlord, Mr. Braun, buttonholed her at the entrance to his apartment house on 7 Aharonson Street. Standing in the doorway he lectured to her sternly about the foolhardiness of her sorties outdoors. Just then a bullet whistled by. Mr. Braun fell dead at my mother's feet.

Odds are Jane doesn't know about Mr. Braun. But she should educate herself about Hassan Bek's snipers, who didn't care about the identity of their numerous random victims. It helps Jane's predatory propaganda not to mention them, to pretend that Jaffa didn't aggressively and continuously attack Tel Aviv, that peaceable Jaffans were dispossessed arbitrarily in villainous circumstances devoid of context.

In a world of cosmopolitan detachment Jane's propaganda works. Toronto festival codirector Cameron Bailey half apologetically conceded that "Tel Aviv is not a simple choice and the city remains contested ground." But if even Tel Aviv is "contested ground," if even its legitimacy is questionable, what are we to say about Israel as a whole?

So much for all those insincerely avowed two-state syrupy sentiments.

It's Not the Settlements, Stupid

Without historical context there can be no real understanding of existential issues – certainly not of essential continuities. That's why those who seek to obfuscate and skew do their utmost to erase telltale fundamental perspectives and present whatever they focus upon as cogent isolated concerns.

Case in point: Obama's fixation on Israeli settlements – whether they be a collection of squatters' makeshift lean-tos on a stony hill in the middle of a barren nowhere or entire populous urban quarters of Jerusalem.

The real issue is a layer deep beneath surface palaver. It's a layer which Arabs implicitly understand, which Jews pretend (or prefer) not to understand and which Obama righteously denies. To paraphrase what Bill Clinton hectored during his first presidential campaign: "It's not the settlements, stupid."

Settlements are mere transitory pretexts, alleged irritants which in fact conceal a far darker but basic truth.

Obama hints at it when he admonishes against creating "new facts on the ground" ahead of the deal he proclaims he's about to concoct. Peace is feasible, he says, providing Israelis effectively stay inanimate and refrain from altering reality beyond the non-border (1949's Armistice Line, aka the Green Line). Otherwise they jeopardize Obama's magic remedy to all that ails the region but which thus far has eluded cure by lesser healers than himself.

His unspoken apparent assumption is that whatever betokens Israeli/Jewish life and vitality perforce undermines harmony and bliss. Bottom line priority: weaken Israeli/Jewish interests.

This has been the Arab subtext since the very advent of Zionism, though at different intervals the casus belli assumed different façades.

Anti-White Paper demonstration, Tel Aviv, 1939.
The banner reads: "We won't surrender."

In all instances the pro forma grievance was that Jews were "changing facts on the ground," just as now.

On occasion, as currently, the outcry centered on settlements, or more specifically on land purchases. (Jews weren't always accused of robbing Arab land. Sometimes their crime was buying stretches of wasteland.) At times it was immigration.

Often, it was both, as in the days of the infamous White Paper, published by Britain just months before the outbreak of WWII, when the Holocaust was about to be kick-started. Germany's Jews were already shorn of citizenship and stateless. Hitler's threats were well recorded, shouted in the world's face and hardly kept a secret.

Besides its draconian curbs on Jewish land ownership, the White Paper issued by Neville Chamberlain's government also set severe limits on Jewish immigration into the country which the League of Nations earmarked for the Jewish people. The White Paper authorized only ten thousand Jews to enter annually for a five-year period. It magnanimously allowed an additional twenty-five thousad quota for the entire five years to provide for "refugee emergencies." Any post-1944 Jewish inflow would hinge on Arab permission.

It must be recalled that Jews were at the time fleeing in all directions to escape Hitler's hell. The White Paper encompassed all the goodwill the international community could reluctantly muster, lest "changes on the ground" occur that would rile the Arabs in and around the Jewish homeland.

The fault wasn't Britain's alone. Obama's then White House predecessor was fully complicit. Franklin Roosevelt unreservedly shared the predispositions of his European counterparts. Likewise, Obama isn't the sole pro-Arab Western leader today. He is unreservedly in line with kindred European Union pompous pontificators. The unholy Allied prewar mindset has been revived.

In his day Hitler tauntingly invited the world's democracies to take his Jews, if they were so fretful about them. He knew that for all their high-minded rhetoric, these countries wouldn't rise to his provocative challenge.

After 1938's *Anschluss*, their representatives met in Evian-les-Bains, on Lake Geneva's French shore, to decide what to do with Nazism's desperate victims, pounding on their gates in search of asylum. They never even called them Jews, lest they incur the führer's wrath.

It turned into a great Jew-rejection fest. Britain bristled at any suggestion of admitting Jews into Eretz Yisrael, mandated to it to administer as the Jewish national home. Progenitors of today's Palestinian terrorists made sure endangered Jews wouldn't be sheltered and His Majesty's government appeasingly assented.

The vast empty spaces of Canada, Australia and New Zealand were likewise off-limits. American humanitarianism consisted of tossing the undesirable hot potato into the international arena, because the Jews weren't wanted in the Land of the Free either.

Indeed FDR toyed with the notion of shipping German Jews to Ethiopia or Central Africa. The UK favored the jungles of Venezuela or Central America. Mussolini changed direction northwards. Instead of exposing Berlin's urbane Jews to the rigors of the tropics, he opined that the Siberian arctic might be a preferable hardship.

The competition was on: Who'll suggest a more remote and less hospitable exile in which to dump those whom the British Foreign Office shamelessly labeled "unwanted Jews"? The motivation wasn't much more beneficent than Hitler's initial choice of Madagascar.

During all that time, it needs be stressed, immigration into British-mandated Eretz Yisrael hadn't stopped. Only Jewish immigration was targeted and impeded. Arab immigration continued unhindered. Itinerant Arab laborers streamed here from the entire Arab-speaking world – from the Maghreb to Syria.

The Jews created what was dubbed locally as "prosperity." Arabs drifted to partake in it. But nobody objected. They were counted as natives. The UN actually recognized as "Palestinian refugees" any

Arabs who sojourned here two years prior to 1948. Much of the Arab population on Israel's coastal plain, for example, is originally Egyptian and arrived with British acquiescence.

Jewish development proved a mega-magnet for Arabs throughout the Mandate era. The recorded population explosion in some Arab villages ranged quite unnaturally between 200 percent and 1,040 percent, according to Professor Moshe Prawer's research into Arab migration here from Lebanon, Syria, Egypt, Libya, etc. The Brits and their allies didn't consider the Arab influx as "changing facts on the ground," possibly because enlightened Jews didn't riot.

The bête noir that once was aliya is today called settlement. But intrinsically the two are one and the same – antagonism toward Jewish presence. The Jews are anathema, as is any habitat for them. If both are curtailed then Jewish existence is undercut. That was and still remains the Arab endgame aim.

Today's unofficial settlement freeze won't satisfy Israel's supposed peace partners, just as the British White Paper proved insufficient for their 1939 forebears. The ultimate White Paper goal was the creation of a single binational state with power sharing according to the proportion of Jews to Arabs as would exist in 1949.

Those 1939 restrictions on Jewish immigration would preclude any "changes on the ground" until then – just what Obama purports to prevent with the ban on Jewish construction in Judea and Samaria.

Nonetheless, the Arab Higher Committee rejected said White Paper, demanding "a complete and final prohibition" on all Jewish immigration and an unequivocal, absolute repudiation of the Jewish national home. Translated into today's diplomatic parlance, this is equivalent to "the unconditional end to all settlement activity" and the refusal to recognize the right of a Jewish state to exist.

What was is what is. It's just not about the settlements.

Tall Tales from the Has-Been Bunch

Anyone familiar with the *Arabian Nights* tales knows they depict a reality comprised of layer upon shadowy layer, one concealed behind another. Cloaked schemers abound, each exploiting another schemer, each duping someone for secret ends. Life is an interminable complex of nefarious conspiracies in which it's best not to trust anyone but to suspect everyone.

In the Arab Middle East, one and all assume you're conning them and you can never prove otherwise. Truth isn't only immaterial; it's downright undesirable. This after all is the region that regarded Nasser as a victor following his 1956 and 1967 debacles. This is the region that spawned the Palestinian persecution scam and which convinced its masses that Israel was behind the 9/11 destruction of the Twin Towers.

By such fanciful yardsticks, it's no stretch for unanimously reelected Fatah chief Mahmoud Abbas (aka Abu Mazen) to claim that he honors his undertakings to eradicate terror while making cozy, affable deals with it and glorifying its perpetrators as role-models – to be emulated by the youths educated in his schools, indoctrinated by his media and preached to in his mosques.

His proven penchant for duplicity makes Abbas eminently worthy of the mantle of his predecessor at the Palestinian Authority helm, Yasser Arafat. Abbas assiduously toes Arafat's footsteps. This can be gleaned from the testimony of Muhammad Dahlan, Arafat's longtime sidekick, who, like his boss, carefully cultivated a reputation for ostensible moderation. Singing Arafat's praises on an interview broadcast from Ramallah on PATV, Dahlan took pains to extol Arafat for "having never turned his back on the armed struggle" against Israel, his lip service to the Oslo process notwithstanding.

Arafat had condemned terror attacks "during daytime, but did the honorable thing at night," Dahlan stressed in his audience's own Arabic idiom. Proficient in their milieu's nuances, Dahlan's listeners understood that "the honorable thing" meant fostering terror and that "at night" meant surreptitiously.

In other words, Dahlan profusely praised Arafat for saying one thing upfront while doing the precise opposite behind the backs of the international community and his peace partners.

No less adept at subterfuge, Abbas postures as Israel's wretched victim. His heart is genuinely on the side of the angels. He seeks to do only good – which he would honestly do, had those impeding Israelis not gotten in his way.

The watching world voluntarily falls for Abbas's fabrications and encouragingly promotes the PA figurehead's pose. Seemingly in the progressive advance guard of the righteous-battle brigade, Abbas convinces keenly credulous suckers that he significantly differs from Hamas jihadists.

When there's nobody else to cast as an interlocutor, it's facile for some Israelis to market the supposed minor miscreant as mankind's miracle maker. After all, Abbas reverently promises, as often as he is required, to suppress incitement within his bailiwick. He's still promising.

That's why no big ruckus was raised anywhere about Abbas's choices for laureates of the PLO's highest medal of heroism – the al-Quds Mark of Honor. Five women were named – at the time all behind Israeli bars – as "a humanitarian gesture," geared to highlight their "sacrifice and suffering as Israel's captives, to raise their morale and pay tribute to them."

The five included Ahlam Tamimi, who participated in the August 9, 2001, attack on Jerusalem's Sbarro pizzeria. She drove the suicide bomber to the eatery where he murdered fifteen persons. Among his victims were seven children and five members of one shattered family.

Another of Abbas's heroines is Amna Muna, intractably unremorseful and the most belligerent bully at the women's security wing in the penitentiary where she was incarcerated. She is the eye-catching Fatah operative who via Internet chats lured sixteen-year-old schoolboy Ophir Rahum from his Ashkelon home to a cruel death outside Ramallah on January 17, 2001.

Of late Abbas inaugurated the Martyr Dalal Mughrabi Girls' School in Hebron. Mughrabi was among eleven terrorists who on March 11, 1978, waylaid a cab and two buses on Israel's coastal highway, murdered thirty-five (among them twelve children) and wounded seventy-one. She presumably is the inspiration for the youngsters who'd be inculcated with her legacy at the institution that bears her name.

In the same vein, remorseless Khaled abu-Usba, one of Mughrabi's two surviving accomplices (he was released in 1985's Jibril deal) was accorded a hero's welcome at the August 2009 Fatah convention in Bethlehem.

Abbas's Fatah is lauded worldwide for apparent pragmatism.

Abu-Usba's atrocity undoubtedly stirred pleasurable nostalgia among the mostly geriatric delegates to the first Fatah convention in twenty years. The majority were politically over the hill and tainted by corruption. Abbas wouldn't have summoned this elderly lot had he not been threatened by Hamas and Fatah's own militant younger generation.

This has-been bunch is hardly likely to recognize Israel as a Jewish state with legitimate sovereign presence here. It's least likely to drop insistence on the "right of return" – the "right" to obliterate Israel via inundation by untold millions of hostile Arabs. Indeed this bunch is too feeble and frightened to negotiate, much less end warfare.

The only ace up its sleeve is the deceased Arafat's charisma. No wonder all sides to Fatah's rife domestic disputes lay claim to his moral authority. Fatah cofounder Farouk Kadumi – who significantly brands the two-state solution "just a temporary phase" – showed al-Jazeera TV what he asserted were protocols of a three-way collusion by Abbas, Dahlan and Israel's then prime minister Ariel Sharon to assassinate Arafat.

To counter Kadumi's accusation, Abbas recruited the "Face of Terror," Bassam Abu-Sharif, Arafat's consigliere. But did Abu-Sharif deny the calumny? Heck, no! Tall tales of a plot to murder Arafat are too good to pass up in a setting where fact and fiction are inherently indistinguishable. Since no one would anyhow believe Arafat died a natural death, better just blame all foul play on Israel.

According to Abu-Sharif's 1002nd *Arabian Nights* tale, he knows for a fact that Israeli agents clandestinely substituted poison for medications Arafat was taking. Moreover, the lethal Israeli concoction was deliberately brewed especially for this purpose by a leading Israeli pharmaceutical firm.

Nobody asked how Abu-Sharif came to possess this information, whether he can back it up or why he chose to divulge it only years after Arafat died. Instead, all Fatah delegates – without a single redeeming skeptic among them – raised their hands in favor of a resolution proclaiming that Israel is culpable for Arafat's demise. The convention unanimously demanded an international inquiry into Israel's role in terminating the Nobel Peace laureate.

The canard became gospel. Invaluable energy was expended on it at the expense of tackling real problems.

Scheherazade herself couldn't have come up with a more convoluted plot for the 1002nd tale. Its fantastic twists and turns certainly won't lead where Barack Obama and additional assorted foreign meddlers cynically assure us – road map in hand – that it will. Where the culture of mendacity reigns, trustworthy accords cannot grow.

(Trans)Jordan *Is* Palestine

If anyone can lay claim to consummate mastery of the thriving art of history-forging it's the Jordanians. Their entire state, nationhood and very identity are counterfeit. Had the international community not been sympathetically predisposed to lap up the lie, Jordan obviously couldn't pull it off. Its wholesale fabrication hinges on a world that contentedly collaborates in hoodwinking itself.

So deceit blithely marches on.

Among its twists and turns is the artificially concocted kingdom's decision to strip untold numbers of Palestinians of Jordanian citizenship. Those who were Jordanian for decades suddenly aren't. It's like the infamous Soviet encyclopedias' loose-leaf pages, which were removed and replaced with the latest authoritative versions of what once was. The past is ever malleable in the service of mutating agendas.

The aim, according to Jordanian interior minister Nayef al-Kadi, was to preempt the possibility of anyone resurrecting reminders that Jordan is part and parcel of what's called Palestine. Jordan is indeed the largest chunk thereof. That being the case, Palestinians – whether born east or west of the puny Jordan River – are Jordan's natural citizens (regardless of whatever name it or they adopt). Al-Kadi, under his monarch's orders, set out to underscore the falsehood that "Jordan is not Palestine just as Palestine is not Jordan."

Thereby, both monarch and minions hope, no future peace deal could rubber-stamp Jordanian domicile for so-called Palestinians. Instead they'd be driven to overrun Israel and turn it into the *third* Arab state in the original jurisdiction of the post-WWI British mandate over Palestine.

Otherwise Jordan would forfeit all proceeds from the gargantuan deception it labored so hard to market to a world so eager to be deceived – i.e., the synthetic Jordanian and Palestinian ethnicities, along with the notion that these recent-vintage nationalities are dissimilar from each other and deserve self-determination in separate homelands: Jordan and Palestine.

This cock-and-bull contention begot the image of the stateless Palestinians – aggrieved indigenous inhabitants, striving desperately to throw off the yoke of foreign (Jewish) occupation.

Until 1948 Palestine was synonymous with the Hebrew Eretz Yisrael. The "Palestinian" epithet was largely reserved for Jews and used by them. Local Arabs preferred allegiance to Greater Syria or Iraq.

Golda Meir used to quip: "I am a Palestinian, but don't like the name. Palestine is a name the Romans gave Eretz Yisrael with the expressed purpose of infuriating defeated Jews.... Why should we use a spiteful name meant to humiliate us? ...Christendom inherited the name from Rome and the British chose to call the land they mandated Palestine. Local Arabs picked it up as their supposed nation's supposed ancient name, though they couldn't even pronounce it correctly, and turned it into Filastin, a fictional entity."

Palestine/Filastin never had an independent existence, cultural uniqueness, linguistic distinctiveness or religious idiosyncrasy to differentiate it from the surrounding Arab milieu.

Moreover, the British Mandate in Palestine extended over both banks of the Jordan. In 1921, 78 percent of what the League of Nations designated as "the national home of the Jewish people" was ripped off and presented as a gift to Abdullah, son of Sharif Hussein bin-Ali, Mecca's Hashemite emir (also self-proclaimed caliph of all Muslims).

Sharif Hussein bin-Ali, caliph of all Muslims and emir of Mecca

Hussein later (1924) lost control of Islam's holiest city and surrounding Hejaz to a rival clan, the Saudis. Had he won, we'd be speaking today of Hashemite Arabia. As is, we're saddled with Saudi Arabia and Hashemite Jordan.

Consistently striving to recompense their Hashemite lackeys, the Brits enthroned Abdullah's younger brother Faisal as king of Greater Syria in 1920. After the French uncooperatively expelled Faisal from Damascus that same year, London manufactured for him a make-believe realm called Iraq.

His grandson Faisal II was deposed, executed and his corpse dragged through Baghdad's streets in 1958, but England's unnatural Iraqi fusion remains and continues to disturb the world.

Abdullah sought the title of emir of Palestine. Britain made him settle for Transjordan. No Transjordanian nation appears in human chronicles. It was conceived on Palestinian soil by Perfidious Albion. That was the *first* division of Palestine.

On April 24, 1950, Transjordan annexed the territory it had occupied since the Arab invasion of newborn Israel in 1948, called it the "West Bank" and thereafter declared itself the Hashemite Kingdom of Jordan. The Arab League threatened to boot out Jordan for the deed. Only Britain and Pakistan approved of the annexation.

Jordan's leaders, including the late King Hussein, stressed over and over in numerous pronouncements that "Jordan and Palestine are one and the same." So did Palestinian leaders, including Arafat. The Palestinian Covenant, in fact, covets all of Jordan – precisely because it's Palestine.

Yet eventually it became expedient, PR-wise, to claim the reverse and assert that Palestine exists exclusively west of the mini-river, justifying the campaign for a *second* Palestinian Arab state, to be wedged between Israel and Jordan and actually called Palestine.

Fearing that his Palestinian subjects would topple their imported Hashemite rulers, Hussein kicked out the PLO in Black September,

1970. Too bad. Had Hussein failed, Arafat would have taken over Amman and nobody could today deny that Palestine is divided among Jews and Arabs, with the Arabs holding nearly four-fifths thereof.

Now Hussein's son Abdullah II seeks to rewrite history once more in the well-trodden Jordanian tradition.

His father dropped the claim to what was branded the West Bank but didn't revive the ludicrous moniker of Transjordan. After seventeen years of annexation (1950–67) the Jordan trademark gained global acceptance. It rang authentic. Why then return to the more obvious fake?

Jordan's population, though, is overwhelmingly Palestinian. The only exceptions are Bedouins who accompanied Abdullah I from Hejaz. Like the Hashemites, they're foreigners. Gallingly these outsiders presume to delegitimize the natives. Expectedly, governments and human-rights NGOs worldwide maintain polite silence.

Jordan was born of fraud, which it's fated thereafter to prop up via unremitting retroactive repairs to the past – even the distant past. Not too many years back, Jordan TV aired a documentary on Jerusalem portraying ancient Jebusites as Arabs.

Of course, were the Hebrews not the People of the Book, those Jerusalem-area Canaanites known as Jebusites would have never made their exceedingly fleeting appearance on the pages of history or on JTV.

For anyone who forgot the brief biblical references, the Jebusites were the folks from whom King David conquered a wee hamlet he later turned into his capital. The books of Judges and Ezra indicate they intermarried and assimilated among the Israelites.

Posthumously Arabizing these Jebusites ostensibly establishes an Arab claim to Zion. JTV concomitantly magnified the Jebusites' contribution to mankind to proportions that would have doubtless astounded them.

However, JTV altogether expunged Jews from Jerusalem's annals, save for one abrupt but indispensable appearance in the *judenrein* city. Villainous Jews arrived abruptly, out of nowhere, and stayed just long enough to crucify Jesus, who is described as "a Palestinian Arab prophet" – an epithet that would certainly have taken him by surprise.

JTV even treated us to recipes from the Jebusite kitchen. These would have altogether floored the long-lost Jebusites, as it appears that their favorite ingredients were tomatoes and chili peppers, which, alas, only reached the Old World 2,500 years later, when Spaniards brought them back from America.

Perhaps, however, the enterprising Jebusites beat Columbus there, thus establishing an Arab claim to the Western Hemisphere. Any claim that Jordan isn't Palestine is just as unimpeachable.

Self-Exiled by Guilt

Those little neglected news stories that rarely make front-page headlines and never receive airtime are often the most telling of all. It's through them that deliberately suppressed fundamental truths occasionally surface. It's there that big lies are sometimes, albeit inadvertently, exposed.

Scant attention was paid to Palestinian president Mahmoud Abbas's revelations on Al-Palestinia TV. Abbas talked about his youth in Safed, from whence he routinely claims his family was forcibly driven out by Israeli troops in 1948. Abbas revels in his supposed refugee status. It's his stock-in-trade on the Arab scene and the international arena. The pitiable pose of an aggrieved victim confers ostensible moral authority upon his cause.

This pose, moreover, becomes a basic Arab tenet – the crucial claim for justifying terror against Israel and for refusing to relinquish the so-called "Right of Return" by refugees to what are described as homes robbed from them by violent interloping Jewish conquistadores. Biased world opinion willingly and gladly falls for the Palestinian freedom-fighter fable.

But foolhardy carelessness – or trust that nobody listens to intra-Arab discourse – occasionally pulls off the painstakingly fabricated mask. That's what happened to Abbas (aka Abu Mazen). Fatah's cofounder reminisced at length about his Safed origins and haphazardly let the truth slip out.

"Until the *nakba* ("calamity" in Arabic – the loaded moniker for Israeli independence), he recounted, his family "was well-off in Safed." When Abbas was thirteen, "we left on foot at night to the Jordan River.... Eventually we settled in Damascus.... My father had money, and he spent his money methodically. After a year, when the money ran out, we began to work.

"People were motivated to run away.... They feared retribution from Zionist terrorist organizations – particularly from the Safed ones. Those of us from Safed especially feared that the Jews harbored old desires to avenge what happened during the 1929 uprising. This was in the memory of our families and parents.... They realized the balance of forces was shifting and therefore the whole town was abandoned on the basis of this rationale – saving our lives and our belongings."

So here it is from the mouth of the PA's head honcho himself. He and no other verifies that nobody expelled Safed's Arabs. Their exile was voluntary, propelled by their extreme consciousness of guilt and expectation that Jews would be ruled by the same blood-feud conventions that prevail in Arab culture. Unrealistically they anticipated that Jews would do to them precisely what the Arabs had done to Safed's Jews. If that was their premise, they indeed had cause to panic.

The "uprising" Abbas alluded to was one among the serial pogroms instigated by infamous Jerusalem mufti Haj Amin al-Husseini, who's still revered throughout the Arab world. He was a Berlin-resident avid Nazi collaborator during WWII and a wanted war criminal postwar.

In August 1929 al-Husseini rallied Arabs to slaughter Jews on trumped-up allegations of Jewish takeover attempts at the Temple Mount. Sixty-seven members of the ancient Jewish community of

The shelled Jewish Quarter of Safed during the 1948 Arab onslaught

Hebron were hideously hacked to death. That was the most notorious massacre, but others were perpetrated throughout the country. In the equally ancient Jewish community of Safed, twenty-one were butchered no less gruesomely (a cat was stuffed into one old woman's disemboweled abdomen). A young woman due to be married the next day and a child were cold-bloodedly shot dead by Arab constables whom British Mandatory officers assigned to watch over the majority of Safed's Jews who sought safety in the police courtyard.

The British proposed that all Safed Jews be evacuated "for their own safety," as was the case in Hebron. The offer was vehemently refused. Thereafter, principally during the 1936–39 mufti-led rampages, the Hagana and Safed's own Jewish resistance group Irgun Zeva'i Le'umi cells protected the town's two thousand Jews.

Nevertheless, in the ill-fated evening of August 13, 1936, Arab marauders managed to infiltrate and invade the modest Unger home in the old Jewish Quarter, just as the family ate supper. They murdered the father, Alter – a thirty-six-year-old Torah scribe – his daughters Yaffa and Hava (aged nine and seven respectively) and the six-year-old son, Avraham.

In his book *Safed Annals* author Natan Shor includes the following eyewitness account from one of the first neighbors who soon chanced by:

> The boys heard groans from one of the houses. We entered and in the middle of a dark room – furnished only by a table, a broken chair and a bookcase crammed with mostly religious volumes – lay a man's body. His skull was bashed in. Half the head was missing. We saw only a beard, part of a nose and the right eye.... The corpse lay in a pool of blood and brain matter....
>
> In the next room amid the dishes, lay three little bloodied lifeless children. Two of them were still open-eyed. An old

woman, the grandmother, ran around from room to room, crazed with grief. The mother, herself wounded (probably left for dead), went from child to child. She didn't yell or wail. Staring intently, she repeated quietly over and over in Yiddish: "If it were only me instead of you." Her hand bled profusely and an amputated finger hung by a strip of skin.

Such was the uprising for which Abbas's kinfolk assumed they deserved just reckoning. Ironically, Jews were alarmed by the Arab exodus, figuring it presaged a formidable onslaught by invading Arab armies (which indeed came).

In many areas (Haifa, for instance) Jews begged and pleaded with local Arabs to stay. But Arabs in Safed and elsewhere – heeding their leaders' exhortations to pull out and hounded by fears arising from their own vengeful traditions (but not Jewish ones) – did what was prudent in light of their surmise that Jews would behave according to Arab codes.

On the eve of the April 16, 1948, British withdrawal from Safed, the Mandatory authorities turned over the town's police facilities and Mount Canaan's strategically dominant military fort to the Arabs. They offered to escort all Jews out of town "for their own safety." As in 1929, the Jews refused unequivocally, though memories of the horrific carnage should have inspired more dread among them than among the fleeing Abasses.

Why wasn't Abu-Mazen's pivotal testimony accorded due resonance in our press? Why did Israel's mainstream media largely ignore Abbas's own recollections? Perhaps most editors aren't interested in the ideological underpinnings of the war against their own people. Preserving the myth of Israeli fault is de rigueur, a hallmark of enlightenment.

Nothing must be allowed to dent the potent-cum-fraudulent Palestinian refugee narrative, not even the memories of the Palestinian headliner, to say nothing of Jewish memories.

The latter are altogether dispensable. Hence Safed residents recently had to petition their own municipality not to demolish the old Unger home but preserve it as a commemorative historic site.

In the Footsteps of Sam Lewis's Suck-Ups

Sometime at the very start of 1982 I attended a function at the American embassy in Tel Aviv, which would have been entirely forgettable except that rarely was I since as nauseated as then.

I came away revolted by the spectacle of my Israeli colleagues eagerly milling around Ambassador Sam Lewis, seeking his attention and trying to outdo each other in heaping mockery and contempt upon their own prime minister. Brutal jokes at Menachem Begin's expense came fast and furious. Lewis visibly appreciated them and laughed along condescendingly.

It was one of the sorriest displays of Israeli self-debasement I had until then witnessed.

But in time I came to regard it as typical of the fawning eagerness to curry favor with foreign bigwigs. Kowtowing to the exceedingly well-connected and widely courted Lewis wasn't merely ingratiating. It also served the local Left's visceral anti-Begin politics. Undisguised American displeasure with him seemed a serendipitous source of support.

It was after Begin had serially disobeyed Washington. First he dared destroy the Iraqi nuclear reactor. Though America should have profusely thanked Israel for the service, Secretary of Defense Caspar Weinberger (to my shame a distant relative of my father's) was livid. Hence the previously contracted delivery of fighter jets to Israel was "suspended."

Later Israel bombed the PLO's Beirut headquarters and more aircraft deliveries were put on hold. Then the bill extending Israeli law to the Golan was enacted. The US responded by reassessing its strategic cooperation agreement with Israel.

Begin decided not to take his lumps. He summoned Lewis and subjected him to the most undiplomatic dressing-down any US diplomat probably ever received from an ally. Begin bristled at the very notion of American diktats. "Are we a vassal state?" he demanded, and went on to stress that Israel is neither a banana republic nor a bunch of "fourteen-year-old boys who have to have their knuckles slapped" for misbehavior.

Begin was on a roll. He told Lewis that Israel would not be intimidated by threats of punishment and that these would fall on deaf ears. He vowed not to allow "the sword of Damocles to hang over Israel's head…. Jews have survived without a strategic cooperation memorandum with America for thirty-seven hundred years and can live without it for another thirty-seven hundred years."

The Golan legislation, Begin stressed, would not be annulled. This earful was immediately released verbatim by the PM's office for publication, so the populace would know its government drew red lines and stood by them.

However, Israel's left-dominated media never lost an opportunity to lay bare its obsequiousness. It reacted with the shock of a stern cleric to outright unpardonable blasphemy. But more than it was genuinely upset, it exploited Begin's candid indignation as yet another pretext to pillory him. National pride was already then perceived as reactionary and uncool, especially when it clashed with post-Zionist dogma.

How like the reaction by most of our subservient scribblers and talking heads to then president of France Nicolas Sarkozy's unsolicited recommendation that Prime Minister Binyamin Netanyahu kick out Foreign Minister Avigdor Lieberman and replace him with Tzipi Livni. No matter whether we like or dislike Lieberman, it's at instances like these that no consideration ought to feature in our internal discourse other than national pride.

Put in the context of Sarkozy's infamous big mouth, his insolence toward Lieberman was no big deal. Sarkozy apparently appointed himself freelance caustic critic of far more prominent figures on the world stage than our foreign minister. The meek retort by Netanyahu – the ostensible heir to Begin's mantle – is of greater concern.

Yet most disconcerting of all is the alacrity with which current Israeli commentators – fully in the footsteps of Sam Lewis's suck-ups of yesteryear – seize any chance to further their agenda. In some cases the triumphant gloating at Lieberman's humiliation was tangible. To that end it was excusable to portray Sarkozy's scorn as gospel.

Such glee is nowadays frequently afforded our pundits, including many employees at the state's own broadcasting authority – the one involuntarily subsidized by you and me. Not a day goes by without some pronouncement from the Obama court about how Israel must comply with Washington's decree to cease all "construction in the settlements" – including in much of Jerusalem.

Netanyahu's response – on those rare occasions when any is at all heard – is as wan as it was in Paris. He appears timid and wishy-washy. His heart is in the right place but he is too nervous to utter a fitting rejoinder. Trepidation may be embellished as signifying prudent restraint, as not breaching diplomatic protocol Begin-style, as keeping a cool head and, calculatingly, a tight lip.

Ah, if it were only so.

Unfortunately there's too much cause to suspect that Netanyahu is irresolute. He may not quake in his boots but he is too insecure vis-à-vis Obama's barefaced arrogance and Israel's own homegrown hecklers. Netanyahu's passivity would be bad enough were this a fixed, non-fluctuating situation. The problem is that it isn't.

The more Netanyahu consents to taking it on the chin, the more audacious Obama gets and the more any head of government anywhere feels empowered to chime in and add his or her two cents' worth. Even the relatively friendly Angela Merkel couldn't resist getting in on the act. Obama strikes the tone, while others sing along and relish harmony at Israel's expense.

British government headliners appear united solely by their obsession with fifty housing units in the Jerusalem suburb of Geva Binyamin (aka Adam), five kilometers northeast of Israel's capital. It boggles the mind to think that world stability hinges on the project not being completed.

Nevertheless, this is the consistent international de rigueur mantra. It is what none-too-impartial NGOs abroad haughtily hector. It is what a slew of accomplice "peace-promoting" local NGOs (which derive their funding from European and other less-than-friendly overseas benefactors) trendily reiterate. It is what the Israeli coterie of tendentious left-wing news purveyors unquestioningly chants.

Under these circumstances, the pushy presumptuousness toward Israel becomes inevitable. Israel earned the disdain it encounters everywhere. Foreign governments take liberties against Israeli sovereignty that would be inconceivable against any other independent country. It's doubtful any other state anywhere would be treated with similar disrespect – not just by inimical leaders like Obama, but even by emissaries like George Mitchell was. Ours is to do their bidding even at our palpable peril.

The more Netanyahu delays forthrightly defying such international chutzpa, the more he invites it. There are times when seemly circumspection is contraindicated. Begin by now would have called the American ambassador to order and sent an unequivocal message to said ambassador's boss, even at the risk of local sycophants rushing to brownnose the latter-day Sam Lewis.

Poster Child of Razzmatazz Land

The only thing I ever admired about Michael Jackson was his doll collection. He had a hoard of vintage 1930s-era composition Shirley Temples that I shamelessly envy.

Otherwise, I confess to being underwhelmed. That probably marks me as hopelessly out of sync with most of humanity – to judge by the media-hyped hysteria about the self-inflicted demise of yet another showbiz oddball. So sorry to be a killjoy at the time of an obvious international mourning fest.

Sarah, age two and a half, with her very first antique doll

That said, I did heave a great sigh of relief upon learning that the live-in cardiologist who attended to the King of Pop at his deathbed wasn't a Jew. That was all the Jewish people needed – another deicide to be blamed on us. When it comes to Jews, there are no individual wrongdoers. The fault is insidiously collective.

Just imagine if the eccentric who sang "Jew me, sue me" and "kick me, kike me" was actually supplied drugs by a "kike" MD. It would have been another irresistible pretext for innuendo.

Just imagine the inevitable subtle accusations swelling into unrestrained rants about the Jewish vendetta against the frail saint who sought solace in Bahrain, who perhaps soulfully sympathized with Islam, who surrounded himself with guards from the milieu of Louis Farrakhan (of "Judaism-is-a-gutter-religion" and "Hitler-was-a-great-man" fame), whose family friends are Jesse Jackson (of "Hymietown" fame) and Al Sharpton (of the Crown Heights pogrom fame).

The hypothetical ramifications are frightening, especially given that Neverland's bizarre misshapen kid-wannabe was the ultimate icon of the image-is-all-that-counts mindset. The real Michael never mattered – apparently also not to himself – and hence his obsessive self-mutilation in search of supposed beauty. Grotesquely sculpted by cosmetic surgeons, he was the perfect poster child of razzmatazz land, where truth mustn't interfere with the mass fantasy, fiction is serially superior to reality and appearance trumps substance.

Jacko dulled his mind with chemical cocktails rather than endure the aches and hurts suffered by lesser mortals. The substances he used to soothe whatever unsettled him weren't substantially different from the kitschy catchphrases which serve as the proverbial painkillers in our geopolitical reality. Facile formulations for peace on earth and goodwill to all villains and despots are just as common among respectable unthinking denizens in the world's democracies as prescribed narcotics are in Hollywood. They are just as addictive, no less imbecilic and every bit as dangerous.

Like their stoned superstars, vast multitudes of fashion-following quasi-junkies are lulled into an artificial calm. It's too difficult to exert indolent gray matter, study history's none-too-simple lessons and come to terms with the realization that instant remedies can't be prescribed for all trials and tribulations. Not every crisis can be magically wished away, managed or even minimized. Some afflictions demand struggle but struggle isn't what the Jackson crowd countenances.

The strife-shy inclinations of a self-delusional pseudo-free world, led by a sappy-slushy Obama-entranced America, are lapped up with undisguised delight by Tehran and its satellites. The American president purveys sweet cure-alls to his citizenry and cloyingly seeks to impress the ayatollahs with his evenhandedness. However, no matter what his message, he breeds nothing but contempt among his would-be Iranian interlocutors. They'll extort exorbitant prices for even condescending to civil conversation.

Not intoxicated themselves, they recognize that Obama's America – hooked on superficial solutions – is bereft of moral fortitude. They know that when push comes to shove, Obama's diplomatic raison d'être is to make nice in order to purchase a modicum of their cooperation. In return Obama will do little more than kick up a loud fuss about their nukes, presumably on condition these only be directed against Israel.

And Obama will make Israel look bad. It will seem to deserve threats and punishment. It will be judged as bringing misfortune and menace upon itself. Small price to fork out for Iranian compliance with obligatory Obama-esque stage-setting.

Obama's premise is that paying with an Israeli coin will eventually buy an ayatollah dialogue of sorts. The dialogue will be marketed to America and Europe as progress. After all, "keeping the channels of communication open" is a narcotic worth sacrificing Israel for. In a world of shallow façades, propping up the pretense is the name of the game.

In that world, regardless of how ruthlessly they crush the pro-democracy movement, Tehran's tyrants will be appeased. The totalitarian regime for which Ahmadinejad fronts is assured preferential treatment to that accorded irritant Israel – the antithesis to Obama-brand opium for the masses.

Ironically, Obama will undermine precisely those moderate factions in the region to whom his beguiling rhetoric is ostensibly geared to appeal. The so-called temperate Palestinians in Mahmoud Abbas's entourage can posture as forces to be reckoned with only because Israel buttresses them. By weakening Israel, Obama won't strengthen those who depend on Israel. Willy-nilly Obama will render Abu Mazen increasingly vulnerable to Hamas predations. Obama functions as the de facto enabler for Iran's proxies.

During the entire Obama presidency Israel is guaranteed to be universally deserted and to remain chillingly alone. For the sake of sedating America, Obama will offer real perks to the Arab/Muslim fanatics and will try to coerce Israel into real concessions that will undercut its survival prospects.

This reality is bitter enough to cause many Israelis to themselves seek the seductive comfort of blunted cognition. Dealing with the real hardships of our predicament may be too much. Escaping torments, unremitting adversity, treachery and defamation is ever tempting. It's not easy to acknowledge existential peril. Being unpopular is agonizing. Jackson craved the safety of acceptance, the bliss offered by potent psychogenic tonics – to the point of deliberately deadening all discordant sensations.

Nevertheless, Jackson – like other celebs, e.g., Anna Nicole Smith – aren't held responsible for their choices and resultant downfalls. It's as if they're not masters of their fates and not liable for their failures. According to conventional narratives, they're at the mercy of merciless manipulators.

Just like world opinion.

News consumers aren't held accountable for their cerebral sluggishness. They're not expected to think but to routinely run with the herd. That's why they fall for anti-Israel machinations and why we ought to be thankful that the pill-pushing doc wasn't Jewish.

A Jew would have never enjoyed the leeway accorded Jackson when he resorted to slurs every bit as offensive as the dreaded N-word. All Jackson had to do to get away with his "Jew me" and "kike me" lyrics was to chirp that he's "not anti-Semitic because I'm not a racist person. I could never be a racist. I love all races." That sufficed for those besotted with him. In the same razzle-dazzle reality no more is demanded of King-of-Political-Pop Obama.

Drenching Little Srulik

When I grew up and actually got to meet and even strike up a friendship with my childhood idol Dosh (the late Israeli cartoonist and illustrator Kariel Gardosh), I asked him which, to his mind, was his most enduring political caricature. For that, he replied, we need return to December 1956 – approximately a month after the Sinai Campaign and the Soviet invasion of Hungary.

Dosh noticed that while the international community was seething about Israel's feisty self-defense, it wasn't overly perturbed about the human rights and self-determination brazenly crushed beneath heavy military armor right in central Europe.

The hypocrisy, Dosh recalled, was hardly surprising but nevertheless galling, particularly the shamelessness of it. So he compressed it all into one frame. In the background a house labeled

Dosh's quintessential 1956 caricature, showing UN secretary general as a fireman directing his hose at Srulik, while Hungary burns

Hungary is going up in flames. In the foreground UN Secretary-General Dag Hammarskjöld, in firefighter gear, wields a hose labeled UN. But he's not dousing the blaze. He's drenching little Israel – Dosh's iconic sandal-clad Srulik – who stands soaked, angry and perplexed as he's subjected to more wet punishment.

Dosh produced way more dramatic and memorable cartoons but he estimated that the situation portrayed in this one will always stay topical. He predicted that Israel will always be the world's whipping boy, thrashed for the misdeeds of others and used for diversionary tactics. Instead of dealing with urgent crises and genuinely alarming dangers, the powers that be will rage at Israel to draw attention away from their own dereliction and cowardice.

"The old czars," Dosh noted, "used to say 'beat the Jews and save Russia.' Today it's 'beat the Jews and save the world.'" He reckoned this would "stay true even when nobody remembers Hammarskjöld."

If Dosh only knew how right he was. Today he'd probably have produced a very similar pen-and-ink commentary but with Iran burning and Barack Obama extinguishing…Israel. The more things change, the more they stay the same.

As pro-democracy demonstrators were killed in Tehran and as its ayatollahs furthered their designs to arm themselves with nukes, the leader of the free world harped on Israeli settlements. You can almost understand where he came from. Iran is a tough customer and crazy too. It's tempting not to rile it and to deflect criticism by focusing on some lonely remote outposts in the middle of Judea and Samaria's barren moonscape.

Not only isn't Israel scary like Iran, it'll broadmindedly collaborate in an effort to appease its detractors. How facile it therefore is to claim that peace and bliss on earth hinge on tearing down a few Jewish tents, rickety lean-tos, ramshackle sheds and decrepit trailers. It's true heroism to take them on in the guise of securing global propriety. It's plain to see that no greater peril plagues humanity – if we only avert our gaze from Iran, that is.

Accordingly, Obama announced for all to hear: "I take a wait-and-see approach. It is not productive, given the history of US-Iranian relations, to be seen as meddling in Iranian elections."

Of course it's one thing to entertain such notions, but quite another to broadcast them out loud. All sorts of perceptions may prevail in the Oval Office and shape policy, so long as they're not ballyhooed. Blabbermouth statecraft, however, is a bad idea. Noisy hype doesn't go unnoticed, especially not in the nuance-sensitive Middle East.

Obama may arrogantly consider himself super clever, but his overtly declared nonintervention is equivalent to…intervention. Neutrality is often complicity with the status quo.

Obama's error is eerily reminiscent of the series of egregious errors toward Tehran during the term of Jimmy Carter, the past president most like Obama, though hardly as radical.

In his memoirs, Khomeini's first foreign minister, Ebrahim Yazdi, writes that "the Shah was doomed the minute Carter entered the White House." The novice president indiscreetly sent all the wrong signals, beginning with an exceedingly public cold shoulder to the shah. The mullahs were heartened and exuded confidence. Increasingly shaken, Mohammad Reza Pahlavi sought to ingratiate himself to Carter by relaxing restrictions on opposition agitators. That further emboldened the religious fanatics and spawned unrest. Carter admonished the shah against quelling the disturbances by force.

Willy-nilly, Carter's bungling was instrumental in installing a reactionary, repressive theocracy in Tehran. Under the banner of freedom, Carter helped the forces of medieval darkness. The shah was a goner and the ayatollahs repaid Carter by holding fifty-two American embassy staffers hostage for 444 days until he was replaced by Ronald Reagan.

Carter's indisputable legacy was the bloodshed of the Iran-Iraq War, the carnage at the Buenos Aires Jewish Community Center and Israeli embassy, the burgeoning of Hezbollah and Hamas, the co-option of Syria/Lebanon and Gaza into Iran's evil sphere, massive-scale worldwide terror mongering and lately nuclear ambitions and rhetoric about wiping Israel off the map.

During the entire embassy-standoff fiasco, strikingly ineffectual Carter dithered piteously. Yet he compensated for inaction on one front by hyperactivity on another. As per the Dosh depiction, he turned the water jets on…Israel.

Carter's entire diplomatic energy reserves were misspent on pressuring Menachem Begin at Camp David, and quite ruthlessly so. The Georgia ex-peanut farmer's latent anti-Semitism would finally manifest itself with the publication of his book *Palestine: Peace Not Apartheid*. His misguided liberalism in international affairs led Carter to bolster the worst despots in our time while lashing out at one of the most intrinsically democratic of societies anywhere – Israel.

Unrepentant, same said Carter hobnobbed with Gaza's terror kingpins just as Iranians protested against ayatollah tyranny. He spuriously censured Israel for treating Gazans "more like animals than human beings.… Never before in history has a large community been savaged by bombs and missiles and then deprived of the means to repair itself.… This abuse must cease. The crimes must be investigated. The wall must be brought down, and the basic right of freedom must come to you," he told Hamastan's ayatollah proxies, without a word about Israel's pullback from Gaza, the uprooting of twenty-one settlements and the atrocities that Gaza subsequently unleashed on Israel.

Carter is Obama's mentor and Obama is the new Carter.

Their motto is: in democracy's name, be kind to democracy's most rabid enemies and be nasty to embattled democrats. Hence, while it's "not productive" for Obama to meddle in Iran, it's imperative he meddle in Israel. Déjà vu. As in Carter's administration, a lopsided artificial balance must be struck in pseudo-sophisticated statesmanship.

In other words: no matter where fires flare uncontrollably, the fire hoses will be aimed at Israel. This is why Dosh's caricature remains ever relevant – just as he predicted.

Haggling over the Price

As anecdote has it, George Bernard Shaw once asked an attractive socialite whether she'd sleep with him for a million pounds. After she answered in the affirmative, he offered her a mere ten shillings. Outraged, she railed: "What do you take me for? A prostitute?"

Shaw reputedly replied: "We've already determined that. We're just haggling over the price."

Now substitute Barack Obama for Shaw and our own Binyamin Netanyahu for Shaw's peeved female interlocutor.

We're not saying that Bibi is a prostitute, not even in the loosest polemic sense. Indeed, given our current political setting, he's perhaps the best prime minister we can hope for. He's the lesser of available evils. What we're saying is that he had willy-nilly cast himself in the prostitute's role when agreeing to a Palestinian state, albeit demilitarized (demilitarization being eminently reversible).

Netanyahu established the principle that his principles are for sale and all that's left is to fix the conditions.

It's not that Netanyahu blithely sold out his ideological virtue. He's under seemingly inexorable pressure to demonstrate "moderation." However, moderation isn't all it's cracked up to be and in itself is hardly what we should automatically aspire to. It may work in certain circumstances but bomb in others. Moderation, moreover, isn't necessarily synonymous with pragmatism.

And pragmatism isn't always wise and mustn't be confused with levelheadedness. History is replete with examples of calamitous and cowardly choices paraded as pragmatic. All too often the road to disaster is paved with pragmatic considerations. Conversely sometimes bold and nonconformist responses prove in retrospect to have been actually pragmatic. On the eve of WWII it was hawkish Churchill who was realistic and popular dove Chamberlain who was the dupe.

Pragmatism is akin to focusing on specific potholes in our national path rather than sometimes lifting our eyes from the ground to scan the horizon, survey the sweep of the land and behold the full track ahead. Pragmatism is getting bogged down in details and neglecting the whole. It's quibbling about issues and forgetting the basics.

That's what Ariel Sharon did in 2003, when he wouldn't reject the road map to supposed peace. Instead he composed fourteen reservations – like Netanyahu's reservations vis-à-vis a Palestinian state. But who today remembers Sharon's footnotes? America disdainfully ignored his fourteen objections. These mattered temporarily only in our internal self-deceptive discourse. Same goes for Netanyahu's Palestinian state footnotes.

The blood-soaked map continues to obligate us despite Sharon's provisos. Similarly, the Palestinian state will continue to plague us after the limitations Netanyahu set for it are discarded – as they surely will be. Sharon's stipulations are down history's unforgiving, all-devouring sinkhole. It would have been wiser to tear up the disastrous map (postfactum deemed holy gospel) than to accept it with conditions (postfactum deemed illegitimate).

Some of us benighted sorts said so in real time but were maligned as rabid fiery-eyed nutcases, foaming at the mouth for good measure. We were roundly derided for recalling how in 1967 nobody in the White House could find the 1957 document spelling out US assurances that Egypt won't blockade the Tiran Straits again. American infidelity made the Six-Day War unavoidable. Washington could have preempted that showdown and its derivative so-called "occupation."

Anyone who ever counted on clever formulations and American promises wasn't a pragmatist but a fool. Remember US undertakings not to deal with the PLO? Count on Obama to just as cynically overlook more recent declarations against powwowing with Hamas.

Obama, we must bear in mind, is less sympathetic to our cause than even his least savory predecessors. Hence his feigned ignorance of Bush's understandings with Sharon regarding settlement blocks. Assurances Obama might offer Netanyahu on a Palestinian state would be just as fleeting.

Obama after all has indulgently redefined terrorism as pesky "extremism." The corollary is that Israel's emphasis on its enemies' terrorist proclivities instead of on Jewish rights is wasted breath. It only serves to magnify the inimical trendy perception that we're in the wrong and that those who would annihilate us are desperate insurgents against injustice.

Instead of being reduced to prostitute status, we're better off going back to basics, proclaiming loud and clear that the Arabs only conjured Palestinian nationality in order to stake rival claims to ours; that a Palestinian state never existed (i.e., we certainly didn't conquer and subjugate it); that *we* were attacked; that we didn't drive out hapless refugees (who themselves started the war); that they caused their own downfall by plotting genocide and ethnic cleansing against us; that our only sin is surviving. We might as well remind the world of the Nazi legacy of Pan-Arab/Palestinian hero Haj Amin al-Husseini.

Arabs launched a war against the two-state solution and brazenly now continue that very war under the two-state banner. If the world misrepresents this bloody dispute as being about a Palestinian state, we must protest that it's really about denying the right of a *Jewish* state to exist. Otherwise, to please our critics, we concede the Palestinian argument.

Israel's latest misguided position – about natural growth in the settlements – is equally damaging. It's counterproductive to stutter about the right of Jews to reside everywhere in the 22 percent of Eretz Yisrael west of the Jordan River. The remaining 78 percent – east of the river – should satisfy the aspirations of Arabs calling themselves Palestinians (resorting to an epithet invented by the Romans to humiliate defeated Judea). That 78 percent has been renamed Jordan, primarily to further Arab irredentist designs to wrest from Jews the little left them – slice by slice.

No Obama can imperiously deny us our rights in our homeland – just as Titus Vespasianus couldn't. When we humbly implore to be permitted to make room in select settlements for baby Jews, we seem to confirm that our very presence is offensive, that we're interlopers, that Jews may not move to the Jerusalem suburb of Ma'ale Adumim. We only beg that supplicant parents already in Ma'ale Adumim be please allowed to keep their babies there and that Obama let them build nurseries for said newborns, even if Obama doesn't welcome their birth.

We gain as much respect via ignominious compromises as did the woman whose asking price George Bernard Shaw attempted to lower. As soon as we turn our existential struggle into something that resembles negotiations about the prostitute's remuneration, we forfeit everything because promises made to a prostitute are never kept. No one owes her a thing.

The assumption is that everything she does is illicit, that at most she can expect a little condescending pity mixed with disgust, that she resides outside normative society and cannot expect what others perceive as their natural due. Most of all she can be endlessly pushed around and her prices pushed down. Just like Israel.

Nitpickers That We Are

Barack Obama's intentions when delivering his over-long, cloying and history-warping Cairo University speech may have been good. He may have genuinely imagined himself on a messianic mission to win Muslim hearts by virtue of his own (hitherto expediently downplayed) Muslim background.

His references to colonialism and past treatment of Arabs as cold-war proxies (never mind their own cynical exploitation of the clout handed them thereby) no doubt appealed equally to politically correct European postmodernists. Anything that takes the West down a peg and exalts the Third World is in great vogue.

That, coupled with the seemingly sincere stance of the speaker and his superstar can't-set-a-foot-wrong invulnerability, makes his assertions stick excruciatingly in the craw of chronically uncool, non-cheerleader types. It's hard to swallow so much schmaltz and saccharine, washed down with so much honey and olive oil.

Try as some of us benighted nausea-prone sorts might, we couldn't sprout fairy wings and dance merrily in the light projected forth from the halo of the White House resident.

Nitpickers that we are, we couldn't stop harping on incidentals such as the slapdash equivalence Obama drew between the Holocaust and the Palestinian "pain of dislocation," and between mass murder and settlement construction (much of Jerusalem included).

We couldn't chant his mantra that Palestinian "displacement" was "brought by Israel's founding" (fully in line with deceptive Arab narratives). We couldn't gracefully accept blame for "daily humiliations that come with occupation" or for Gaza's "humanitarian crisis."

Azzam Pasha (front left) and Haj Amin al-Husseini (front middle) on the steps of the Arab League headquarters in Cairo, 1948

Unable to partake in the stylish hoopla and pretend that Obama spouted novel insightful revelations, we couldn't extinguish some unmodified memories. No matter how much we're urged to beat our breasts in agonizing contrition, we know Israelis never set out to dispossess anyone. We likewise know that designs existed on the Arab side not only to dispossess all Jews in embryonic yet-to-be-born Israel, but if possible to annihilate every last one of them.

On May 1, 1948, two weeks before Israel's birth, Arab League Secretary-General Azzam Pasha warned, "If the Zionists dare establish a state, the massacres we would unleash will dwarf anything which Genghis Khan and Hitler perpetrated."

Obama should know Arabs became displaced in combat they initiated for the expressed purpose of displacing Jews.

It's bad if he doesn't realize this. It's abysmally worse if he deliberately feigns ignorance of the 1947–48 expulsions by Arabs of Jews in this country from both ancient and new communities, with all the attendant carnage Azzam Pasha promised and which was already then – before Israel's establishment – maliciously drilled into the Arab mentality.

On its first day, defenseless newborn Israel was ruthlessly attacked by seven Arab armies. So-called Palestinians ended up subjecting themselves to a minuscule portion of the catastrophe they planned for Israelis. They got their just deserts. Israel only caused the problem by not adhering to the Arab script for its own demise. Though tragically outnumbered and outgunned, Israel gallingly repulsed the concerted Arab invasion. That was Israel's one and only cardinal offense. So, Obama, pardon us for living.

Prior to Israel's creation, Arabs refused any compromise that left Jews even an unviable toehold, like the deathtrap patchwork between Tel Aviv and Netanya. Obama disingenuously avoided mentioning that the Arabs could have had their Palestinian state, but didn't want it. They wanted Israel destroyed. They instigated bloody sabotage of the UN's 1947 partition resolution (which they now wish implemented). Had the Arabs not launched their war, they wouldn't have lost. There would have been no refugees and no pretext for unremitting discontent.

The same goes for their discomforts at roadblocks and their distress in Gaza. Had they not launched a terror war against Israel, no checkpoints, barriers or limitations on Gazan crossings would have been necessary. These originated from the need to protect Israelis from free-roaming terrorists. Arabs inflicted this too on themselves, yet outside onlookers – Obama foremost – accept and promote the poor pitiful Palestinian underdog pose.

By likening Palestinians to America's black slaves, Obama inculcated a shocking canard into the minds of his adulating audiences worldwide. He didn't criticize the professed motivations of the terrorists (or mere "extremists" in his idiom), only the ineffectiveness of their methods. "Resistance through violence," he intoned, "does not succeed." Had it succeeded, it might perhaps receive his blessing.

Obama rendered the perception of terrorists as freedom-fighters an axiomatic premise. He amplified this key Arab propaganda postulate – that terror was provoked by the *nakba*, the Arab homegrown "calamity" and insidious moniker for Jewish self-determination. *Nakba* is the lead entry in the Arab lexicon of Israel's delegitimization and its ongoing effect on the Arab psyche is potent.

Arabs demand confession of crime and auto-demonization from Israel. Thereafter, presumably, aspiring Arab exterminators might let some Jews subsist as tainted interlopers in their sphere (which they regard as their *Lebensraum*, after the example of the Third Reich). By playing along, Obama drastically diminished peace prospects rather than enhanced them. Why would vehemence against Israel subside when the leader of the free world validates it?

Essentially Obama requires Israelis to acknowledge culpability or be pilloried as obstructionists. Yet wouldn't Israeli self-denunciation serve as justification for Israel's eventual elimination? Admission of guilt would hardly make fanatical hate abate. If anything, it would encourage millions of brainwashed Arabs, spuriously claiming refugee status, to inundate and eradicate the Jewish state.

Had Obama earnestly intended to become a harbinger of change, the last thing he'd have claimed was that Israel spawned the Palestinian problem. He would have stressed that hate predated Israel, that Arabs fulminated with genocidal antagonism even as Jews began marring the perfection of a depopulating desert ringed by putrid malaria-ridden swamps. "Butcher the Jews" was the clarion call – already in the early 1920s – of the revered pan-Arab would-be führer Haj Amin al-Husseini, who would in time gain infamy as an avid Nazi-collaborator, a Berlin resident during WWII, a Holocaust accomplice and a wanted war criminal postwar.

Obama should have emphasized that the so-called Palestinian misfortune was bred by lethal Arab lies – from cynical incitement to slaughter in 1929 because Jews purportedly plotted domination of the Temple Mount (to which, according to brazen Arab fabrication, Jews anyway have absolutely no historic/religious ties) to the latest spate of intifadas fueled by the identical calumnies.

Change isn't flattery but courage to state the truth: Palestine is an irredentist contrivance. Arabs only discovered (and initially rejected) the European appellation (of anti-Judaic Roman origins) after the British Mandate began.

But the more a lie is allowed to fester, the more it takes hold. Over time it becomes a given, not only in the seething Middle East but also among intellectually indolent respectable folks elsewhere. Truth is fragile. Obama failed to sustain it. If anything, he severely undercut it. He granted falsehoods and semi-falsehoods the sort of incomparable resonance that wouldn't prevent the clash of civilizations, but would hasten it.

Not a Spiritual Santa

From the outset it was unrealistic, if not altogether foolish, to look for any show of emotional empathy or heartfelt contrition from the German pope during his historic address at Yad Vashem. Those who harbored such expectations didn't base them on Benedict XVI's actual personality but on a kindly spiritual Santa, a figment of their wishful thinking. Josef Alois Ratzinger, however, is a product of his time and upbringing. It would have been out of character for him to conduct himself otherwise. He conformed to his predisposition and didn't break conventions, as we perhaps kidded ourselves that he might.

This has nothing to do with whether or not he was forced to join the Hitlerjugend or with his conscription (willing or not) into Nazi military service. It perhaps has more to do with his postwar milieu, when coercion was no longer a pretext. The worldview of this devotedly religious, ultraconservative youth was shaped in American-occupied Bavaria.

There, the church that guided Ratzinger made it its mission to shirk charges of collective German guilt. It became Church doctrine to assert that guilt was an individual issue to be judged by God. Accordingly, churches throughout post-Holocaust Germany held prayers of forgiveness for all "who had gone astray."

After that, the past was to be sidelined – the quicker the better.

Germans avidly did their darndest to misremember. The US Army's Information Control Division conducted opinion polls in November 1945 which showed that only 20 percent of Germans considered their country responsible for the war. Repeat polling in January 1948 showed no perceptible change. Germans were neither ashamed nor repentant.

Moreover, the church in effect did its utmost to foil denazification, perceiving it as leftist and atheist. Nazis were tolerantly regarded as redeemable and deserving of absolution and a second chance. Clerics under whom the young Ratzinger studied, instructed Catholics not to assist Allied denazification tribunals. The Church itself came to the aid of former Nazi officials by backing up their contentions that they were small-time functionaries at the bottom rungs of the Third Reich hierarchy. This enabled many Nazi hotshots both to escape justice and to remain influential in the civilian frameworks of the "New Germany."

Thus many Third Reich stalwarts were acquitted and remained the honchos who called the shots day-to-day also in the "New Germany."

Before long, the convenient mythology of German victimhood

and lack of any culpability arose. Holocaust atrocities were committed by indeterminate "others," called Nazis. Something bad happened about which nobody knew and for which nobody is blameworthy. That essentially was the recurrent refrain of Benedict's frosty homily at Auschwitz-Birkenau in 2006. Anyone who recalled his clichés then couldn't have been surprised by his insensitive omissions at Yad Vashem three years later.

If any doubt lingered about how snugly this pontiff fits into the moral mold of his native land, his assertions at the largest German death camp eliminated it. According to Benedict, Germans "were used and abused" by "a ring of criminals."

Like most of his smug compatriots, he evidently subscribes to a laundered version of history, where the Holocaust is reduced to a crime without readily identifiable perpetrators. Moreover, these anonymous felons "ultimately wanted to tear up the taproot of the Christian faith." Ergo, 1.5 million Jewish children were martyred in the context of an onslaught on Christianity.

To hear the bishop of Rome, no occupied country colluded in deporting its Jews, none spawned greedy looters and collaborators, while the occupiers themselves were an alien band of no distinct ethnicity, known generically as Nazis, or "a ring of criminals."

Even Germans mustn't be required to assume collective onus for them. Sanitized history portrays Germany as yet another pitiably occupied nation. The Allies "liberated" – not vanquished – it. Germans prefer to bellyache about their suffering, avoiding excessive emphasis on the fact that without millions of ardent followers and enthusiastic accomplices, no "ring of criminals" could have sadistically slaughtered multitudes.

With blitzkrieg intensity, bloodstained Germany was transformed into spotless progressive New Germany, which goes out of its way to profess bigheartedness and beneficence. The pope, as he described himself, is indeed "a son of Germany."

For Germans collectively, WWII's calculated, systemized, industrialized bloodletting constituted something akin to reform school. Dutiful Germans recited their lessons, did their homework, sat for their exams and graduated with honors. What more can Jews demand of them? They paid their dues. They emerged edified from the cataclysm.

By their yardstick, Jews didn't equally purify themselves nor rise to Germany's ethical standards, overcome the distasteful past as elegantly as all Europeans, surmount residual unpleasantness and let bygones be bygones. Hence, even Germans feel free to carp about Israeli self-defense and urge Israel's return to the Auschwitz borders (as dovish Abba Eban dubbed the 1949 armistice lines).

Benedict's righteous platitudes and missed opportunities at Birkenau presaged more of the same at Yad Vashem. If nothing else, he demonstrated unwavering consistency.

Standing at Birkenau – 95 percent of whose inmates were Jews – he listed the various nationalities of Auschwitz prisoners, as if the tragedy were identical and the proportions equal. He managed not to point out that Jews were exterminated like vermin, not in a violent fit but in painstakingly premeditated fashion – orderly, methodical and mass-production-style. They weren't even a warring side.

In the same vein, at Yad Vashem, he couldn't bring himself to admit that Holocaust victims were "murdered." This meticulous scholar certainly understood the difference between "killed" and "murdered" (hence his afterthought attempted correction before departure).

But at least both in Poland and Jerusalem Benedict at all referred to Jews. In 2005, while condemning global terrorism, he lamented bloodshed in Britain, Egypt, and Turkey. For some reason, Israel wasn't included. Subsequent attempts to whitewash the oversight only made matters worse. The Vatican contended that Benedict alluded only to "recent incidents." Yet a suicide bombing in Netanya on July 11, 2005, came *after* the July 7 targeting of London's mass transit passengers and the human toll in Netanya was greater than that of the Turkish outrage which followed later.

Even if this betrayed a subconscious tendency to discount Jewish lives, we can nevertheless take facetious satisfaction in noting that things have improved. Eventually, in obligatory circumstances, Jews were accorded obligatory papal mention. It's progress and in our existence that's nothing to scoff at, especially so far as Jews are concerned.

On more serious reflection, though, our lesson from the visit – whose importance we exaggerated, as only affection-craving Jews can – is that we ought to know the characters at play well but to care about their utterances and opinions of us a whole lot less.

We really shouldn't bother about what the pope pontificated here, to which precise phraseology he resorted or whether he inched closer to an apology. We don't need his approval. As David Ben-Gurion maintained decades ago: "It doesn't matter what the goyim say, but what the Jews do."

Don't Dream On

Dreams, when they serve as wish-fulfillment vehicles, are hard to give up. They become sources of comfort and confidence – even if, all too often, false ones. They are the gossamer pedestals on which dreamers base their prestige and self-possession, even when these contradict empirical evidence and coolheaded realism.

Jewish history is replete with examples of making believe that desires are fact. From early on, expressionist icon Max Liebermann (no relation to Israel's foreign minister) – the most renown painter of Weimar Republic days – should have known better than to expect genuine German recognition regardless of his Jewishness.

Yet a seminal signal was already dispatched in 1879 when his *Twelve-Year-Old Jesus in the Temple with the Scholars* was exhibited at the Munich International Art Fair. German critics excoriated the Berlin-born Jew's gall to focus on a New Testament theme. Liebermann was pilloried in the press and condemning him became so de rigueur that even the Bavarian parliament, egged on by the Crown Prince, couldn't resist censuring him.

But dreams endure. Liebermann only pressed harder in his quest for German approval. In order not to offend hostile opinion, he thereafter avoided religious motifs and revamped the Semitic-looking Jesus of his controversial work. The child's dark locks were repainted blond, the profile became more Nordic and hand gestures were modified. Jewish origins befitted neither the artist nor his subject. Authenticity was consciously subverted to facilitate the façade.

Are we here and now any better? Don't we fool ourselves as much?

Liebermann sacrificed his artistic freedom and personal integrity. We sacrifice our national honor, heritage and security. But are these sacrifices so dissimilar in essence? Don't we crave acceptance every bit as much as Liebermann did? For all of Zionism's avowed aim to remold the delusionary Jewish psyche, self-deception is entrenched in the Jewish state. Instead of trusting our senses, we prefer sweet imaginings. We are disturbed by what our eyes and ears report. We are soothed by fantasy.

We have been pretending for many years that we won Palestinian recognition, though cognitively we know the PLO Charter calling for Israel's destruction was never abrogated.

Palestinian Authority websites, official communiqués and school curriculums all attest that the charter/covenant lives on with all clauses intact – just as they were before the sham spectacle staged in

Gaza to impress the visiting Bill Clinton on December 14, 1998. On that occasion articles which "contradicted the exchange of letters with the Israeli government on September 1993" (Oslo) were supposedly nullified by a show of hands (with votes uncounted) at a Palestinian Central Council session attended by the visibly gratified US president.

That charade followed a string of previous evasions of undertakings to abolish explicit exhortations for Israel's obliteration. In effect, the PA periodically promised amendments without ever making actual changes.

Genocidal intent was declared years before the 1967 pretext for the myth that enmity to Israel arose from post–Six-Day War "occupation." The destroy-Israel refrain was already central to the "Palestinian Constitution" drafted in 1963 by Ahmed Shukeiri, the PLO's first chairman. It was officially adopted in 1964.

The charter's second article incidentally states: "Palestine, with the boundaries it had during the British Mandate, is an indivisible territorial unit." Translation: no fragment for Israel, while Jordan (comprising nearly 80 percent of the Mandate territory) is Palestine according to the Palestinians, who nevertheless posture as stateless before the international community.

Following are other choice charter selections:

> **Article 9:** Armed struggle is the only way to liberate Palestine. Thus it is the overall strategy, not merely a tactical phase.
> **Article 15:** The liberation of Palestine, from an Arab viewpoint, is a national duty and it attempts to repel Zionist and imperialist aggression against the Arab homeland, and aims at the elimination of Zionism in Palestine.
> **Article 19:** The partition of Palestine in 1947 and the establishment of Israel are entirely illegal, regardless of the passage of time.
> **Article 22:** Zionism is a political movement organically

associated with international imperialism.... It is racist and fanatic in its nature, aggressive, expansionist, and colonial in its aims, and fascist in its methods. Israel is the instrument of the Zionist movement, and geographical base for world imperialism placed strategically in the midst of the Arab homeland to combat the hopes of the Arab nation for liberation, unity, and progress. Israel is a constant source of threat vis-à-vis peace in the Middle East and the whole world. Since the liberation of Palestine will destroy the Zionist and imperialist presence and will contribute to the establishment of peace in the Middle East, the Palestinian people look for support of all the progressive and peaceful forces and urge them all, irrespective of their affiliations and beliefs, to offer the Palestinian people all aid and support in their just struggle for the liberation of their homeland.

Article 33: This Charter shall not be amended save by a majority of two-thirds of the total membership of the National Congress of the Palestine Liberation Organization at a special session convened for that purpose.

Was a two-thirds majority achieved for the Clinton extravaganza? It's immaterial. Purportedly moderate Fatah argues that it's unbound by the ceremonial vote and to hardly moderate Hamas it's altogether utter anathema.

The 1988 farce, ironically, was produced for the benefit of then prime minister Binyamin Netanyahu, who insisted the charter be altered. All this should caution Netanyahu. He now rightly notes the lack of Palestinian acceptance of a Jewish state.

The danger is that Netanyahu would merely invite another elaborate con. The Palestinian penchant for deception is unmatched. Palestinians are yet to abide by any agreement they signed. Netanyahu's present challenge is not to be bamboozled even if Obama leans on him and collaborates with Mahmoud Abbas in a bid to lull Israelis to dream on.

We love to dream but awakenings can be mercilessly rude. German patriot Liebermann died in 1935, never realizing that next door to his Wannsee villa the Nazis would in 1942 decide on the Final Solution and that in 1943 his widow Martha would commit suicide there to escape deportation to Theresienstadt.

Yet Liebermann survived long enough to see how hollow his coveted recognition as a German was and how summarily it was withdrawn. He served as president of the Prussian Academy of Arts until forced out in 1933. "I sought to serve German art with all my strength," he wrote in his resignation letter. "My conviction is that art is unrelated to politics or descent."

That conviction was a dream. Liebermann acknowledged its shattering in a letter to poet Haim Nahman Bialik in Tel Aviv: "You perhaps recall the discussions we had on this subject, while I was working on your etching, during which I tried to explain why I distance myself from Zionism. I now think otherwise. As difficult as it was for me, I awakened from the dream I dreamt my whole life."

The Craftiest of Sophists

It's doubtful Palestinian Authority president Mahmoud Abbas (Abu Mazen) ever delved into Protagoras's philosophic slyness when he was enrolled at Moscow's communist-era Russian University for Friendship between People (aka the People's Friendship University of Russia, also aka the Patrice Lumumba Friendship University).

As best befits Friendship U's academic ambience, Abbas specialized in revising history – an endeavor which in 1982 ripened into a PhD dissertation that both denied the Holocaust yet blamed Zionists for it. Two years later Dr. Abbas further expanded and embellished his "research."

He never apologized for his brazen falsifications and never retracted so much as a single negligible nuance thereof.

But though Abbas probably never heard of Protagoras, he might as well have taken lessons from the old master himself on how to outsmart an adversary. It's hard to imagine a greater virtuoso practitioner of Protagorean tactics than Abbas – a proven whiz at having everything both ways. Win – you win. Lose – you also win.

The original Protagoras, after whom Plato named one of his most famous dialogues, was the foremost exponent of distortive dialectics in ancient Greece. It was the finely honed forte of thinkers known collectively as the Old Sophists. So great was Protagoras's reputation for guile that he was eagerly sought as a teacher of shifty polemics. His tutorials didn't come cheap. According to Plato, Protagoras made more than Phidias and ten other sculptors put together.

This spurred one of Protagoras's students to elude exorbitant tuition fees by contracting an agreement that exempted him from payment until he won his first legal case. Since the student never took up litigation, Protagoras sued him – confident of victory no matter how the trial went. If the ruling favored Protagoras, he'd collect the debt owed him. If Protagoras lost, his student would pay up by virtue of having won a legal case. The student felt equally self-assured. A favorable ruling meant he's not delinquent, while losing his case freed him from having to fork anything over.

Utterly bewildered, the judges decided to adjourn for one hundred years.

Such shenanigans, of course, would hardly wow anyone in our region. We regularly witness far more outrageous flip-flops of logic and scruples – like the "two-state" formulation. No one can accuse Abbas of reneging on anything. Didn't he (sort of) recognize Israel?

Admittedly, he did refrain from acknowledging it as a Jewish state, but that was for fear of waiving the right to Arabize it. It's okay by Abbas if the name Israel is temporarily applied to the third Arab state (after Jordan and "Palestine") in historic Eretz Yisrael (correspondingly roughly to the original British Mandate territory). This doesn't preclude overrunning it with millions of "repatriated" Arab refugees. The name will be changed later by the resultant Arab majority. No need to quibble about it prematurely.

"We don't accept the term 'Jewish state' and insist on achieving all our rights," Abbas announced unequivocally in Ramallah. "We say that Israel is a state and the Israelis have the right to call themselves whatever they wish. But I don't accept this. We told the Israelis that we only recognize the State of Israel…never a Jewish state."

While Protagoras and his artful dodger student both would be hard put to unsnarl the above tangle, they'd readily recognize Abbas as one of their own and salute him as the craftiest of sophists. Abbas's primary ruse is in convincing foreigners that the Middle East dispute can be settled by erasing Israel's 1967 victory to facilitate the establishment of a heretofore never-existent Palestinian state.

Simultaneously in internal Arab discourse it's obvious that the "occupation" and clamoring for a Palestinian state are nothing but pretexts to persist in a conflict that dates back to the mid-nineteenth century, and to delegitimize any Jewish entity in this land. From Abbas's perspective, the real grievance isn't the absence of yet another Arab state in original Palestine but the survival therein of the single Jewish state.

Leftist Israeli wishful thinking and yearnings for simplistic solutions helped market the deception that territorial concessions are all that's required. However, the Palestinians leave no room for a Jewish presence.

The second clause of their constitution (not a Hamas-wrought document but one authored by supposedly respectable statesmen, headed by Fatah's own Nabil Sha'ath) describes Palestinians as part of the "Islamic nation." Clause 5 specifies Islam as the state's established religion. Clause 7 bases all legislation on Islam.

The Palestinian state (initially slated for Gaza, Judea and Samaria) is to be *judenrein* and Muslim. Jordan, comprising nearly 80 percent of original Palestine, already is *judenrein* (by law) and Muslim.

That leaves the tiny remnant which Abbas would allow to provisionally be known as Israel. It wouldn't be Jewish but an indeterminate amorphous concoction, which already includes a sizable Arab irredentist minority, and which is to be further inundated by untold millions of hostile Arabs claiming spurious refugee status.

With that in mind, Protagoras's disciple offered to resume peace talks with Israel on the basis of the 2002 Saudi initiative, the two-state stratagem and that tattered American "road map."

"The [Saudi] peace initiative is no longer an Arab initiative," Abbas stressed with Protagorian cunning. "It has become part of the road map, which has been endorsed by the Quartet [the US, EU, UN and Russia], and as such it's an internationally recognized peace plan. We don't want to impose an Arab-Islamic peace vision on the Israelis, but this is an international plan."

A mantra to make Protagoras proud.

The Saudi plan to overwhelm Israel with Arab "returnees" was indeed embraced by the international community (no skin off European and American noses). It may appear innocuous to the uninitiated. Others don't mind its catastrophic consequences for Israel.

The world enthusiastically endorses the inbuilt asymmetry that obliges Israel to recognize a second Arab-Palestinian state while Arabs refuse to accept the legitimacy of one ethnic Jewish state. This lopsidedness is based on the premise that Israel is an occupier (in its own homeland), while migrant/conquistador Arabs are downtrodden natives.

Abbas can thus welsh on his undeniable road map commitments, yet maintain that he fulfills them to the letter. If he gets away with it – as the international community is quite content to let him – then he becomes an Arab hero.

If Israel, however, won't fully acquiesce to his prevarications, he'll pose as the wronged, piteously pleading weakling. Israeli vocal locals would avidly corroborate his assertions of helplessness, while the international community would offer unstinting succor.

Abbas can't lose.

He's safe so long as no one gets wise to his sophist wiles and looks up Aristotle's warnings against the Protagoras pattern of "making the weaker arguments sound stronger" and the false sound true.

The May Day Massacre

There's no telling where the final ideological resting place of intellectually restless Yosef Haim Brenner – one of the Second Aliya luminaries and founding giants of modern Hebrew literature – would have been had he not been slain before reaching his fortieth birthday. He might have evolved into a nationalist like initially leftist Moshe Shamir or followed his socialist leanings to the farthest radical fringe. Speculations are moot. Brenner was a full deck of cards from which any hand could have been dealt. Nothing was irrevocably predetermined when Arab marauders took his life on May 2, 1921.

As it was, they murdered a thinker quite fascinated by Arabs. Not that they cared much. Ironically, nowadays the Right – tendentiously almost always dubbed "the extreme Right" – is regarded as Zionism's firebrand, the component of our body politic which, alas, most incenses our enemies. The Left, in contrast, is cast – chiefly by its own hardly impartial spokespersons – in the role of the peacenik of the equation, the accommodating, "sane," pacifying side.

Arabs hardly subscribe to the current bias of Israel's own left-dominated media and academia. They never really did. As Brenner's tragic fate undeniably illustrates, to our enemies a Jew is a Jew is a Jew. Our enemies are equal opportunity assassins. They spill Jewish blood without discrimination, without first bothering to verify the political orientations of prospective victims.

Brenner was perhaps the most famous casualty of one of the twentieth century's forerunner Arab intifadas – the gory prototype of what we witness today and which our would-be annihilators and their gullible (and not-so-gullible) domestic and foreign cheerleaders insist is mere response to Israeli occupation.

There was no occupation when the 1921 intifada erupted on May 1. On that hot day the British police permitted a group of Labor Zionists to hold a May Day parade in then tiny Tel Aviv but denied the same privilege to Jewish communists, who rallied anyway in Neve Shalom, the second-earliest Jewish neighborhood adjacent to Jaffa. The two groups of leftist Jews collided and exchanged a few blows.

But while the Brits energetically chased several communists through Neve Shalom's winding narrow lanes, they doggedly turned a blind eye to the thousands of Arabs massing in Jaffa, all brandishing clubs, knives, hatchets and metal pipes and hysterically chanting *"Itbach el-Yahud"* (Slaughter the Jews).

With no British presence to cool their ardor, rioters began attacking Jewish passersby. The only representatives of the law were members of Jaffa's Arab constabulary. But rather than quell the rampage, they

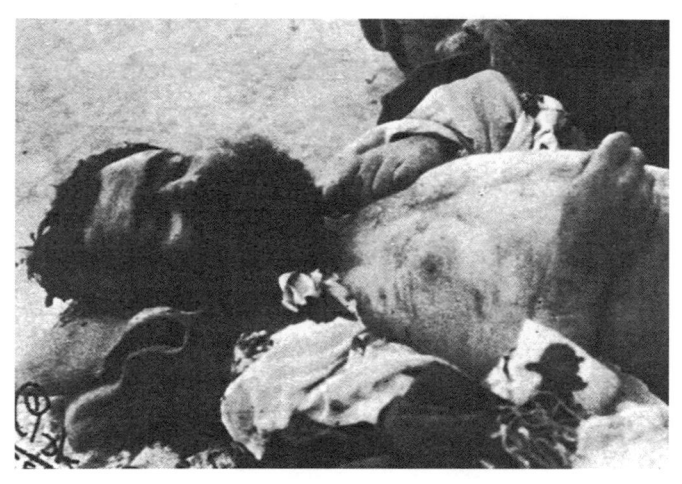

Body of murdered author Yosef Haim Brenner

helped turn it into "a full-scale pogrom," according to Yitzhak Ben-Zvi, who three decades later would become Israel's second president.

In a May 11, 1921, letter of protest to British high commissioner Sir Herbert Samuel, Ben-Zvi charged that "the Arab policemen themselves led the onslaught on the Jewish Immigrants Hostel in Jaffa's Ajami quarter. They shot Jews with weapons supplied them by the government." Sounds familiar?

Ben-Zvi continued: "Rather than disperse the rioters, the police encouraged them and distributed firearms to the incited rabble. They ignited the flame of murder, fanned by confidence that the government sides with them and that they can massacre Jews with impunity."

The hostel provided temporary shelter to newcomers who had just come off the boats at Jaffa's primitive port. Dozens were rooming there when the mobs tried to burst into the courtyard. After repeated unsuccessful attempts to break down the gate, Jaffa's senior Arab police officer, Tewfik Sa'id Bey, assured the besieged Jews that he had come to restore order and rescue them.

Trapped and unarmed, the relieved immigrants let him in. To their horror he tossed hand grenades at them and ushered in the screaming throng baying for their blood. Fourteen Jewish lodgers were hideously butchered and scores wounded.

The gruesome orgy spread quickly, like wildfire. It soon reached the outskirts of nearby Abu Kabir, a settlement of Arab migrants from Egypt. Where south Tel Aviv's teeming Derech Kibbutz Galuyot now stretches, the Jewish Yitzker family at the time set up a modest dairy farm – in seeming idyllic coexistence with the neighbors. The pessimistic brooding Brenner boarded there with two other authors – Yosef Luidor, twenty-eight, and Zvi Gugig, twenty-five. All three writers were home that fateful May Day, as was farm owner Yehuda Yitzker, fifty-four, and his teenage son, Avraham. The women and younger children traveled to town for the socialist celebrations.

When the dreadful scale of the Jaffa mayhem became apparent, Yitzker's son-in-law Zvi Schatz, also a literati, hired a car and came out to take everyone at the homestead to safety. Yitzker refused to budge and Brenner backed him. Unable to convince anyone, Schatz stayed with them.

The next morning another car was dispatched from Tel Aviv. Five mutilated corpses were discovered on the pathway outside the house. Luidor's body still remains missing to this day.

The mobs would have invaded Tel Aviv too had units of the Jewish Legion (formed by Ze'ev Jabotinsky and Yosef Trumpeldor in WWI) not intervened in time. The British lost no time in expelling the Legion for preventing more carnage. London soon backed down from its Balfour Declaration undertakings and issued the first of several anti-Jewish White Papers that would follow every Arab terror offensive. As is still the case, Arab aggression handsomely pays off.

In his letter Ben-Zvi noted that "the rioters were never disarmed" and that the British "never so much as referred to what happened as 'murder and looting' but as 'regrettable clashes,' which they sought to contain with 'moral persuasion.' Over twenty Jews were arrested to convey the impression that this was no anti-Jewish attack but a chance conflict."

Reminiscent of today's artificially evenhanded prattle about the "cycle of violence"? The more things change, the more they stay the same.

It goes against our ingrained wishful thinking to acknowledge that enduring Arab animosity has nothing to do with the desperation which the Jewish state's birth supposedly fomented among so-called Palestinians; with the occupation which supposedly represses them or even with the supposed aspiration to found a Palestinian state which the Jews supposedly foil. In 1921 there were no traces of the above pretexts – so prevalent in the manipulative Arab narrative, so popular among progressive sorts here and almost universally accepted as gospel abroad.

Brenner, who considered it paramount to revolutionize both the Jew and the Jewish lot, was slaughtered – as were other Jews before and after him – for no other reason than being Jewish.

Today this remains an essential underlying truth, unamended by the twists and turns of our survival-against-the-odds saga in this land. If we mulishly deny that Jew-hatred is the moving force behind hostilities still unleashed against us, we only fool ourselves. We turn ourselves into the dupes of a genocidal enemy's cynical propaganda machine. Suckers ultimately become easy prey.

The Forward Position

My mom was never big on surprises, especially when it came to birthday gifts. The surest way not to miss the mark, she reckoned, was to straight-out inquire what I wanted. Just before I turned nine, I asked her for a volume of poet Natan Alterman's *Seventh Column*. My wish was granted and the brown hardcover anthology has remained one of my most cherished possessions ever since.

Davar, the defunct Labor daily, put the seventh column of its front page at Alterman's disposal and he editorialized in verse on the current events of the day (yes, there was a market once for literate commentary). The quality of Alterman's output hasn't lost its flavor over the decades and its crisp cleverness never ceases to astound.

But beyond that, his stanzas are a voice from the past, genuine testimony to the zeitgeist of Israel's earliest days. Here's a window to how things were perceived in real time – often in stark contrast to the distortive rewriting of history and the conventional wisdom of intellectual milieus here and abroad.

Alterman, regrettably, is almost forgotten nowadays. One former education minister, Yossi Sarid, proposed that the works of "Palestinian National Poet" Mahmoud Darwish be included in our public school curriculum (though Darwish unrepentantly preached genocide and/or ethnic cleansing against this country's Jews).

In the name of standoffish pluralism and moral-relativist enlightenment, another former education minister, Yuli Tamir of Labor, saw fit to enrich said curriculum with the *nakba* (Arabic for catastrophe – the propagandist Arab moniker for Israeli independence).

Sadly, even scandalously, Israeli children aren't taught the poems Alterman published in *Davar* just before and after that first Independence Day in 1948. It's obviously a sign of our postmodernist environment in which not only are there no absolute truths, virtues or values, but our smart set doesn't even accord Israel's case equal hearing with that of its mortal enemies' manipulative narrative.

How can we then complain if foreigners – unfamiliar even with our map, tortuous borders and diminutive size – fall for the slanderous portrayal of tiny, beleaguered Israel as an ogre expansionist empire, born in sin and designed to dispossess peace-loving, blameless victims?

Few authentic texts serve better than the rhythmic relics of Alterman's *Seventh Column* to transmit the truth across the years – that sense of acute danger that enveloped the embryonic state at its birth and the gritty come-what-may resolve of the few against the many.

Just before Israel regained its sovereignty after nearly two millennia, Alterman published a column in rhyme entitled *The Forward Position* (my translation, alas, cannot begin to impart the austere beauty and cadence of the original Hebrew):

> Between the Jordan and the sea
> Stand six hundred thousand people.
> Jews, young and old,
> One mass, hairs bristling, watchful and silent.
> And reverberating in the starlight
> Is the thud of iron beaten by hammer.
> They forge armor and guns
> And the heavens witness and keep mum.
>
> And the State Department telegraphs in code,
> Remarkably soliciting expert advice
> On whether it's possible this time to betray,
> Without paying treachery's price –
> And signal Husseini in secret,
> And honor at his altar sacrifice,

And surrender and scorn the UN writ.
But it's not easy to actualize

Because between the sea and Jordan stand
Six hundred thousand people,
Jews, young and old,
Who'll form a hurdle of flint.
Upon a starlit barricade
Their pounding hammers buttress
One of the final fortifications
Of a collapsing, indifferent world.

And the hatchers of deceit know
That this fortification will not be easily vanquished.
That the quintessence of a universal struggle
On this barrier rests.
If liberty isn't surrendered – while loyalty is sold out
As tribute to its enemy –
Then this forward position will be remembered
For shielding freedom from the trampling crush.

Remembered will be the stand of
The six hundred thousand people,
Jews, young and old.
And fortunate is he who saw and felt
How their star-adorned night,
Full of the din of armor and hammers,
Arose strong in the midst of intrigue and ambush.
And the world will bow down and keep silent.

Little Israel still constitutes that very same "final fortification." It is still at the vanguard of the fight for freedom. Indeed Israel is practically the only state committed to that struggle in earnest, doing what other nations, their occasional lip-service notwithstanding, fail to do. And for our pains, we're still as unappreciated, censored and even punished. What was, still is.

Israel remains the proverbial canary in the world's coal mine. What befalls us will in time haunt all democracies, yet these democracies seem intent on chasing off and choking the killjoy canary. The world remains the same "collapsing, indifferent world" which Alterman deplored.

True, Israel is no longer as helpless as in its neonatal days, but if anything, it's berated for not being as weak and as at the mercy of others as some – ostensible friends included – would like.

For all our growth and incomparably improved circumstances since that early perilous period, Israel remains infinitesimal vis-à-vis the hostile Arab/Muslim multitudes who wish (in Darwish's words) to expunge us "from all memory." Israel remains as pesky, illegitimate and disposable in the eyes of much of the international community as it was then.

We still face would-be destroyers while around us intrigues and plots of betrayal swirl, rendering Alterman's *The Forward Position* as relevant as when it first saw print. Just substitute nearly seven million Jews for six hundred thousand.

In essence, our War of Independence continues unabated. In individual terms the duration of renascent Jewish self-determination so far equals almost a lifetime, but by history's scale it's a flash. There were ups and downs, flare-ups and lulls, but our existential war is unconcluded – save only for sporadic rounds.

It's nothing we can control. Former PM Ehud Olmert offered PA president Mahmoud Abbas everything. Nevertheless Olmert's egregious concessions were unceremoniously spurned. By his own testimony, Olmert was willing to cede that little extra beyond the 98 percent which Ehud Barak proposed during his own (disastrous) stint as premier (1999–2001). Yet in both cases the deal-breaker was the adamant refusal, first by Arafat and then by his successor, to formally end the conflict and recognize the right of the Jewish people to sovereignty.

When push came to shove, our survival-jeopardizing territorial generosity failed to buy us the peace and acceptance we crave. The enemy, still baying for our blood, strives to shrink our toehold, yet retain the right to obliterate us.

We don't readily like to admit this truth. Back in 1948 self-deception was rare. Today it's bon ton. The immutable bottom line, however, is that over six decades on we remain threatened, vigilant in that same vulnerable forward position and fighting for our lives – even if we wish we didn't have to.

First Peacenik, Forgotten Founder

Is a penchant for useless information nature or nurture? Whenever I speculate about a likely inborn inclination, I recall how my mother always made sure I learned the origin of every street name in any address we ever lived at. So when my parents bought an apartment on Tel Aviv's leafy Yosef Eliyahu Street (near the Mann Auditorium), I was sure to become the only kid around who could expound about who Yosef Eliyahu was.

For me he quickly became not only the most familiar of Tel Aviv's founders but the one with whom I had somehow developed an almost personal affinity, despite the fact that he was born in 1870 and died in 1934. Posthumously, he became part of my childhood.

Thus, as Tel Aviv marked its centenary, what could be more natural than to recall my own favorite founder?

Yosef Eliyahu Chelouche was the second son of Aharon Chelouche, one of nineteenth-century Jaffa's foremost Jewish community leaders. Aharon was a baby when his family sailed from its native Algiers to Eretz Yisrael in 1839. Two of Aharon's brothers perished in the perilous journey – Yosef and Eliyahu. They were commemorated in their nephew's name.

Yosef Eliyahu's entrepreneurial spirit couldn't have found a better outlet than the Zionist revival. A manufacturer and a builder, he constructed over half of Ahuzat Bayit's sixty earliest homes – thirty-two in all. His most famous project was Gymnasia Herzliya – Tel-Aviv's first school and its first public edifice.

His own home stood on the corner of Rehov Herzl and Sderot Rothschild. Across the boulevard and three houses up the block was future mayor Meir Dizengoff's dwelling, where thirty-nine years later Israel would be declared independent.

The boulevard itself wasn't a preplanned aesthetic feature. The twelve acres purchased in 1909 for Ahuzat Bayit were a desolate windswept wasteland. In his memoirs Yosef Eliyahu would recall it as "a sea of sand, a barren desert with powdery yellow mountains and hills, where jackals howled."

The pyramidal mounds with their unstable, continuously shifting slip faces were pronounced unsuitable for construction. To level off the area, teams of pioneers used wheelbarrows to move tons of sand from the highest points and deposit them in the gullies bellow. The deepest ditch cut across Ahuzat Bayit exactly where Sderot Rothschild would stretch. Filled with so much soft sand, it was judged unsafe to support structures. Instead it was covered with topsoil and lined with trees.

But the most frightening description of the dunes from which Tel Aviv would rise appears in Yosef Eliyahu's 1931 autobiography. In 1880 ten-year-old Yosef Eliyahu was lured out of Jaffa's winding

Yosef Eliyahu Chelouche (seated on the right, bearded) with his wife and children. The eldest boy standing in the center back row is Moshe Chelouche, who served as Tel Aviv mayor when he grew up.

alleyways by his father's Arab acquaintance and marched through the undulating shadeless wilderness beyond.

It was a horrendous, almost impassable and seemingly interminable tract, without landmarks or signs of habitation. The kidnapped Yosef Eliyahu's feet kept sinking in the sand, he was thirsty, beaten and terrified. At night, however, salvation came to Yosef Eliyahu as a silhouetted figure on a donkey approached. It was Yisrael Simhon, guard of the Montifiore Orange Grove, near where Azrielli Center currently dominates Tel Aviv's skyline.

To his last day, despite decades of distinguished public service, Yosef Eliyahu was known as the "abducted child." The barren expanse through which he was forcibly dragged now lies beneath bustling downtown east-central Tel Aviv, intersected by Israel's busiest traffic arteries.

His early trauma notwithstanding, Yosef Eliyahu tirelessly campaigned for coexistence. He was perhaps the first peacenik. In 1913, to counter already rife Judeophobia and incendiary agitation in the Arab press, Yosef Eliyahu, along with other Arabic-speaking Tel Avivians, founded Hamagen (the shield), an organization dedicated to persuading Arabs that they and the Jews share economic and cultural interests and can only improve each other's lot.

Yosef Eliyahu published an Arabic-language daily in Jaffa, *Saut el-Othmania* (Voice of the Ottomans), and cultivated close contacts with leading local Arabs in the hope of stemming already-rampant hatemongering.

The wanton massacre unleashed by Jaffa's Arabs in 1921 not only cost the lives of forty-nine Jews and wounded 150 others, but it also caused the untimely demise of Jaffa's Jewish community, while concomitantly bolstering its upstart offspring. Adversity turned Tel Aviv into an energetic, attractive and autonomous urban alternative. The carnage should have disheartened Yosef Eliyahu, but he wouldn't abandon his peace quest.

It seemed mission impossible after Yom Kippur 1928, when notorious Jerusalem mufti Haj Amin al-Husseini raised a shrill cry over a flimsy cloth partition positioned to segregate male and female worshippers at the Western Wall. The British lost no time in tearing down the offensive screen. Jewish opinion of all political shades was outraged.

On October 6, 1928, Yosef Eliyahu published an article entitled "To the Arabs," his last-ditch plea for sanity. He wrote:

> You crudely disrupted and battered congregants who came to pour out their souls to their Father in Heaven at the place and date holiest to them.... Then you declared holy war against your victims charging they assailed your holy shrines.... You prepare for outright bloodbath and jihad against the infidel desecrators.

> What desecration? ...How can such absurdity be allowed to foment religious hostilities between Jews and Muslims? My good brothers, you are manipulated by wily politicians.... How can anyone begrudge Jews the pitiable remnant that is their Western Wall, the sole relic of the brokenhearted?

But the mufti's disciples didn't heed Yosef Eliyahu. Their premeditated harassment grew increasingly violent, till trumped-up tales of Jewish takeover attempts at the Temple Mount sent Arabs rioting countrywide on August 23, 1929. The slaughter lasted an entire week.

The rampages began in Jerusalem but the most notorious carnage took place in Hebron, where sixty-seven men, women and children were gruesomely hacked to death in homicidal frenzy. Hebron's centuries-old Jewish community was dispossessed. Smaller Jewish enclaves in Gaza, Jenin, Tulkarm and Nablus were likewise dislodged.

This is significant to us now. The visceral enmity, which Yosef Eliyahu sought to defuse, long predated Jewish independence or the Six-Day War. It predated all Arab narratives about having been victimized by so-called Israeli occupation. Yosef Eliyahu didn't live to see Israeli sovereignty but he did witness the preexisting bloodcurdling libel.

Yosef Eliyahu didn't survive long enough to realize just how monstrously his outstretched hand was rebuffed. He died before the blood-soaked 1936–39 mufti-led and Nazi-financed Arab uprising, as well as the mufti's Hitler-endorsed residence in WWII Berlin – where he avidly collaborated in perpetrating the Holocaust.

Knowing what Yosef Eliyahu couldn't imagine in his darkest nightmares, we can put his failed peace overtures into perspective and realize the futility of well-intentioned naiveté.

Yosef Eliyahu described vicious incitement that inflamed passions when Jews clung to a mere strip of empty desert, reclaimed it and called it Tel Aviv. The world prefers to ignore the sources of hate and portray the Zionist accomplishment – embodied by the metropolis that Tel Aviv became after a century of blood, sweat and tears – as the root of regional evil. If anything, the forgotten legacy of the forgotten founder is anything but irrelevant, useless information.

Saving Labor from Itself

The requiem for Labor may be premature. Nevertheless, its demise is inevitable if it fails to save itself from itself.

What's at stake isn't merely Labor's misfortune but that of our entire body politic, which must be able to count on two responsible mainstream mainstay alternatives. Kadima – an opportunistic concoction, without a weighty past, a promising future or any true adhesive to bind its cynical mélange of expedient self-seekers – isn't one.

Labor is Kadima's indirect victim. Parasitic Kadima didn't bite into the Likud but it devoured the Left. That said, Labor wasn't just temporarily harmed. It had been steadily declining throughout the decade and won't get back to what it once was until its hotshots first understand what made them such easy prey to Kadima's predations.

Obviously a party claiming to be socialist cannot afford to alienate the common man. This transcends the fact that Labor has paradoxically become the party of big business, of the millionaires and billionaires and their emulators who aspire to sidestep pesky Jewish travails and struggles, live high on the hog and pretend they're in Davos all year round. Belittled plebeians are uncannily perceptive. They see right through the hypocrisy.

Indeed the commoners' estrangement from Labor's preachy elites isn't just on pocketbook issues. The proletariat which Laborites profess to represent is patriotic and retains commonsense self-preservation instincts. The jetsetters hadn't entirely debilitated the basic existential logic of regular folks – once the hallmark of Labor under its mutating monikers.

What started out as Poalei Zion (Zion's Workers) and became MAPAI (Hebrew acronym for Workers Party of Eretz Yisrael) eventually opted to ditch all reference to Zion or the Land of Israel. Thus Labor began losing its soul.

The 1977 electoral upset that brought the Likud to power gave further impetus to Labor's psycho-political disintegration. Shimon Peres, isolated after his political defeat, became Yossi Sarid's and Yossi Beilin's virtual captive. Far to his left, both eventually meandered to Meretz, yet at the time the Yossis became Peres's sole sounding-boards and filters to the outside world.

Transformed, Peres later brazenly hoodwinked his party into the Oslo fiasco but the party (which he ultimately abandoned for Kadima's allure) remains unrepentant, as if deliberately doing its darndest to achieve irrelevance and turn its face backwards in order to avoid today's reality. If anything, Labor's excesses flirt with post-Zionism.

David Ben-Gurion, Labor's greatest-ever leader, must have spun in his grave when Education Minister Yuli Tamir (of Labor) included the *nakba* (Arabic for calamity – the Arab propaganda-loaded moniker for Israeli independence) in the Jewish state's school curriculum. Intuitively that grates against ordinary Israelis' sense of justice.

Labor will never regain its standing of old until it again acknowledges the mass sentiment, which survives despite the left-dominated media's shrill cacophony. Failure to realize this will marginalize Labor and leave it to vie with Meretz for the same mini-constituency.

If Labor forgets to put the Jewish connection to the Jewish homeland atop its agenda, it'll be lost. This doesn't oblige it to espouse the ideals of the Eretz Yisrael Movement (which ironically arose from its own ranks following the Six-Day War). It needn't avoid pragmatic remedies, but it mustn't paint Jews in Judea as occupiers.

Labor must be as vehemently and passionately insistent on our rights as Ben-Gurion sincerely was, even though he countenanced territorial compromise when that seemed the sole alternative. When consenting to the partition plan that left embryonic Israel in an untenable puny patchwork, he gave up what wasn't then in his possession. Yet subsequently Ben-Gurion resolutely hung on to land liberated in the bloody War of Independence which the Arabs foisted upon Israel.

And he didn't agree to partition jubilantly. On July 15, 1937, while recommending partition, he wrote: "The Jewish people have always regarded, and will continue to regard the whole of Eretz Yisrael as a single country which is theirs in a national sense and will become theirs once again. No Jew will accept partition as a just and rightful solution."

Soon afterward, he told the Twentieth Zionist Congress: "No Jew is entitled to give up the right of the Jewish nation to the land. It is not in the authority of any Jew or of any Jewish body; it is not even in the authority of the entire nation alive today to give up any part of the land.... Even if, at any point, Jews choose to decline it, they have no right to deprive future generations of it. Our right to the entire land exists and stands forever."

This isn't about territorial divisions but about the enduring link, the collective memory that binds us and returned us here. Ben-Gurion knew that the Jewish people didn't surrender its link to its geographic cradle during two millennia of unimaginable persecution. That the sovereign Jewish state should weaken if not altogether break that link would have been unthinkable under Ben-Gurion's Mapai, for all its manifold faults.

What is nationhood after all if not collective memory? Ben-Gurion knew it well.

Testifying before UNSCOP in 1947, he noted:

> Three hundred years ago, a ship called the Mayflower left for the New World.... This was a great event in the history of England and America. But I would like to know: Is there a single Englishman who knows the exact date and hour of the Mayflower's launch? How much do American children – or grownups – know about this historic trip? Do they know how many people were in the boat? Their names? What they wore? What they ate? Their path of travel? What happened to them on the way? Where they landed?
>
> More than 3,300 years before the Mayflower set sail, the Jews left Egypt. Any Jewish child, whether in America or Russia, Yemen or Germany, knows that his forefathers left Egypt at dawn on the 15th of Nisan. What did they wear? Their belts were tied and their staffs were in their hands. They ate matzos, and arrived at the Red Sea after seven days.
>
> He knows the path of their journey.... The child can even quote the family names from the Torah. Jews worldwide still eat matza for seven days from the fifteenth of Nisan, and retell the story of the Exodus, concluding with the fervent wish "Next Year in Jerusalem." This is the nature of the Jewish people.

Until we hear today's Laborites enunciate the same sentiments as forthrightly, as genuinely, as unambiguously and as proudly as Ben-Gurion did, they won't win back the people's hearts. Until Labor retreats from the post-Zionist brink and retakes the Zionist high-ground, it'll continue losing ground.

That'd be a tragic shame because a viable Labor is vital for Israeli democracy. Labor deserves to be rescued from its own bungling radicals-cum-apparatchiks.

Ma'alesh, Inshallah, Bukrah, Bakshish

Years ago – when peace with Egypt was new and relatively warmer – I was plenty angry with my paper for forcing me to file my copy from Cairo by telex rather than phone. I was sent there on a news assignment way back when – among the broad lower strata of Egyptian society (as distinct from the razor-thin so-called intelligentsia) – peace with Israel hadn't yet been thoroughly delegitimized.

Neither cell-phones nor the Internet were around. Now-obsolete technologies like the telex were staple and old-fashioned landlines were indispensable. All my colleagues from other Israeli papers – and there were considerably more dailies then than currently – were authorized to phone in their stories. The *Jerusalem Post*, although handicapped by the earliest deadline (due to its out-of-Tel-Aviv base), was the sole exception. My editors wouldn't even hear of footing the bill for long-distance telephone communications.

They had made arrangements with the Reuters bureau in Cairo which entailed my arriving there in person each evening, handing in my written material and having the local teletypist transmit it to the *Post*. Traveling alone at night from our well-secured hotel to Reuters raised safety issues. One-way by taxi was supposed to take an hour, though I was warned that I'd better plan for no less than an hour and a half.

My bosses became the immediate laughing stock of the entire Israeli press delegation. However, the ribbing the *Post* took came to a very abrupt halt when we needed to dispatch our first report. No phone line worked. Despite unstinting help from the Israeli VIPs and well-intentioned (though excruciatingly lethargic) assistance from Egyptian Foreign Ministry personnel, it was like flogging a dead horse.

Reliable phone connections couldn't be established. This trouble persisted night after nerve-racking night, with only occasional short-lived patchy successes, allowing a lucky individual to briefly – sometimes – get through.

I became a sudden star among my colleagues. I had an ostensibly viable alternative. In no time it was decided that I'd become a pool writer and that my English-language pieces would be relayed to other Israeli papers as well. The upside was that I had company on those long, forbidding, after-dark cab adventures.

But another rude culture shock awaited us at the end of the ride. Reuters's Egyptian teletype operators were a nonchalant bunch. There was no hostility, just no rush.

We explained that we were up against deadlines, to which the inevitable reply came with a shrug of the shoulder and the word *"ma'alesh."* We soon learned that it denoted something approximating "Who cares? What's the big deal? So what? Don't take it too seriously."

On my absolute best behavior and controlling myself stringently, I spoke for the entire group (because of my English and the *Post*'s prepaid deal with Reuters). I explained what must be done and by when. The man in charge, chewing on some late-night nourishment, nodded and uttered *"inshallah"* – God willing.

I was hardly heartened. I thought the task was straightforward enough to be attempted without divine intervention.

I again noted the urgency of our business, stressing that this item must go to print soon, but nothing seemed to inspire the crew to action. In near desperation, I asked the telex chief when the text would at last be processed. *"Bukrah,"* he answered. That meant "tomorrow."

What's the point of rehashing yesteryear's bygone exasperation? Because it's eminently relevant today. Our disparate mindsets – leastways emanating from cultural diversity and work-ethic incompatibility – are still conspicuously potent.

The languor displayed by Egyptian employees at a busy Western news agency isn't all that different from the languor of Egyptian uniformed personnel charged with safeguarding the Philadelphi Corridor (between Egypt and Gaza) – and that's assuming unadulterated goodwill, which shouldn't be one bit assumed.

The aid of European/American gadgetry, know-how and officious kibitzing won't curtail illicit missile imports. Moreover, foreigners can be counted upon to prefer the side which intimidates Westerners most and demands least of them.

Israeli gripes about assorted violations will only expose the failures of outsiders who won't relish risk nor want to admit failure. Israel will be stuck with the wretched consequences, for which nobody will take responsibility.

Forgotten or deliberately downplayed is the fact that Egypt is largely to blame for allowing Iran's lackeys to arm Gaza to its teeth. Had Egypt lived up to its obligations to hinder Hamastan's gunrunning, there would have been no need for Israel's offensive and no need for Egypt to posture as the honest broker.

All this should caution us not to put our trust in Egypt (the "staff of hollow reed," as per Isaiah 36:6), which had already let us down more than once. Egypt in the best of circumstances is never as good as its word, its sincerity or lack thereof notwithstanding. Even if Cairo's powers that be were unreservedly determined to preserve calm – which is much more than a little questionable – odds are that nothing would change.

Northern Sinai's Bedouins are scarcely likely to toe Cairo's line – regardless of who rules the capital's roost. Lawlessness and smuggling are the Bedouins' livelihood and their insubordination continues unchecked. Any attempts to control them are met by violent resistance. Whichever international agreements might conceivably bind Cairo make no impression on the tribal gangs that de facto rule Sinai.

Similarly unimpressed is Egyptian bureaucracy. Its super-snarled red tape effectively obstructs all governmental executive decisions.

Even topmost policy edicts are unrecognizably ground down as they're subjected to arbitrary whims imposed along the way by inflated cadres of sluggish officials.

The bottom of the bureaucratic pyramid is the most troubling of all. True, the peace treaty with Egypt caps the numbers of its troopers at the border, but much more significant is the nature of these men. They are woefully underpaid and hence eminently bribable. For a handful of dollars, Egyptian officers will turn a blind eye to Hamas military contraband, regardless of diplomatic undertakings. *Bakshish*, after all, greases all Egyptian wheels.

Not unexpectedly it was only *bakshish* which at the time resuscitated those prearranged Reuters telex services. In the end, after recurring maddening rounds of *ma'alesh*, *inshallah*, *bukrah*, we finally resorted to *bakshish*.

The clock was ticking. Deadline was literally minutes away. We all coughed up some foreign exchange, greased the head honcho's palm and in return he allowed me to sit at his teletypewriter and punch its keys myself.

There may be a lesson here for the Israeli collective. The only job we can rely on is the one we ourselves do.

Judah Macabee Was Your Father

Happy days – the Israeli movie *Waltz with Bashir* raked in the tributes. Having done us proud and won the Golden Globe, it in turn became an Oscar contender. Already under its belt was the Israel Film Academy's Ophir. It was singled out as the best animation feature by

LA's film critics and was an unexpected box-office hit in its theatrical release in America.

This presumably should have made us ever-so-joyful. The much-maligned Jewish state, after all, craves honors – even when they effectively dishonor it.

To figure this out we might recall the Hanover-born philosopher Theodor Lessing, who was assassinated by Hitler's agents in 1933. The man who delved into the warped Jewish psyche and produced the still eminently germane volume entitled *Der jüdische Selbsthass* (Jewish self-hatred) deserves attention, especially as Israelis daily disprove his optimistic prognosis.

Born into an assimilationist family, Lessing converted to Christianity – as was the vogue among his contemporary up-and-coming young German-Jewish sophisticates. But then, deeply affected by anti-Semitism and passionately moved by the Zionist ethos of Jewish national revival, he recanted, returned to Judaism, visited pre-independence Israel and theorized that only in its environment of a healthy normal Jewish existence could Jews stop hating themselves.

That's how much he knew!

Back then, three years before the Third Reich's birth (and, as it emerged, three years before his own unnatural death), he took it upon himself to painfully pick at the most intractable of Jewish scabs – the maddening capacity of Jews to loathe themselves, or, more precisely, to loathe their fellow Jews. He ascribed this inclination to two millennia of abnormal persecuted existence. He assumed that the normalization, which Zionism took upon itself to achieve, would eradicate the aberration. It was a sound hypothesis, except that perhaps Lessing and Zionism underestimated the profound psychological deformity which two thousand years of anomaly wrought.

That crossed my mind when *Waltz* won the Globe. In concept and execution this peculiar animated hybrid perhaps breaks with convention, but its central thematic core is every bit as predictable, cravenly conformist and run-of-the-mill as nearly all Israeli flicks of the past few decades.

Local filmmakers uniformly revel in portraying Israelis as jaded, essentially unpleasant (if not altogether repulsive), justifiably insecure, rightfully apologetic, malaise-ridden, terminally devoid of vitality, corroded within and/or wretchedly wrecked by self-reproach.

The Arab is revealed as the antithesis to the inherently disagreeable, fatigued, befuddled, farcical, foolish and/or pathetic Israeli. Arabs are devoted patriots, confident in their cause, outspoken in their righteous indignation, vindicated in their umbrage, noble, proud, tough, young, vigorous and deserving of victory.

Some occasional counterfeit cardboard dichotomies are tolerable – freedom of expression and all that rot. However, when simplistic falsehoods become the single premise, then the overbearing presence of pressure by manipulative groupthink must at least be suspected. The utter lack of deviation from this one homogeneous portraiture style testifies to the imposition of ideological diktats – obviously in the name of democracy and artistic free will.

Misgivings are further intensified when we realize how many of these one-dimensional productions are subsidized by the Education Ministry's Israel Film Fund. Portions of our hard-earned incomes go – as taxes collected from you and me – to underwrite either outright slander of the Jewish state or, at best, unsympathetic depictions of a bumbling imbecilic entity.

No government dares reduce officialdom's largesse to Israel's self-appointed creative ambassadors, who blithely batter their country's image at any available film festival abroad. Hand-in-hand with omnipotent media cliques, our artistes vehemently orchestrate intimidating reputation-trashing onslaughts which no higher-up or administration in recent memory could withstand.

And so – willing or not – we bankroll them and, at our expense, they relish in thumbing their avant-garde noses at the "benighted" aggregate of ordinary Israelis who are denied other homegrown cinematic fare, certainly anything Zionist.

Since nothing pro-Israeli can win accolades at Cannes or Berlin, the preferences of overseas nabobs must be pandered to in our filmmakers' quest for fame and fortune. Thus, in order to bask in the limelight of enlightened foreign approval, Israelis enhance the fraudulent Arab narrative. Pleasing the enemy is the one surefire way to make it in Israeli showbiz.

This state of affairs, after more than six decades of Jewish sovereignty, would have shocked the Zionist in Lessing. Nevertheless, Lessing the scholar would have easily been able to fit the Israeli strain of "the old Jewish disease" into his painstakingly compiled typology of self-hating Jews.

In essence Lessing noted that Jews are unique in their self-deprecation, yet it's such second nature that they seldom acknowledge the condition. Non-Jews would never dream of harboring such scorn for themselves.

Excessively moralistic and idiosyncratically contrary, Jewish intellectuals are predisposed to self-blame, even when not remotely guilty of whatever inequity they ascribe to their people.

This meshes flawlessly with the historically honed and religiously indoctrinated propensity of non-Jews to scapegoat Jews. But über-brainy Jewish suck-ups, stopping at nothing in order to ingratiate themselves, invariably praise those who despise and target them.

They demonstrate an inexhaustible aptitude for understanding visceral antagonism toward themselves and identifying with their antagonists' rationale. It's a combination of the Jewish intellectuals' contempt for their own kind and their hankering to be accepted by those who abhor them. That, in a nutshell, is the Jew's predilection for forsaking his own heritage and his longing for another identity.

Israel's artistic/intellectual milieu dovetails with alarming precision into Lessing's diagnosis of Jewish psychopathology. Its seasoned

Theodor Lessing

hotshots and neophyte pretenders alike yearn for approbation from globalized multiculturalism's makers and breakers, the dispensers of politically correct postmodernist endorsement. And since the latter, for a myriad of unsaintly motives, choose to subscribe to "Palestinian" historiography, Israel's eager-to-curry-favor intelligentsia must cozy up to the Palestinians.

Thereby, latter-day Israelis paradoxically parallel Lessing's peers, who courted esteem by renouncing their roots. Like their cerebral forerunners, they too enlist to battle the Jewish nation, creed and civilization.

Lessing didn't imagine that what he dubbed "auto-antisemitism" could continue within the self-governing Zionist creation. The affliction which tainted his own generation with self-hate, he reasoned, was fated to disappear. While initially Zionism gained impetus from the rejection Jews suffered, the complex-free generation born into a liberated Jewish state "would be Zionist because it feels Jewish, not because it is injured by its Jewishness."

Remember, Lessing urged fellow Jews, "Judah Macabee was your father. Queen Esther was your mother. You are a link in the chain of Saul, David and Moses. Don't betray your destiny. Follow it."

But both foremost and upstart Israeli highbrows would undoubtedly mock such exhortation as preposterously naïve, uncool and dangerously reactionary. They would anyway never deign to read Lessing.

Anything Zionist is backward and irrelevant for self-seeking post-

Zionists, although – irony of ironies – they uncannily mimic the very self-reviling Jews whom Lessing so rigorously analyzed.

Obama's Conquest and Beilin's Confession

Ever since the Vietnam misadventure, a postmodern revolution had been looming in America. Barack Obama's tour de force is its clincher. American campuses have been mass-producing smug, politically correct poseurs and slogan-spouting self-assured groupthink conformists for decades. Converging circumstances enabled the postmodernists who indoctrinate America's younger minds to conquer its highest political bastions as well.

To us in Israel none of this is new, except that here postmodernists are called post-Zionists.

Their underlying assumption is the absence of objective truths, justice or ethical absolutes. Nothing is black and white – just subjective shades of gray on a landscape of moral relativism.

All cultures are of equal merit. The worst despotic societies aren't more villainous than societies which, their imperfections notwithstanding, sanctify civil liberties. Indeed the postmodern inclination is to downplay autocratic repression while simultaneously casting doubt on the freedoms of the world's most egalitarian systems.

Bottom line: democracies are in essence little better than the tyrannies which challenge them.

The operative conclusion is that rather than fight for their righteous causes, democracies must acknowledge inherent guilt for the state of the world, make amends, shrink inwardly and, where possible, appease and buy respites.

This is an all-encompassing mindset. It manifests itself even in stateside liberal aversion for offshore oil drilling and nuclear power. At heart is the belief that America shouldn't expand its own fuel supplies, but should go green, pump up car tires, recycle restaurant grease, hype windmill farms and practice what Al Gore preaches.

The perception of American culpability leads to prescriptions for retrenchment versus growth and for contraction of global American superpower influence. This, in turn, leads directly to a conciliatory attitude toward the nuclear ambitions of Mahmoud Ahmadinejad.

As if the 1930s never were – as if Neville Chamberlain never sold out at Munich – Obama has already categorized Iran as puny and insignificant. If we minimize the probability of conflict – to say nothing of outright genocidal attack – make nice to the most bellicose of potentates, try to understand what gets them riled, talk things out, meet them "halfway," pressure their intended victims, then maybe the bad guys will reform and the nightmare will dissipate.

We Israelis have been there, seen that.

As the world proletarian revolution expired with a whimper, well-heeled Western radicals discovered the Third World – downtrodden, but, as stylish mythology would have it, spiritually superior.

The sufferings of the Jewish people, it goes without saying, never aroused significant sympathy. As ever, Jews constituted fashionable foe, whereas pro-Arab sentiments – especially under the Palestinian label – became de rigueur. Trendy Israeli left-wingers eagerly jumped at the opportunity of luxuriating in the ambience of European enlightenment and winning coveted approval and acceptance.

Thus originated Israel's unique brand of postmodernity. It evinces no qualms about jeopardizing the self-determination of the ancient Jewish people, while at the same time espousing the notion of self-determination for Palestinians, whose nationhood is a recent invention, cynically calculated to counterbalance renascent Jewish sovereignty.

For Israeli "progressives" – who freely avail themselves of the benefits of Jewish broadmindedness and democracy – anything that basically furthers the interests of the Jewish state, and steels it against unmitigated assaults, is anathema.

We have paid the price on our buses, streets and marketplaces and can expect more bloodbaths unless we somehow manage to reason out of the box that post-Zionist groupthink foisted upon us.

That of course would be a tall order even if Israelis for now avoid Peace Now's endorsed choices. Our judiciary, academia and above all media still exclusively chant left-wing mantras. They'll make successful government near impossible for anyone they viscerally hate (like Binyamin Netanyahu) and they'll let their darlings get away with anything.

It was mind-boggling to gauge the zero-resonance to Yossi Beilin's unambiguous confession that he cooked up the Oslo fiasco clandestinely, sans authority, even behind Shimon Peres's back, and that he had conducted his negotiations in clear contravention of the prohibition in effect at the time against contact with the PLO, when it was appropriately designated a terrorist enemy.

In an October 31, 2008, *Yediot Aharonot* interview Beilin unabashedly admitted that during the Oslo process, he "had to do things behind people's backs. I was deputy foreign minister. The foreign minister and prime minister [Peres and Rabin respectively] didn't know that I was conducting talks with the PLO until I decided to inform them."

This should have generated a furious political maelstrom. Our opinion-molders should have been scandalized. Our entire public discourse should have reverberated with outrage. But nobody was appalled. Nobody reeled. It was the season of the Rabin assassination anniversary and the media yet again exploited the occasion to whack its political opponents, as is unfailingly its annual rite.

Thus, one day post-interview, Israel Radio's weekend news magazine ignored what Beilin voluntarily owned up to. Moderator Pe'erli Shahar instead strove to resurrect the pre-assassination rally in Jerusalem. She bellyached about "those at the Zion Square balcony... who stayed silent despite posters of Rabin in SS uniform." It doesn't matter how thoroughly a lie is refuted, if it's repeated frequently, consistently and melodramatically.

One would assume that by now every Israeli knows that "the posters" were a single A4 page (21 cm x 29.7 cm, or 8.3" x 11.7"), not conceivably visible to Netanyahu while addressing a mass audience from the second story. Moreover, the small homemade photomontage was the handiwork of Shin Bet agent-provocateur Avishai Raviv, who goaded and guided assassin Yigal Amir.

But who cares about truth when falsehood is so satisfying?

Who cares about serious dangers when frivolities serve as diversionary tactics? Just as Oslo's illegitimate birth didn't preoccupy Israel's press, so its American counterpart preferred to dwell on Sarah Palin's wardrobe instead of focusing on Obama's frighteningly ultra-radical milieu.

In our postmodern reality, truth is conditional, a malleable function of interpretation. Facts are blithely ignored if counterproductive to groupthink choirmasters. What counts is the buzzword's efficacy, not its relevance and certainly not its veracity. Sadly, gone are the days – both here and in the US – when more than a few rare news outlets tolerated dissident opinion and when refusing to run with the pack was the hallmark of professional integrity.

Manipulative, brainwashed and arrogant reporters cluster expediently and cozily in the shelter of shallow consensus without critically evaluating its catchphrases. Individual insight and independent criticism are lost in pursuit of advantageous cohesiveness. Views outside this comfort zone are unlikely so long as the overriding motivations of news purveyors are to avoid embarrassment and/or to continue currying favor with the powers that be.

This is the essence of groupthink, the underpinning on which postmodernity and post-Zionism are erected. Cadres of dutiful mouthpieces, whose homogeneity of associations and ideology is striking, maintain this construct. Without effective defiance from genuinely introspective and analytic freethinkers – and without according such journalists fair space and airtime – nothing can upset postmodern groupthink.

Pius's Pious Pretension

I've got a terrible confession to make – I don't want to go to heaven. It's not that I don't relish rewards in the afterlife. It's just that if Pope Pius XII is there, especially if exalted to saintly status courtesy of his current Vatican successor, then in the immortal words of Huck Finn: "I can't see no advantage in going where" the former Eugenio Pacelli purportedly went.

Like Huck, I'd rather be where Tom Sawyer ends up, because with Tom there's never any pious pretension of infallibility.

But in Pius's case sanctimonious affectation enveloped profound immorality – like failing to advise staunch Catholics in Germany, Poland and elsewhere throughout WWII's Europe that it's not exceedingly nice to condemn ordinary folks to extermination merely because they were born to Jewish parents (or even a single Jewish grandparent). Characteristically, Pius and his adherents proffered handy excuses – prime among them that Pius's expedient "neutrality" saved his church from Nazi retribution (even if said church worships an altruistic, *self-sacrificing* Christ).

British author John Cornwell, a committed Catholic and one-time candidate for the priesthood, aimed to prove Pius's innocence in face of charges that he had betrayed the Jews during their darkest hours. Cornwell was even allowed to peruse bits of the secret Vatican archives, the vast bulk of which the Holy See still refuses to open to scrutiny.

Even the 1999 Vatican-appointed International Catholic-Jewish Historical Commission was denied full access. Only pre-1923 papers were made available. In reaction, the commission suspended its work in 2001, after producing no findings on the papacy during the Holocaust.

Following exhaustive research, Cornwell related, "By the middle of 1997, I was in a state of moral shock. The material I had gathered amounted not to an exoneration but to an indictment.... The evidence was explosive. It showed for the first time that Pacelli was patently, and by the proof of his own words, anti-Jewish. It revealed that he had helped Hitler to power and at the same time undermined potential Catholic resistance in Germany. It showed that he had implicitly denied and trivialized the Holocaust, despite having reliable knowledge of its true extent. And, worse, that he was a hypocrite, for after the war he had retrospectively taken undue credit for speaking out boldly against the Nazi persecution of the Jews."

Cornwell's full account can be read in his spellbinding 1999 book, significantly entitled *Hitler's Pope*.

The Vatican was up in arms upon its publication and, while it couldn't issue a Muslim-style death fatwa, it proceeded to launch a veritable crusade against the hapless author. No effort was spared to discredit him. Today, years after the event, the Internet still bristles with anti-Cornwell vituperation. By 2004 it got so bad that Cornwell partially undercut the thrust of his momentous effort but nevertheless afterward reaffirmed his earlier contentions in new editions of his book.

Despite all the commotion and emotion, though, the would-be disciples of St. Pius couldn't put the genie back in the bottle.

It's out there for all to read, both in an abridged version online and in the well-annotated hard copy, making it therefore superfluous to revisit the wartime conduct of Hitler's pope in this column. Less, however, is known about Pius's postwar record, when the excuse of fearing Hitlerian vengeance could no longer serve him. After V-E Day, obviously free of Fascist and Third Reich intimidation, Pius's deeds had to attest to his innermost predispositions.

It's thus particularly telling that on November 20, 1946 – according to a letter exposed in 2005 by *Corriere dela Sera* – Pius forbade the return of Jewish children and babies who were baptized by French Catholics during the Holocaust. These tots were variously hidden and their baptisms were hardly voluntary. Nevertheless, Pius ordered the youngsters "be kept in Catholic custody."

Perhaps even more significant is the fact that Vatican City and its many extraterritorial buildings in Rome became protective semi-official asylums for numerous wanted war criminals.

The virtual exodus to Arab destinations and the Americas of Nazis and their collaborators would have been impossible were the highest Vatican echelons genuinely faultless or clueless. Ecclesiastical networks helped in the initial escape, subsequent concealment, creation of fake identities, acquisition of forged documentation, travel arrangements, financing and resettlement. It was a massive undertaking, unlikely without at least tacit papal consent.

Prewar, Austrian cleric Alois Hudal was ordained a bishop by Cardinal Pacelli and later embarrassed the Vatican with his unabashedly ardent pro-Nazi pamphlets. Postwar, as Vatican representative to German-speaking internees in Italy, Hudal facilitated the flight of Adolf Eichmann, Franz Stangl, Gustav Wagner, Alois Brunner and many more of the bloodiest butchers.

Declassified US Army Counterintelligence Corps reports explained how Church-aided ratlines – underground smuggling systems – worked. The Croatian case is instructive.

Father Krunoslav Draganovic, secretary of the Confraternity of San Girolamo in Rome, was in contact with Pius and senior Vatican Secretariat of State officials. Although Draganovic was infamous for avid Ustasha (Croatia's Nazi-clone movement) sympathies, the Vatican officially requested he be permitted to visit Ustashi POWs.

Draganovic and his San Girolamo priests, whose ratline was larger than Hudal's, moved the Ustashis from Trieste, to Rome, to Genoa, and on to neutral countries – primarily Argentina – where they lived out their days unpunished and unnoticed. Virtually the entire Ustasha leadership got away.

A more corrosive yet largely inconspicuous postwar papal intrusion manifested itself in occupied Germany. The Vatican placed itself at the vanguard of attempts to foil Germany's denazification.

German Catholics were directed not to cooperate with Allied denazification tribunals, while the Church supplied Nazi businessmen and civil-servants with testimony to the effect that they were mere nominal party-members, small cogs in the machine. Thus many Third Reich stalwarts were acquitted and remained the honchos who called the shots in daily life (see Tom Bower's *Blind Eye to Murder*).

This time too Pius invoked an excuse – fear of Communism. Nazis evidently were less objectionable than Bolsheviks, who in Pius's mind were inextricably associated with Jews. The dual antipathy was already expressed soon after WWI, when Archbishop Pacelli was dispatched to Munich as a papal nuncio.

Cornwall discovered a letter from Pacelli describing a group of revolutionaries who sought to exploit postwar chaos. Their "filth" was "completely nauseating," Pacelli wrote, and the palace where they gathered was "resounding with screams, vile language, profanities. Absolute hell…and in the midst of all this, a gang of young women, of dubious appearance, Jews like all the rest of them, hanging around in all the offices with provocative demeanor and suggestive smiles." Another Jew was "pale, dirty, with vacant eyes, hoarse voice, vulgar, repulsive, with a face that is both intelligent and sly."

Pius XII

For Cornwell, "this association of Jewishness with Bolshevism confirms that Pacelli, from his early 40s, nourished a suspicion of and contempt for the Jews for political reasons. But the repeated references to the Jewishness of these individuals, along with the catalogue of stereotypical epithets deploring their physical and moral repulsiveness, betray a scorn and revulsion consistent with anti-Semitism."

Long Live MAPAI

Israel is a weird place. We relish extremes. During our socialist phase – under the pre-state and early-state hegemony of Mapai (yesteryear's acronym for the Israel Labor Party) – we voluntarily were the USSR's ideological quasi-outpost, albeit a democratic-cum-erratic one. Young Israel was tied to Mother Russia by sentimental bonds, yet was quite unwilling to endure Communist hardships.

However, with socialism as their rallying banner, then-ruling elites forced returning Israelis, for instance, to muck up fridges purchased abroad because only used goods were allowed in without exorbitant tariffs. Why import fridges? Because in the heyday of state control (for which many of our headliners and self-acclaimed experts now profess nostalgia), you had to wait your turn for a locally produced appliance. If you couldn't pull the right strings or exploit useful connections, it could have taken years.

The wait for a telephone was more excruciating. It was a privilege for which you shelled out plenty while the well-placed apparatchik pretended to do you a favor.

Those were the wonderful days in which if you dared bring to Israel a reel-to-reel audio recorder, you could count on a begrudging customs officer to unwind the tape and measure it. Only so many meters of tape could be imported and no more.

Foreign currency controls led to the blossoming of the black market. Life's hypocrisies were straightforward and predictable. Everyone knew there was a righteous façade and a thriving subterranean reality. Higher-ups sanctimoniously preached to hard-working commoners and berated them for breaching class solidarity. A kid who flaunted a new plaything was denounced as a *bourgani* (bourgeois). No youngster quite knew what *bourgani* meant, but it was a pejorative.

Self-satisfied socialists addressed each other as *haver* (comrade) – which was Bill Clinton's parting epithet for Yitzhak Rabin. Rabin indeed came from sterling socialist stock (his mother, Rosa Cohen, was a solid rock of the Histadrut establishment). While Israelis groaned under stringent bureaucratic restrictions, he kept an illicit bank account in America (even if in the wife's name). The transgression wasn't so awful in itself. It shouldn't have been made an offense to begin with. Rabin, though, did nothing to decriminalize it for Mr. and Ms. Average Israeli, while allowing himself exemption from rules imposed ruthlessly on others.

The exposure of Rabin's lapse contributed to Labor's 1977 defeat. Thereafter Israel began steadily gravitating to the other extreme. Begin's government took hesitant first steps. In time our universities churned out enough free marketers of the Friedman-Thatcher-Reagan mold to speed along the reaction against Marx, Lenin, Borochov, A. D. Gordon, et al.

New-breed socialist converts to no-holds-barred capitalism, mind you, weren't averse to continuing to adhere to old-Left ultra-dovish views and advocate in their infinite wisdom that Israel forthwith divest itself of all its existentially vital strategic assets. Apparently a miniature, vulnerable nine-mile-wide state – crammed into what fellow ultra-dove Abba Eban dubbed the Auschwitz lines – is good for business. What's good for business is perforce good for Israel.

And so, a new fad was born – subscribed to ironically also by sorts who kept pompously attesting to their socialist credentials. Helter-skelter we got uncontrollably globalized and began privatizing everything with frenzy, including even the post office. If once publicly owned concerns were considered preferable, now they're objects of revulsion.

If once bosses couldn't fire the worst incompetents on their payroll, today the most diligent wage earners feel unsafe. Inscrutable "reorganization" can make valuable employees redundant overnight.

That said, one thing remains unalterable: there's an underlying schizophrenic Israeli inclination to boastfulness, coupled curiously with deep-set insecurities and inferiority complexes. As equity markets teeter-tottered worldwide and our bourse nosedived in panic, spectacular hubris manifested. We simultaneously shook in our sandals and sang our own praises for doing things better than Wall Street, for regulating more, for being wiser. Wall Street could come to Rehov Ahad Ha'am for a lesson or two.

The fact is that we possessed inordinate hubris even in Israel's infancy, when we subsisted on handouts and barely emerged from severe austerity and food rationing. Even then, we were know-it-alls, resplendent in progressive socialism, rejecting decadent Western influences and refusing to admit TV to our impoverished land, lest our altruistic youth be corrupted.

No way, we now gloat, would we in the land of red tape make mortgages as easily available as Fannie and Freddie did. Of course, we did manage a bad bubble ourselves about a quarter of a century ago, when bank share values here were disastrously inflated.

True, our government eventually stepped in and effectively saved our entire financial system from imploding. Now, crow local braggarts, the Americans follow in our footsteps, although clearly more clumsily and less efficiently. They emulate what we had already done so precociously in 1985.

How like the supercilious conceit which Ephraim Kishon satirized back in the 1950s, by facetiously proposing a union of equals between Israel and the USA.

The new flag, he envisioned, would feature "two stars instead of fifty" and the two nations would

> merge into a political federation, thereby giving birth – instead of two states, until now unnecessarily and wastefully separated – to a powerful federated unit named Monolithic Alliance, Previously America and Israel (MAPAI).
>
> This natural process of union is fully justified by the closeness of the twin countries, which are separated only by the Mediterranean and the Atlantic.... The area of the federation will extend over 3,632,085 square miles, an increase of 45,000%

for Israel.... It goes without saying that Israel is to guarantee America's present borders.... The armed forces of the two states will also be completely merged. The joint HQ is to reside in Ramat Gan. Israel's armaments industry will most certainly put its entire output at the disposal of the Joint Army... At the personal request of the Finance Minister, the new HQ will publish in the very near future a calming statement to the effect that Israeli officers' pay won't be raised after the union...but the fine for importing low-cost phonograph records from America will be raised.... The new federation is eagerly tearing down the partitions that so far separated the economies of the two states.

And a good thing too. Obviously Israelis are savvier. As Kishon clairvoyantly forecast all those decades ago, our unique-brand old-time socialism is triumphantly vindicated. Any simpleton can see that America belatedly took a leaf out of Israel's book and appeared to quasi-nationalize private enterprises, as Israel (with American underwriting) once bailed out its crashing banks. America mimics *us*!

Oops, on reflection we must concede that in the intervening years Israel rushed to privatize all over the place and über-Americanize with super-capitalist vengeance. Oops, we better consider a wee course correction, a tad of a U-turn to catch up with our other MAPAI half, so we can both be on the same MAPAI page. Long live MAPAI!

Then What's the Alternative?

The days preceding Yom Kippur are devoted to soul-searching and apologies. I have loads to atone for, like irresistible meanness to the two Ehuds (Olmert and Barak), Tzipi and their assorted expedient sidekicks and agenda-pushing boosters. But, as incoming mail indicates, I've also offended (albeit unintentionally and without malice) some readers. So I'll hereby seek to explain, by way of making amends.

Lately there's a marked resurgence of complaints about my failure to supply concrete proposals for how I would run the country. I plead guilty but it's no sin of inadvertent omission or careless neglect. It's not up to me to compose detailed substitute policies for the incontrovertible mess which given inept/delinquent leaders have made of things.

I wasn't elected to high office, possess no clout or access to resources and executive authority. Hence, it's unfair, misleading and intellectually insincere to taunt me to deliver what I patently cannot – and shouldn't be asked to.

To draft decision-making guidelines nobody would ever implement is as much a waste of time as constructing castles in the air. Such pointless pursuits negate or enfeeble efforts to rouse some public opinion against catastrophic schemes, utter bamboozlement, and/or corruption. However, warnings delivered in time can save lives.

That's my reply particularly to those who took me to task after I dared assert (see "The Wooden-Headedness Factor" below) that Oslo was a fiasco on so grand a scale that it met all of Barbara Tuchman's criteria for woodenheaded statecraft and would have merited inclusion (had she only been alive then) in her *March of Folly*. In response, one reader wondered whether I prefer to avoid publicizing my recommendations and another took things a step further and asked, "What have Honig and the settlement fanatics ever offered instead of Oslo?"

These questions aren't new, as isn't the "fanatic" epithet. These galling diversionary gibes appear with cyclical regularity. But besides being specious, such provocations are also exceedingly common in Israeli discourse. They're often resorted to by the intellectually indolent but just as frequently are willfully used to derail relevant discussion. Because the "alternative-baiting" tactic is so widespread, it's exasperatingly effective and dangerous.

Occasionally I attempt to highlight the absurdity and shallow harassment inherent in aggressively demanding to know "what's *your* solution?" The very query suggests to unsuspecting minds that no other available courses of action exist apart from gross mismanagement of our most crucial affairs. Yet there's no obligation to behave like imbeciles. Sometimes it's enough just not to be rash and stupid.

The folk tale about an impoverished peddler from a distant Southeast Asian archipelago illustrates the point. The restless fellow pondered his inauspicious condition, pined for better things and hatched plans to improve his lot. He was intent on taking his wares to a far-off island where they'd be rare and fetch lucrative prices. He was elated by the adventure, the opportunities beyond the horizon and, most of all, by the prospect of breaking loose from a dead-end existence.

He had the minutest details worked out, all except one: the boat that would ferry him and his merchandise across the waters.

The authentically self-delusional among our homegrown purveyors of bliss and peace – those who aren't outright shysters – might recognize him as a fellow dreamer. They too have everything worked out except the most key element – a genuine, able, willing and honorable peace partner.

Our resourceful young entrepreneur eventually concocted a creative contrivance – about as practical as Oslo. He set sail in a discarded old tub. It soon emerged, though, that his makeshift vessel wasn't seaworthy. The visionary seeker of fortune would have drowned, had he not been rescued by passing fishermen. They were bewildered by his senseless risk.

Amazed by their lack of insight, their utter failure to think out of the box, he exclaimed, "How *else* could I go after my dreams?"

Translated into Israeli political parlance, his incredulous retort would be: "Then what's the alternative?" Subtext: if there's nothing but a deathtrap contraption to sail in, you embark on the fateful journey in the deathtrap contraption for lack of any floatable alternative.

Here's the essence of Osloite logic. Perhaps the underhanded negotiators, who illicitly contracted their deal behind the nation's back, might have been excused in 1993 for letting unjustifiable optimism and wishful thinking becloud their judgment. But, many years later, with the benefit of hindsight wisdom – after having witnessed how disastrous Oslo proved to be in every possible sphere – there's no condoning continuing self-deception. At this point obstinate cognitive dissonance can willy-nilly lead to self-destruction.

There'll be no friendly fishermen to pluck Israelis from the Mediterranean should the self-inflicted weakening of Israel reinvigorate genocidal temptations and reinforce Arab proclivity to "throw all the Jews into the sea." Even under very different circumstances a great deal of circumspection is warranted before any vital strategic assets are surrendered in a land as tiny and as vulnerable as ours.

Considering their past treachery, all Arab interlocutors – even if they regale us with honeyed blandishments – should be treated with more than a little suspicion. But we have no sweet flattery to worry about. Our neighbors openly rehash their hate, refuse to recognize Israel's legitimacy as a Jewish state and won't renounce their "right" to inundate it with untold millions of hostile so-called refugees.

That said, I do favor an alternative. It's encapsulated in Ze'ev Jabotinsky's *Iron Wall*. "The peacemongers among us," he wrote in 1923 (before we became ogre "occupiers," indeed twenty-five years before we even won independence), "have induced us to believe that all our troubles are due to misunderstanding.… If we only clarify to the Arabs how moderate our intentions really are, they will immediately extend to us their hand in friendship."

Way back then Jabotinsky judged that "this belief is utterly unfounded," because "there is no likelihood of a voluntary agreement with the Arabs. Those who regard a peace accord as a *sine qua non* [an essential prerequisite] for Zionism may as well say '*non*' and withdraw from Zionism.… There will never be a voluntary peace as long as there remains in Arab hearts a spark of hope to be rid of us. They will refuse to relinquish this hope…because they are not a rabble but a living people. This people will yield only when there is no longer any hope of doing away with us, when our Wall of Iron cannot be breached."

Israel's most imperative alternative is to become stronger, not weaker. By poking holes in our proverbial Iron Wall we invite enmity, not further the prospects of coexistence. Our conscious choice must be *not* to take existential risks. Suicide is not a national option and avoiding it is alternative enough.

There might be something to not taking to the high seas in a leaky tub, even if we terribly crave the crossing, even if alluring promises beckon. There's a lot to be said for just staying alive. Where healthy self-preservation instincts prevail, survival takes precedence over pipe dreams – be they for regional peace or personal prosperity. Staying on dry land is the only option in the absence of a boat. There simply is *no* other alternative.

The Sergei Connection

Among the last follies ascribed to Ariel Sharon, just before his catastrophic stroke, was a promise to Vladimir Putin to hand over the Russian Compound's famed Sergei Building (the sumptuous "Sergei Imperial Guesthouse"). It's smack-dab in the very heart of Jerusalem – in the western part thereof, the one that lies within the Green Line, the one which ostensibly Israel may be allowed to keep after it will have relinquished all it liberated in its 1967 war of self-defense (including Judaism's Holiest of Holies).

Claims for a pound of the Jewish national flesh, it so appears, are being made not only by Arabs. We owe slices of our capital to all sorts of latecomers, conquerors, glory seekers, clout hunters and would-be meddlers in our volatile region.

With friends like Putin, let's not forget, we need no enemies. He actively helps Iran gain the nuclear capability with which to obliterate the Jewish state. Putin supplies Syria with missiles with which to decimate Israel's population centers and down its fighter jets.

Via Damascus, Putin succors Hezbollah and Russian-made rocketry fired from Gaza's Hamastan explodes in Ashkelon. Putin deserves none of the consideration that might perhaps be extraordinarily extended a bosom buddy (though genuine allies wouldn't pursue archaic pretexts for a foothold in another nation's capital and the cradle of its heritage).

Moreover, Putin doesn't politely request a special cordial gesture. A Russian Foreign Ministry-sponsored website names the issue of "Russian property in Jerusalem" as one of the most outstanding bilateral problems between the countries, listing it under the heading of "Getting What Is One's Own" with the further elucidation that "Russia has a number of complaints against Israel." It goes on to assert that there's no contesting "the legitimacy of Russia's claim to the St.

Sergius Metochion and the building of the Russian church mission as well as various other facilities in Jerusalem."

Though no written documentation exists anywhere of Sharon's alleged pledge to Putin, its intrinsic logic and consistency are undeniable. An administration prepared to divest Israel of some parts of Jerusalem won't shrink from surrendering other parts too – even bits of its central downtown, in which nobody would presumably portray our tenure as controversial or precarious.

Given such an ultra-appeasing mindset, it might well be that Sharon was loath to disappoint Putin. But had Sharon and his cohorts fully focused on the ramifications?

The ultimate eviction from the Sergei premises of Israel's Agriculture Ministry and assorted environmental organizations is the least troublesome consequence (the blow to national sovereignty notwithstanding). In Kremlin hands, these holdings would de facto become extraterritorial. What if terrorists were to flee and find refuge therein? Would Israeli troops break into Putin's toehold in the Holy Land?

The precedent, additionally, might stimulate other appetites. The Greek Orthodox Church owns the land on which the Knesset and the prime minister's residence stand. If an Israeli ministry can be evicted, why not the Jewish parliament and the head of government?

All foreigners, it seems, claim to have more cogent claims to Jerusalem than do Jews. As Sharon and sidekicks – with his foreign minister Tzipi Livni prominently among them – demonstrated during disengagement, Jews are portable and disposable.

And how did Russia's unchallengeable claims arise? The Russian Compound was chartered by the Russian Church from the Ottoman Turk rulers of this country in 1858. It was earmarked for the welfare of pilgrims. The Sergei Complex, occupying nine compound acres, was constructed decades afterward by Grand Duke Sergei Alexandrovich (son of Czar Alexander II, brother of infamous Czar Alexander III and uncle to last Czar Nicholas II) to accommodate visiting aristocrats.

Among his other distinctions, Sergei was president of the Imperial Orthodox Palestine Society. Turkish law categorized his property as strictly private and emphatically not a Russian state holding.

Post-Revolution, both the "White" and "Red" Russian churches vied for compound ownership. The Mandatory Brits commandeered the lot. Israel purchased most of the compound from the USSR in 1964, but, being cashed-strapped then, paid the $3.5 million in… oranges. The Sergei Building, church and courtyard weren't included in the deal. Until the Six-Day War they served as the local KGB spy nook.

Putin reportedly refused to so much as countenance the sale of the property due to a deep-seated sentimental connection to Sergei and his legacy. Too bad Livni couldn't exude similar emotional attachment to Sergei's victims.

She, of all homegrown dabblers in statecraft, should have known that the Grand Duke was an avid practitioner of the recurrent Romanov theme: *Beat the Jews and save Russia*. His anti-Semitism was unrivalled even by the rabid anti-Semitism of his royal kinfolk.

In 1891 – merely months after Sergei's Building went up in Jerusalem – his brother appointed him governor-general of Moscow. Sergei's immediate move was to uproot the city's thirty thousand Jews. Moscow was to be "cleansed" in three orderly phases – the poorest and least-veteran Jewish inhabitants ousted first and the richest and longest-residing Jews removed last.

The banishment edict was published on the first day of Passover. The next night police swooped down on Jewish homes, roused entire frightened families and drove thousands of scantily clad men, women and children from their beds to the lock-up where they were crammed into filthy cells. Others hid out in dark alleyways and cemeteries, only to be eventually rounded up and roughed up. All, shorn of their possessions, were later driven out of town like vermin. Many were tortured. The infirm died in transit. Some were dragged in wooden manacles, like outlaws, to do long stretches of hard labor in distant prisons.

Over months and several expulsion installments, Moscow was rendered virtually *judenrein*. While Sergei rejoiced, deported Jews were reduced to utter destitution. In Sergei's Russia, however, they were the lucky ones. Elsewhere, Sergei's clan unleashed gruesome pogroms – painstakingly premeditated as diversionary tactics to quell internal unrest – in which Jews suffered all manner of barbaric butchery, eclipsed only by the horrors of the Holocaust.

This is the Sergei whose individual real estate holding Putin elevates to a sacred national heirloom for all Russians.

But if Putin speaks in terms of national birthright, why not also Israel? Why not demand at least a modicum of quid pro quo – a central sliver of Russia's capital for a central sliver of Israel's capital?

Why not demand that – in return for one ruthless Russian despot's property, for which Putin yearns nostalgically – Putin pay with what Sergei stole from the Jews he robbed and exiled? Moscow's Zaryadye historical district, adjacent to Red Square, was the hub of Muscovite Jewry (particularly the sizable Glebov Yard, site of the then-Jewish ghetto). Why not award that area to Israel in return for Sergei's courtyard?

Putin may balk and assert that Israel isn't heir to the Jews Sergei dispossessed, in which case Israel could note that neither is Putin's Russia heir to Sergei.

That's how a proud foreign minister of the Jewish state and a prime-ministerial aspirant should have reacted. But although Livni may not lack ambition, she proved herself woefully deficient in Jewish pride.

The Wooden-Headedness Factor

Insightful Pulitzer Prize-winning historian Barbara Tuchman died in February 1989, over four years before Shimon Peres, Yossi Beilin and their underhanded crew clandestinely negotiated the Oslo Accords and then dropped them on the heads of all unsuspecting Israelis, including their prime minister. Yitzhak Rabin proved too weak-willed to resist the fait accompli with which he had been presented and on September 13, 1993, he formalized it on the White House lawn.

Barbara Tuchman

Thus Tuchman, alas, missed an example of preposterous statecraft on a scale that would have easily vied with every absurdity she included in her 1984 classic *March of Folly*.

Defining folly as "the pursuit by governments of policies contrary to their own interests," Tuchman demanded that to qualify as folly, each policy examined meet three criteria:

1. "It must have been perceived as counter-productive in its own time."
2. "A feasible alternative course of action must have been available."
3. "The policy in question should be that of a group, not an individual leader, and should persist beyond any one political lifetime." It must be adhered to by "collective government or a succession of rulers in the same office."

Oslo, sadly, meets all of Tuchman's conditions and then some. Rarely in human affairs is it as possible to point to a single inanity as the trigger which radically changed the fortunes of a people – in Israel's case of a beleaguered people, struggling for bare physical survival.

Oslo turned this once-feisty and plucky little nation into an apathetic aggregate that has ceased to seethe about much of anything. It briefly appeared that the Second Lebanon War, Oslo's direct defective descendant, might ignite the extinguished flicker of common sense yet again, but that spark quickly died out.

The Oslo-generated apathy allowed Ehud Barak's rash unilateral flight from Lebanon; the unilateral flight from Gaza and the expulsion of its nine thousand Jews; the relinquishment of the strategically indispensable Philadelphi Corridor; the establishment of Hamastan; the continued funneling of funds and supplies of electricity and goods to Hamastan; the failure to react against the rocketing of Sderot, Ashkelon and beyond; the obsequious acquiescence to PA demands for "goodwill gestures" (such as the unilateral release of convicted terrorists); the in-your-face sedition within Israel's own Arab sector and too much more to mention.

Our tired masses seem to stomach anything. There is somehow an unuttered expectation that if we ignore palpable danger signs, or tolerate them and make nice, they'll go away.

That is Oslo's incontrovertible legacy to the Israeli psyche. Few dare insist on the justice of our cause. Fewer yet know our case. The youngest Israelis are never taught it and remain ignorant to a degree that severely imperils Israel's self-preservation prospects. Increasingly we see ourselves as our enemies portray us and we insert their fraudulent narrative into our school curriculums, art, theater and film. We brainwash and browbeat ourselves but call that enlightenment and broadmindedness.

Pre-Oslo we retaliated for every terror onslaught and refused to give in even when hostages' lives hung in the balance. Today the nation that rescued hijacked passengers at Entebbe debases itself by freeing barbaric mass murderers and it bankrolls the indiscriminate shelling of its own towns. The nation that liberated Jerusalem contemplates relinquishing it.

Oslo's rationale was to purchase a modicum of peace by sacrificing strategically vital territory. Yet our convoluted logic failed the test of simple popular perception. All our sophisticated argumentation notwithstanding, nothing could erase the core intuition that a people ready to surrender its patrimony isn't genuinely attached to it as are native sons to their ancestral soil.

By giving away bits of the Jewish heartland, we imparted the impression here and abroad that we have no roots, claim or connection to this country – that we're not here by right. Israeli concessions underscored the slanderous image of Israelis as interlopers who plead to be allowed to retain a bit of what they usurped.

Oslo conferred legitimacy on the PLO, an organization whose raison d'être was to cleanse this land of our presence. Therein lies the fundamental difference between what Menachem Begin contracted with Egypt and what Rabin was conned into championing. Egypt is a neighboring state with whom we fought a number of wars and with whom we reached accommodation.

By compromising with an organization founded for the explicit purpose of coming in our stead, the Rabin-Peres government undermined Israel's claim not only to territories it freed in the 1967 war of self-defense but to the whole shebang – to the entire state Jews established in 1948.

It's no coincidence that more than at any time since 1948 there are escalating challenges in the international arena to our very right to exist. It's no longer taboo in polite society to suggest that Israel shouldn't be.

That is the greatest long-term harm inflicted by Oslo. Not all Israelis can coherently identify the damage and home in on its corollaries, but, sensing grand national failure, they grow dispirited. Disheartenment inures them to repeated blows. Whereas at Oslo's outset we still counted what Rabin cynically dubbed the "victims of peace," we no longer do so.

The deadly tally exceeds sixteen hundred. Proportionally this is tantamount to eighty thousand fatalities in the US. While Americans remember 9/11's disaster (whose relative toll is equivalent to sixty deaths in Israel), most workaday Israelis don't instantly recognize 9/13 for the disaster it was.

That's how profound is the Oslo-imposed impassivity, exacerbated by journalists and judges who failed to protect the public which depended on them. Although years on it's all too abundantly clear that Oslo is a farcical flop, establishment mouthpieces insist on depicting it as an extraordinary breakthrough. The interminable mind-numbing media mantra is all-pervasive, while the opposition is stymied by an agenda-guided and politically interventionist judiciary, unparalleled anywhere in the free world.

Yet the primary culprits are the politicians who brazenly betrayed our trust – from Tsomet MKs Gonen Segev and Alex Goldfarb (who enabled Rabin to ratify Oslo by selling their votes for a ministerial appointment and a Mitsubishi, respectively) and all the way to Ariel Sharon, Ehud Olmert and Tzipi Livni, who ditched the platform on which they were elected and cheated their voters to implement Oslo's disengagement sequel.

Which brings us back to Tuchman's question: "Why do holders of high office so often act contrary to the way reason points and enlightened self-interest suggests?" Her forthright answer is "wooden-headedness," i.e., both "the refusal to learn from experience" and "the source of self-deception."

Such recurrent wooden-headedness, she argues, is "a factor that plays a remarkably large role in government. It consists of assessing a situation in terms of preconceived fixed notions while ignoring or rejecting any contrary signs. It is acting according to wish, while not allowing oneself to be deflected by the facts."

Though writing before the event, Tuchman incredibly seems to have analyzed the Osloite folly with unerring acumen. "The power to command," she stressed, "frequently causes failure to think."

My People Love to Have It So

> I am convinced from the depth of my heart and to the best of my understanding that this disengagement will strengthen Israel's hold on the territory essential to our existence and will win the blessing and gratitude of those near and far, will lessen enmity, will break besiegement and boycotts and will further us on the path of peace with the Palestinians and all our other neighbors.
> – Ariel Sharon, October 25, 2004

This rosy prognosis – indeed this prophesy of peace and bliss – was delivered from the Knesset podium in that fateful plenum session in which the then prime minister, having deviated 180 degrees from the platform on which he was elected and having cynically ignored the party referendum he insisted upon, formally sought parliamentary approval to uproot all twenty-one Gaza Strip settlements and four in northern Samaria as well.

The latter handful were an arbitrary afterthought, decided upon without any consultation or deliberation and without any perceptible purpose (their land is still under Israeli control), except to signal that nothing is sacrosanct, that the fate imposed on the Gazan settlements is also contemplated for their Judea and Samaria counterparts. So much for the spurious notion that Gush Katif was being sacrificed for the sake of territories adjacent to the state's densely populated soft underbelly.

On August 22, 2005, the last brave Gaza settlement – Netzarim – was cleansed of its Jews. The next day Samaria's Ganim, Kadim, Sa-Nur and Homesh were all emptied out as well.

Sharon was the expulsion's formidable driving force but his gall and guile wouldn't have sufficed without the connivance of his willing enablers. None of Sharon's self-serving sidekicks had the intestinal fortitude then to dissent and none have since beaten their breast in contrition. They sat, saw, nodded, propagandized for the boss and were duly rewarded with political promotion.

They heard Sharon's declaration of intent on December 18, 2003, at the Herzliya Conference, where he unveiled and rationalized his unilateral retreat scheme: "The purpose of the Disengagement Plan is to reduce terror as much as possible, and grant Israeli citizens the maximum level of security."

Sharon's hangers-on helped peddle his palliatives to the anxious populace and he guaranteed that "after disengagement the world will appreciate our goodwill and support us"; "after disengagement all kid gloves will be off"; "after disengagement no terror will be tolerated"; "after disengagement our artillery will pound them for every terrorist mortar shell"; "after disengagement we will have no more obligations to their welfare"; "after disengagement it will be another game with other rules."

Enough time has elapsed to evaluate the prophetic assurances tendered so confidently and authoritatively by Sharon and his coterie of unrepentant accomplices. We now know for sure that not one upbeat prediction materialized.

No real surprise here. Enough among us warned in real time of the inevitable catastrophe, but the tendentious press derided us. Though any levelheaded person should have sensibly shared our eminently reasonable doubts, most of the media cheered the disengagement con – some because it suited their agenda and others because of downright cowardice.

Bottom line: no sound individual can claim Israel's "hold on vital territory" was strengthened – indeed our very right to exist is challenged as never before. Far from having earned "the blessings and esteem of those near and far," Israel is more of an international pariah than prior to the disengagement which undercut its claim to any of the Jewish heartland liberated in the 1967 war of self-defense. No boycotts and blockades were lifted, no hate lessened and no peace furthered.

Neither are Israelis even a negligible smidgen more secure. Quite the contrary. Sharon and crew managed to magnify Ehud Barak's Lebanese folly and demonstrate again that whatever terrain Israel relinquishes is destined to become a terror breeding ground. Just as Hezbollah was invigorated and reinforced in the north, so was Hamas in the south. Having learned that terror pays off, Gazans established Hamastan. The same is only a matter of time in Mahmoud Abbas's residue Ramallah-centered bailiwick.

Instead of encouraging moderation, disengagement emboldened fanatic extremists and they arm themselves to the teeth. Not only is Sderot intimidated by Kassams, but Ashkelon has been attacked by Grads. Urban centers like Beersheba and Ashdod were chillingly targeted. With this kind of peace, who needs war?

There should be an official inquiry into the process that allowed the disastrous disengagement to ever be marketed and foisted on the gullible citizenry. If the malfeasance isn't exposed, we're liable for more of the awful same. Disengagement's central deception cost the entire Israeli collective the strategic deterrent indispensable to its survival and it chipped away at the state's Zionist ideological underpinnings. It substantially and indisputably weakened Israel.

To avoid sequel grandiose diversions from and cover-ups of

personal/political corruption there must be no suppression of what spurred disengagement, of how policy makers fell down on the job, how the judiciary rubber-stamped injustice and countenanced special semi-martial night courts which jailed demonstrating juveniles with outrageous disproportionality, of how democracy's watchdogs and civil libertarians stayed dutifully silent. It would be enlightening to discover how the IDF, police and intelligence services were suborned into submission and collusion in a mass demonization campaign against the political opposition (to the point of disseminating calumnies about plotted coups d'état).

But perhaps the reluctance to delve into dereliction/delinquency inestimably greater and more fundamental than that of the Second Lebanon War resides deeper in our psyche. By now, most Israelis, including plenty who compulsively persist in deluding themselves, sense that any probe into the fiasco that was disengagement will show that the electorate was hoodwinked by the latter-day likes of biblical fraudsters. Jeremiah (6:14) decried those "who facilely heal the shattering wounds of my people, saying 'peace, peace,' and there is no peace."

Above all, the fault isn't only in disengagement's false prophets but also in their credulous clientele – those who uncritically imbibe lies that are easier to stomach than unpleasant truths and grim killjoy conclusions.

"The prophets prophesy falsely and the priests bear rule by their means," Jeremiah reminds us (5:31), but "my people love to have it so." This leads him painfully to the rhetorical question of "what will you do afterwards?"

Buried with Kalonymus

When US Secretary of State Condoleezza Rice visited Israel and reproved us with a sanctimonious schoolmarm's sternness, she pro forma professed to genuinely believe that Jews unlawfully seized "Arab Jerusalem." To facilitate Washington's self-serving cockamamie "two-state vision," it is therefore incumbent upon Jewish trespassers to renounce what isn't theirs and certainly not construct more housing for more unwanted Jews.

But I bet anything that self-righteous Condi never heard of Rabbi Kalonymus the Miracle Maker (Kalonymus Ba'al Ha-ness). He's my direct ancestor. Until 1948, a massive mound of stones marked his final resting place on the Mount of Olives' slopes. The Arabs smashed all that. What was once a conspicuous landmark is now gone. But does unbridled vandalism grant Arabs an unassailable deed of ownership?

My father's family knew for sure of at least two illustrious forebears' graves in this country. One was of Rabbi Elazar Rokeach, the Ashkenazi chief rabbi of Amsterdam, to whom we trace our lineage directly, generation by generation, without omission. He left everything to live in Safed, where he died and was buried in 1741 – a full thirty-five years before American independence.

Kalonymus Haberkasten, another of my paternal grandmother's direct and indisputable forefathers, headed the Ashkenazi community of Jerusalem over two hundred years before Rabbi Elazar left Holland to settle in the Galilee. Kalonymus died in Jerusalem in 1550 and was reputed to have been the holy Ari's teacher.

But his greatest renown came from having saved the then Sephardi Eliyahu Hanavi Synagogue from the bloody consequences of a blood libel. On the last Saturday before Passover, neighboring Arabs dumped the body of a young boy at the synagogue and charged that Jews baked matzos with his blood – a popular calumny that originated in 1144 in Norwich, England, and for spurious spin-offs of which many Jews in diverse corners of the world were to pay with their lives for the ensuing centuries.

Somehow my great-great-great...great-grandfather Kalonymus pulled his day's counterpart to a forensic whodunit sensation, proved the accusers' deceit and foiled the rioters.

Those of us not big on miracles can skip the details. Suffice it to say that tradition ascribes the rescue of congregants and synagogue to Kalonymus and that he was revered equally by Ashkenazim and Sephardim. His bold feat had become a staple of Jerusalem folklore.

But Kalonymus didn't savor his victory. He berated himself for having violated the Sabbath in the course of performing his miracle. To punish himself he requested that no tombstone be erected atop his grave. He was interred on the lower mountain gradient, near Rabbi Ovadia of Bertinoro (the "Bartenura"), and ordinary Jerusalemites passing by would always place stones on his unmarked grave. Over the centuries this folksy homage grew to considerable proportions and was visible from afar.

That was the case until 1948, when Arab occupiers ransacked and defiled the Eliyahu Hanavi synagogue (along with fifty-seven others), ripped out tombstones from the three-thousand-year-old Mount of Olives Jewish cemetery and used them to construct public latrines – the ultimate humiliation and desecration.

At that time they also savagely pulled down the giant stack of stones piled up as Kalonymus's marker during almost four hundred years. This was maximal ethnic cleansing, deliberately calculated to purge Jerusalem of its Jewish past and pretend it was never anything but Arab.

So what if Jews constituted the largest ethnic group in Jerusalem as far back as the first available testimonies and records of the earliest decades of the nineteenth century (borne out by noted travelers like Richardson, Carne and Scholtz)?

226 Debunking the Bull

The first official census of 1844 showed 7,130 Jews and 5,760 Muslims. By 1875 the number of Jews exceeded twelve thousand and the Muslims increased to 7,560. By the twentieth century the Jewish majority was incontrovertible – forty-five thousand Jews and twelve thousand Muslims in 1909. On the eve of the 1948 Arab contravention of the UN partition resolution and the Arab Legion's illegal occupation of east Jerusalem, the city included some one hundred thousand Jews and 36,600 Muslims.

That year, 1948, the Jordanians occupied east Jerusalem illegally. They stayed for nineteen years, expelled all of the Old City's Jews,

Jews expelled from the Old City of Jerusalem after the Arab conquest of 1948

destroyed fifty-eight synagogues, sadistically despoiled the ancient incomparable Jewish pantheon on the Mount of Olives and denied Jews the right to pray at the Western Wall.

But there was no global outrage until in 1967's Six-Day War Israel undid the Arab illegality (and that only following extreme belligerent provocation).

The Arabs' nineteen-year illegality is now perceived as the legality that must be restored. Arab conquest and barbarism must be rewarded and recognized by all decent observers as the status quo ante.

Hence it's forbidden to develop the Ma'ale Hazeitim neighborhood adjacent to Ras-el-Amud and the cemetery that was Jewish for three millennia. Condi surely could not fathom the meaning of three thousand years. For her and her like, Jews lost their rights to the mount when Arabs uprooted its tombstones.

Jewish life near the site that housed the Jewish dead – before the collective memories of assorted admonishing Condis ever began – will, asserts Condi, impede peace. She doesn't care that Ma'ale Hazeitim is located on land purchased by Jews (Moshe Weinberg and Nissan Bek) in the nineteenth century.

Irresponsible Israeli politicians – and this didn't start with the corrupt Sharon and his sleazy sidekick and heir Olmert – managed in their scandalous ineptitude to acknowledge the cynical equivalence between Israeli settlements and Arab suicide-bombers or rocket barrages on innocent families. Inimical foreign statesmen – out to further their interests at our existential expense – deem both home construction and indiscriminate attacks as identical "obstacles to peace."

Imbecilely, Israeli hotshots imbibe and regurgitate the lie that the Land of Israel doesn't belong to Israel and that Jewish revival in the Jewish homeland is sinful occupation. Israel's own misguided headliners had put settlements into deep freeze. So why the ceaseless squawk and the relentless bad press abroad? It's mostly about

Jerusalem. Israeli incompetents helped demonize settlements and, by delegitimizing them, they thereby also rendered entire Jerusalem quarters vulnerable.

The bottom line is that it's no longer permissible by the international community's insincere criteria to build homes for Jews in Jerusalem. The presence in Jerusalem of Kalonymus and his like has been effectively erased. The Jewish state's own defeatism helps paint Jews as late-coming interlopers in the cradle of their nationhood, as usurpers who displaced supposedly indigenous Arabs, who – according to truth-slaying historical revisionism – had once comprised the majority.

The truth lies buried with Kalonymus – shamed and disgraced – in a grave as unmarked and as forgotten as his.

A Masjid Grows in Brooklyn

I was Brooklyn-bound – or so I thought. I took the subway to see a fellow alumna of New York's High School of Music and Art (as today's LaGuardia High School for the Arts was then called). I looked forward to the nostalgic reunion. I hadn't been in NYC for ages and catching up with an old classmate seemed an indispensable component of walking down memory lane.

What's more Kathy still lives at the same address in the cozy middle-class neighborhood where I sometimes visited her way back then. It was common for the house-proud Irish to keep property in the family and hence I'd soon reenter the two-storey red brick home in whose wood-paneled rec room we occasionally whiled away hours.

But when I climbed up the grimy station stairs and surveyed the street, I suspected that some supernatural time-and-space warp had transported me to Islamabad. This couldn't be Brooklyn.

Women strode attired in *hijab*s and male passersby sported all manner of Muslim headgear and long flowing tunics. Kathy met me at the train and astounded me by pointing out long *kurta* shirts as distinguished from a *salwar kameez*. She couldn't help becoming an expert. She's now a member of a fast-dwindling minority because "people are running away. We're among the last holdouts of our generation. My kids have fled."

Pakistani and Bangladeshi groceries lined the main shopping drag and everywhere stickers boldly beckoned: "Discover Jesus in the Quran." An unremarkable low-slung building on the corner of Kathy's own block was now dominated by an oversized green sign, identifying it as *Masjid Nur al-Islam* (the Light of Islam Mosque) and announcing that "Only Allah is worthy of worship and Mohammad is his LAST prophet." Here too Christians were urged to "turn to the Quran" if they are "genuinely faithful to Jesus."

It wasn't hard to identify the remaining non-Muslim residences. Kathy's was typical. A huge American flag fluttered demonstratively in the manicured front yard, accompanied by a large cross on the door and an assortment of patriotic/jingoistic banners. "We're besieged," she explained. "Making a statement is about all we can do. They aren't delighted to see our flag wave. This is enemy territory." Lest I judge her paranoid, Kathy began regaling me with what she knew about the mosque a few doors down her street – still as tree-lined as I remember but somehow less pretty and tidy, even vaguely grubby.

Kathy has compiled a bulging dossier of press clippings and computer-printouts about the masjid that grew in a once heavily Jewish area. Until the mid-nineties, its imam was the late Egyptian-educated Gulshair el-Shukrijumah, dispatched by the Saudis as a Wahabi missionary in 1985 and financed by them thereafter.

The Brooklyn street where the masjid grew

His disciple Clement Rodney Hampton-El, an explosives specialist, possibly helped assemble the bomb detonated in the 1993 World Trade Center attack. He was convicted of plotting to blow up the UN, FBI headquarters and the Holland and Lincoln tunnels. Gulshair acted as interpreter for Omar Abdel-Rahman, the "Blind Sheikh" now serving life for the first WTC bombing, conspiring to use explosives at other NYC landmarks and colluding to assassinate US politicians.

Nabbed operational commander of the 9/11 plot Khalid Sheikh Mohammed fingered Gulshair's eldest son Adnan as having been designated by al-Qaeda and personally approved by Osama bin Laden to lead new terror assaults and serve as successor to Mohammed Atta, with whom Adnan was connected. Adnan received flight training and is dubbed "Jaffar the pilot." He was likewise linked to "Dirty Bomber" Jose Padilla, Hamas and Al-Qaeda fundraiser Adham Hassoun, and terrorist Imran Mandhai (convicted of conspiring to bomb the National Guard armory,

South Florida electrical substations, Jewish-owned businesses and community centers, and Mount Rushmore).

Kathy's ex-neighbor is now a fugitive and subject of a worldwide FBI manhunt. Adnan's brother Nabil, incidentally, uploaded to his webpage an image of Jerusalem ablaze with the caption "Al Quds, we are coming."

But of more immediate concern to Kathy and the few leftover neighborhood natives is the "in-your-face insolence of the immigrants." For years the mosque had been calling the faithful to prayers via a rooftop loudspeaker five times daily. Police intervention persuaded the imam to omit the pre-dawn sonorous summons. Catholic Kathy knows all about "*Allahu Akbar*" and how the muezzin intones it.

"I'm not a bigot," she stresses repeatedly. "This was always a pluralistic live-and-let-live section. The jihadists, however, aren't here to coexist but to conquer. The Jewish community," which once flourished "here, was so different. They weren't on the offensive. They just wanted to be left alone."

She reminded me of her brother Eddie, whose best childhood friend was the son of a nearby orthodox rabbi. During his teens Eddie was regularly recruited by his chum to the *minyan* until he was roused too early one winter morning and exclaimed: "What do you want from me? I'm not even Jewish!"

"This kind of a relationship," Kathy comments, "just isn't possible these days. Muslims call us infidels and want all infidels out. We're threatened."

On the way back, I decided to photograph the masjid, sensing it could make a story. Kathy became frantic. "Don't you dare," she almost yelled. As I slipped the camera back into my handbag, she explained that several weeks before my arrival two journalists, Bos Smith and Paul Williams, photographed a similar Brooklyn mosque, Masjid al-Takwa.

They were grabbed by twenty ninja-uniformed men, shoved into the mosque cellar, held captive and roughly interrogated by the group's henna-bearded leader, Ali Kareem. He released them only after they fibbed that they're interested in converting to Islam. On a subsequent visit to the site they were accosted again and an attempt was made to seize and break their camera. "I don't know who may be watching us now," Kathy warned.

Nevertheless, I perused the notice board near the entrance and learned that enrollment is on for the mosque school (where Gulshair once taught) and that if I hang around I could hear one Abu Yousuf lecture on "protecting yourself from *Shaytan* (Satan) this summer."

Alternatively, I could seek sanctuary from *Shaytan* in Israel. It suddenly seemed way safer than certain Brooklyn nooks.

Where His Heart Is

Speakers of Yiddish and German no doubt remember being cautioned that their conduct reflects on how they were reared. When their behavior failed to meet expectations, the predictable admonishing question always was "where is your *Kinderstube*?" Literally *Kinderstube* means the children's room or nursery. Over time it had come to be semi-synonymous with propriety because it denoted upbringing – the scene where value systems are nurtured.

A politician's *Kinderstube* should never be regarded as immutable predestination that automatically determines his future course. Any person can change, renounce or even resent what had been inculcated into him early on. Nothing is absolutely foreordained. But the lack of any clear departure from an early environment must be judged noteworthy, especially when it's subsequently accompanied by steady increments of more of the same.

That's why all those who downplay Barack Obama's contact with Islam – even if only superficial – miss the point. So do those who reject the focus on his later and ongoing associations and denigrate it as a conspiracy to smear.

Obama's associations matter all the more in the absence of any real record. They become the sole available gauge to the man who presumes to lead the free world. Were it not for this presumption, no one would bother about him. Because for better or worse he shapes our fates, it's legitimate to resort to all available clues to figure out what colors his perceptions.

This isn't about Obama's circumstances of birth – over which he had no control – nor about his religion or his Indonesian schooling. These can't and shouldn't tar him for life. Ayaan Hirsi Ali showed the world how a resolute individual can surmount any amount of brainwashing. Obama endured nothing as harrowing or adverse as Ayaan, yet he hasn't evinced anything like the courageous fortitude and intellectual independence of this African woman, born into a Muslim family.

Thus, while it's obvious that she had freed herself from seminal indoctrination, the same assumption can't be made for Obama even if in his case formative influences were hardly as constrictive or overwhelming. In Obama's case we must suspect that *Kinderstube* impressions linger and continue to mold attitudes and proclivities – whether subliminally or consciously.

Most of the time a president's background belongs in the background but it can abruptly become extremely relevant – for better or worse. Harry Truman's Jewish past-partner in the haberdashery business – Eddie Jacobson – is credited with having been pivotal in persuading him to recognize newborn Israel.

When the free world's leader faces tough choices, his seemingly incidental predispositions may be crucial in swinging him one way or another. They load his psychological or ideological dice. They make him more likely to oppose or support what others may not.

The tendency to draw on one's life experiences is universal and inescapable. Hence the spotlight on Obama's *Kinderstube* and subsequent sociopolitical meanderings isn't powered by bigotry.

The emphasis on Obama's interactions and relations is hardly a function of his being different but of his being so much the same, subject to biases and prejudices no less pervasive than those which propelled some of America's WASP patricians into positions incontrovertibly and coldheartedly inimical to the most basic of Jewish existential interests. They were raised in social surroundings which in the very least were unsympathetic toward the Jews whom the native sons were conditioned to dislike.

The Judeophobic *Kinderstube* came cruelly into play as the Holocaust loomed menacingly over Europe. Franklin Delano Roosevelt's administration barred America's gates before Jews desperately seeking asylum from Hitler's hell (among many examples – the 1939 denial of haven to 907 refugees aboard the liner *St. Louis* and the refusal to allow into the US twenty thousand unaccompanied Jewish children).

FDR's America dismissed reports of Nazi Final Solution plans, regularly repressed news of actual extermination, foiled the April 19–29, 1943, Bermuda conference on the slaughter of Europe's Jews and refused adamantly to bomb the railways to Auschwitz and its crematoria (though nearby factories had been attacked repeatedly).

Roosevelt's Secretary of State Cordell Hull, Undersecretary Sumner Welles and Assistant Secretary Breckinridge Long – all resplendent in impeccable Anglo-Saxon names and credentials – couldn't have been more obstructionist. FDR's personal friend, Long, was the most notorious of all. On October 3, 1940, he noted in his diary that the president "was 100% in accord" with his own policy of "postpone and postpone and postpone" the granting of visas to Jews.

In a damning 1943 indictment – after preparations to funnel funds to Europe to underpin rescue efforts were deliberately impeded – the US Treasury charged that the State Department was "guilty not only of gross procrastination and willful failure to act, but even of willful attempts to prevent action from being taken to rescue Jews from Hitler."

That's how deadly *Kinderstube* can be. That's why, mindful of Ahmadinejad's neo-Hitlerian threats, it's incumbent upon Jews not to pooh-pooh any prominent American's *Kinderstube* – not just the *Kinderstube* of a half-black politico with an Arab name and Muslim links.

It's not intolerance of skin color or cultural origins which prompts scrutiny of the company Obama keeps – from Reverend Jeremiah Wright and William Ayers to PLO propagandist Rashid Khalidi and Palestinian activist Ali Abunimah. The contention that Obama is penalized for the sins of others – be it Wright's demagoguery or Ayers's bombing plots – is disingenuous because more than one problematic affiliation is involved.

The sheer confluence of questionable connections creates a weighty preponderance of evidence about Obama's milieu, his subjective antipathies, sympathies and likely leanings. This is far more pertinent a concern than whether Obama is Muslim by Islamic tradition, whether he ever practiced Islam or whether according to Muslim criteria he's an apostate.

Incomparably more germane is the disclosure that Obama's erstwhile Middle East policy advisor, inveterate Israel-basher Robert Malley, routinely engaged in talks with Hamas. The fact that Malley became a political embarrassment, and had to therefore resign, doesn't lessen the significance of the extremist radical sphere to which Obama consistently gravitates and which, contrary to expedient rhetoric, delineates his affinities, orientations and inclinations.

Obama's milieu amplifies his receptiveness to the Arab/Islamist "narrative" and indicates where his heart is. This shouldn't only perturb Israelis and Jews.

Kinderstube eventually evolves into *Weltanschauung* (one's worldview, or mindset).

Three Days and Sixty Years

One of the best books anywhere about the lead-up to Israel's independence is perhaps the most unlikely, least attractive and inordinately trivia-laden little volume imaginable. It was composed by a man considered to have been one of old Mapai's particularly lackluster functionary figures – Ze'ev Sherf. The pinnacle of his career was his brief elevation to the post of finance minister in 1968.

In actual fact, however, his greater distinction was to have served as Israel's first-ever cabinet secretary, a position that grew out of his appointment in December 1947 to head the committee charged with all practical preparations for Israel's declaration of independence and with the establishment of a working administration ready to take over authority as soon as the British Mandatory forces departed.

Sherf in effect was the state's bureaucratic midwife, carrying out the unheroic but indispensable tasks that are later forgotten and taken for granted. As such, Sherf possessed an accumulation of seemingly tedious incidental material, the sort which is really the most telling and vital of all. In 1959 he collected these esoteric minutiae into a thin Hebrew hardcover entitled *Three Days*. It listed in extraordinary detail every move in the three days that preceded independence; its culmination was the actual declaration at the tiny Tel Aviv Museum auditorium in what previously was the home of the city's first mayor, Meir Dizengoff, on 16 Sderot Rothschild.

The venue was no one's top choice. Jerusalem was besieged, while Tel Aviv's Habima Theater was ruled out precisely because it was bigger and could accommodate more participants. Even a marginally larger affair was reckoned undesirable for fear that publicity about when and where the Jewish state's birth was slated to be announced would invite Egyptian air strikes. It was, therefore, thought advisable to keep everything hush-hush, make do with fewer honorary guests and cram them all into a minuscule hall (although the secrecy was quickly breached anyhow, in keeping with local proclivities).

The invitation (including a request to keep it confidential) was mimeographed and sent unsigned. The declaration itself was placed for safekeeping in a bank's basement vault, lest it be destroyed by enemy bombardments.

Only one hour before the ceremony was the declaration's final wording at last approved – after nitpicking objections over every single syllable and turn of phrase. A laborious version authored by Moshe Sharett was roundly rejected and the debates continued until David Ben-Gurion took the text home, trimmed, honed and rewrote everything himself. He accepted Bechor Sheetrit's proposal to commence the declaration by noting that it was in Eretz Yisrael that the Jewish nation was born.

Caught between religious delegates who demanded mention of the Almighty and Marxists who'd hear nothing of the sort, Ben-Gurion's compromise was to affirm "our trust in the Rock of Israel."

Contrary to popular misconceptions, the declaration never features the word "democracy" and only cursorily lists assorted fundamental individual freedoms "in the light of the vision of the prophets of Israel." Considering the meticulous attention to every nuance, this omission was no accident.

Ben-Gurion repeatedly argued that "this declaration is no constitution," and that the terse reference to civil liberties was required by the General Assembly partition resolution. "We inserted the basic elements demanded of us by the UN," he explained to members of the Provisional People's Council (the embryonic parliament).

Ben-Gurion also decreed that the new state's borders would remain unspecified. Again he reiterated that "this is a declaration of independence. The Americans declared independence without stipulating to which territory it would apply."

"Suppose," Ben-Gurion conjectured, "the Arabs launch a war against us. If we then foil their plans to destroy us and, for instance,

Crowds gathering outside 16 Sderot Rothschild in Tel Aviv as Israel's declaration of independence was read out – this despite the secrecy that enveloped the ceremony

capture the western Galilee and the road to Jerusalem, these then would become part of the state – assuming of course our strength suffices to pull us through. Why should we obligate ourselves not to hold on to what the enemy forces us to fight for?"

Ben-Gurion's far-sightedness was gutsy. Bloody battles already raged and Gush Etzion fell just at the very hour in which the secretary who typed the declaration (the parchment-like scroll was inscribed after the event) rushed down (on her own initiative) to the nearest neighborhood stationery store to buy blue paper with which to wrap the pages, to "dress them up," as she described it.

The newborn state possessed no resources or military hardware. Its population of six hundred thousand also comprised the old, the infirm and the very young. The risk was enormous but the spirit and grit were no less colossal.

How different Israel is sixty years on. Its population has multiplied more than tenfold and its military power exceeds anything Ben-Gurion could rationally have dreamed of. But there's no feisty Ben-Gurion at Israel's helm. Ehud Olmert, the premier who presided over the state's sixtieth birthday bash, intones that "we are tired of fighting, we are tired of being courageous, we're tired of winning, we are tired of defeating our enemies."

Olmert and his crew perceive the cradle of our history through the spectacles of the nation's worst genocidal enemies – as holdings which we arbitrarily invaded. To Olmert they're a burdensome legacy to be ditched at the earliest opportunity. He maintains that it's preferable to appease none-too-sympathetic world opinion than to steadfastly struggle. Olmert didn't merely bow to pressure from abroad when he agreed to outfit Fatah's "good terrorists" with firepower and armored vehicles (which, he admits, will inevitably fall into the hands of Hamas's "bad terrorists").

The culprit isn't external coercion. It resides in defeatist mindsets, which overcompensate by earmarking NIS 100 million to celebrate six decades of Israeli independence with pomp, pageantry, circumstance, spectacles, fireworks and crass street entertainment galore.

Sherf, whose documentation no one will bother to air out on the state's birthday, recounted that at four o'clock on the fateful Friday afternoon sixty years ago, "no foreign flags were lowered, our national banners weren't hoisted, celebratory shots weren't fired, the army didn't march, speeches weren't delivered…in barely thirty-two minutes was declared the liberty of the nation subjugated for 1,887 years."

Following Ben-Gurion's proclamation, "Hatikva" was played by the orchestra in the building's upper story (there simply wasn't enough room below), "and as the sounds descended from above, it was as if the heavens had opened up…. Everyone stood silent, motionless and listened to the wondrous hymn, emanating from an unseen place."

Vague and Not Uncommon

Few of my past columns have elicited as much hate mail as a recent one on perfidious Swiss neutrality. Several messages, oozing with particular vitriol, were signed by Arab names. The authors of others purported to be Swiss. Though in cyberspace nothing should be taken at face value, some of what supposedly originated on the Alpine moral high ground did have that ring of authenticity – like the one which affirmed the precedence of Swiss interests over "some goddamned foreigners," i.e., Jews. "No wonder we Swiss don't like your people," the writer summed up.

Dejecting as it may be, the Swiss – or enough of them who share the above sentiments – aren't alone. Europeans by and large still don't and never did like "our people." In generations past there was nothing disreputable about Jew-phobia.

It was indeed often customary and casually accepted in polite society and the intelligentsia. Today, anti-Semitism (the term coined in the late nineteenth century by German journalist Wilhelm Mahr and applied exclusively to Jews – contrary to disingenuous Arab affectations) is no longer overtly respectable.

Especially among politically correct circles, anti-Semitism has gone underground and donned new disguises. The Holocaust – even when denied or deliberately dwarfed – has given anti-Semitism an unpleasant aftertaste. Yet this too is used to berate Jews. They allegedly brandish accusations of anti-Semitism with manipulative intent to silence all criticism, particularly of the Jewish state. Such circuitous reasoning eventually turns Jew-haters into righteous persecuted underdogs, while Jews are cast as exploitive ferocious hounds.

Like it or not, where shallow pop culture predominates, so does an equally superficial yet all-pervasive pop conscience. By the diktats of the global village's smart set, it's bon ton in the very least to deplore "Israeli excesses." That's the stamp of broadmindedness expected of any upstanding person of general goodwill and forward-thinking inclinations. It's an indispensable accessory for the liberal image. Only extraordinary nonconformists, chronic oddballs, maverick dissenters or American evangelicals dare say different, at their own peril. Graduates of fine universities or indolent media consumers are unlikely to avoid the anti-Israel bug.

Reviling the Jewish state is today just as proper and urbane as turning sophisticated noses at Jews was for T. S. Eliot and his prewar milieu. Reacting to verses like "The rats are underneath the piles/The Jew is underneath the lot," Eliot's friend Leonard Woolf (Virginia's devoted Jewish husband) described him as only "slightly anti-Semitic in the sort of vague way which is not uncommon."

That vague anti-Semitism is just as "not uncommon" in Europe's current widespread de rigueur demonization of Israel. Shimon Stein, Israel's former ambassador to Berlin, noted that for some elements in German society "Israel's existence is hardly self-evident." He discerns "consistent erosion" in how Israel is perceived among the progeny of the Holocaust's perpetrators. In recent decades "Israel is depicted as diabolically evil," while German governments increasingly acquiesce to EU censure of Israel. Memories of made-in-Germany genocide no longer suffice to underwrite a "special relationship" with the state the Jewish remnant founded.

A recent *SAT1* poll showed that 52 percent of Germans recognize no "significant obligation to the Jewish state." Many Germans, moreover, frown at special relations either on the grounds of "Jewish extortion," or because of the imperialistic sins they ascribe to the Jewish state. Or both.

The mind-blowing upshot is that the children of murderers, sadists, collaborators, bureaucrats, robbers – those who didn't see, those who didn't want to know, those who saw and knew but didn't act – now consider themselves morally superior. They now presume to haughtily preach to the children of the slain, gassed, burned, shot, buried alive, starved, tortured, degraded, dehumanized, enslaved, dispossessed, bereaved and orphaned.

In our topsy-turvy reality nothing is unthinkable. Germany is now extensively regarded in all European countries as the continent's leader, while Israel is deemed a pariah. Descendants of the world's worst guys parade as good guys and they arrogantly portray descendants of the most downtrodden as flagrantly deficient of virtue.

A 2008 BBC poll found that Israel is the world's second most unpopular country, just a tad behind Iran and marginally more detested than Pakistan. Runner-up status is little consolation even if one year earlier, in a similar BBC poll, Israel topped the list of countries deemed to have "the most negative influence on the world."

In 2003 the EU citizenry voted Israel "the greatest danger to world peace" and the same happened in 2000 when Ehud Barak headed Israel's most conciliatory government until then.

It's not Jewish deeds which are the root cause of the abhorrence – not in this twenty-first century, nor in the twentieth, thirteenth, eighth, first or BCE.

Jews always did and still do attract abuse – even when they call themselves Israelis. From time immemorial they found themselves in the eye of whatever storm was brewing. They didn't rouse the tempest but it always revolved around them. From the dawn of history Jews were civilization's codifiers of ethics and harbingers of progress. That in itself was enough to render them unbearable irritants, for which they paid horrifically.

Europeans who decades ago shouted "Jews to Palestine," and showed no mercy to those who didn't flee in time, now shout "Jews out of Palestine." With Jews unwanted anywhere, the bottom line precludes any Jewish survival. This, beyond all else, is what should be uppermost in our minds during Holocaust Memorial Day.

So long as Hitler merely targeted Jews, the world didn't mind. Germany was battled only when it aggressed against others. Throughout, no one fought to save Jews. Their rescue was WWII's belated byproduct. If Ahmadinejad guarantees to only nuke Jews, then the rest of the world could learn to somehow tolerate Iran's bomb. A Jewish-only target is almost a plausible compromise.

The more things change, the more they stay the same.

Here is where Israelis' dulled self-preservation instincts must take over. If we blame ourselves to curry favor with cynical maligners, to make them like us, to secure their approval and good press – if we obsess about their opinion of us – then we're goners. If we don't overcome our awe of not-uncommon Judeophobes – vague or otherwise – then our two-thousand-year-old hope is tragically lost.

Where Penitents Stand

Rare is the temptation to turn over any of one's finite column space to another's op-ed ruminations. But Gilad Sharon's *Yediot Aharonot* piece "It's All about Hatred" is one such irresistible exception.

Every sentence by Ariel Sharon's younger son deserves to be chiseled in stone. Gilad's straightforward truths should be resonated at home and abroad – often, loud and unequivocally.

What Gilad wrote should become no less than the mantra of Israeli diplomacy and PR. That, however, was rendered improbable when Gilad's own dad – whose sentiments were once identical to what Gilad now expounds – cynically performed an abrupt about-face for which he never bothered to account.

The senior Sharon's disengagement folly not only callously displaced nine thousand Israeli patriots, not only poisoned the souls of soldiers and policemen, not only presented Jews as portable interlopers, not only emboldened genocidal enemies, not only brought Hamas to power, not only turned Gaza into an armed-to-the-teeth military encampment, not only exposed greater and greater stretches of the Israeli hinterland to terrorist rocket barrages, but it also distorted the very truth of which Gilad reminds us.

Perhaps the gravest and most abiding sin committed by the father – along with his accomplice sons and self-serving entourage – was to lead too many Israelis to lose faith in the justice of their cause and to worship the Golden Calf encapsulated in Arik's blandishments, extolling disengagement's boon-to-come.

On October 25, 2004, as he urged the Knesset to approve the reckless withdrawal, Gilad's father assured the nation that "this disengagement will strengthen Israel's hold on the territory essential to our existence and will win the blessing and gratitude of those near and far, will lessen enmity, will break besiegement and boycotts and will further us on the path of peace with the Palestinians and all our other neighbors."

The shattered shards of these sham inducements now tumble menacingly all around us. Not only wasn't a syllable of Sharon's enticing promises fulfilled, but the exact opposite came to pass, just as his all-too-prescient political critics – disparagingly smeared as "rebels" – had warned to no avail. We aren't now back where we started, we're incalculably worse off.

And now Gilad, judged by some to have powerfully influenced his father's ideological reverse, mocks the notion that "the moment the conflict between us and the Palestinians would be resolved, the reason for the Arab and Muslim world's hostility towards us will disappear.... This conviction is naïve and false – the Palestinian issue is the pretext; a means used to slam Israel. It is not the problem.

"The Arab world never reconciled itself to our existence as a Jewish state in the Mideastern space. The only Arab maps where the State of Israel appears are military maps. When it comes to the maps used in geography classes at schools, we do not exist.... If the Palestinian issue bothered Arab states so much, what stopped them from establishing a Palestinian state before 1967 and the Six-Day War? ...Terrorism against Jews in Israel started more than 120 years ago, much before the Six-Day War and the War of Independence; before we were accused of expulsion or occupation."

Gilad goes on to demolish popular canards ascribing terrorism to economic misery. The perpetrator of the Mercaz Harav slaughter of schoolboys, he notes, came from well-to-do circumstances, as did the 9/11 crew. They were driven, Gilad deduces, not by distress but by hate, by the fact that "radical Islamic fanaticism...is unwilling to accept the West and its way of life and culture, and seeks to enforce its dark and zealous beliefs on all global residents through any means available."

The Sharon scion advises Americans and Europeans "to realize that pressuring Israel to make concessions would not bring them the calm they so covet and would not allow them to go back to a life of hedonistic euphoria. Giving in to terrorism and violence doesn't appease the aggressor, as was proven by Hitler, but rather, only encourages it.... People around the world and around here too [sh]ould realize that the zealot demon who emerged from the bottle cannot be compromised with. We can only push it back into the bottle with strength and determination and bury it deeply in the sands of the Arabian Peninsula."

Only extraordinary self-control can keep Gilad's readers from throwing his belated common sense back in his face. Where was he in 2005 when Israel – under the father he himself unstintingly supported – gave in to terrorism and appeased the aggressor? Why did Gilad allow his remorseless dad to quash all opposition with steamroller ruthlessness in order to compromise with the zealot demon? Why does Gilad not explicitly address what disengagement was?

The likelihood that Gilad didn't just suddenly experience an epiphany puts his family's great transgression in a much more sinister light. If Gilad believed all along in what he now preaches – indeed if in his heart of hearts his father clung to the same views – then disengagement's sin wasn't the product of a sincere doctrinal conversion.

If this is what the Sharons thought throughout, then they willfully hoodwinked the populace and crushed its spirit to advance egocentric schemes – like extricating themselves from their legal travails. By implementing Peace Now's agenda, they made themselves indispensable enough to the Left to benefit from its sway in the media and the judicial establishment.

But why pick at that still-festering open wound? Jewish tradition avers that "where penitents stand, those who have never wronged cannot stand." In other words, repentance is worthier than absolute righteousness. Who, therefore, are we to quibble if Gilad effectively confesses the error of his ways (even if he doesn't quite beat his breast in specific contrition)?

It will suffice us if he now comes out and, without pussyfooting, expressly joins the outcry against the further survival-jeopardizing surrenders touted by Arik's assorted ex-collaborators. Actively striving to prevent follow-up "disengagements" would be the least Gilad can do to begin to make amends.

About the Author

Sarah Honig is a veteran columnist and senior editorial writer. During her decades-long history at the *Jerusalem Post*, she served for many years as its political correspondent (a position she also held at the now-defunct *Davar*), headed the *Post*'s Tel Aviv bureau and wrote daily analyses of the political scene, along with in-depth features.

Sarah was born in Israel and reared both in Israel and the United States. She was educated at the High School of Music and Art in New York City and at Tel Aviv University.

She began work as a reporter for the *Jerusalem Post* while still a student. From the inception of the aliya movement in the USSR, Sarah was the leading reporter covering Soviet Jewry's struggle, often breaking the stories which were then picked up by news outlets throughout the world.

In the early 1980s Sarah became the *Post*'s senior political correspondent. She produced a weekly column on the intricacies of Israeli politics, "Insider Dealings." From 1991 to 2001 she was the *Post*'s often nonconformist political analyst who spiritedly offered unusual perspectives and spotlighted the background behind the headlines.

Currently Sarah is a columnist and senior editorial writer at the *Jerusalem Post*, contributing daily editorials on a broad variety of topics. Sarah's column "Another Tack," covering Israel and world affairs, has been appearing since 1999.

www.sarahhonig.com